Sanskrit Education and Literature in Ancient and Medieval Tamil Nadu
— An Epigraphical Study —

Reconstructing Indian History & Culture
(ISSN 0971-3824)

1. Society in Ancient India; by Sures Chandra Banerji.
2. Political Thought in Ancient India; by G.P. Singh.
3. Early Indian Historical Tradition and Archaeology; by G.P. Singh.
4. Vasantotsava: The Spring Festivals of India; by Leona M. Anderson.
5. Ecological Readings in the Veda; by M. Vannucci.
6. Vṛndāvana in Vaiṣṇava Literature; by Maura Corcoran.
7. Social History of the Tamils (1707-1947); by P. Subramanian.
8. Ancient Indian Coinage; by Rekha Jain.
9. Buddhism and Socio-Economic Life of Eastern India; by Bimal Chandra Mohapatra.
10. Chandragupta Maurya; by P.L. Bhargava.
11. Mṛtyu: Concept of Death in Indian Traditions; by Gian Giuseppe Filippi.
12. Yama: The Glorious Lord of the Other World; by Kusum P. Merh.
13. Sacred Complex of Ujjain; by D.K. Samanta.
14. Vedic View of the Earth; by S.R.N. Murthy.
15. Society in the Atharvaveda; by B.S. Kharade.
16. Orissan History, Culture and Archaeology; by S. Pradhan.
17. Education in Ancient India; by Mitali Chatterjee.
18. Surà: The Liquor and the Vedic Sacrifice; by M.B. Kolhatkar.
19. Human Ecology in the Vedas; by Marta Vannucci.
20. Governance in Ancient India; by Anupa Chandra Pandey.
21. The Cultural Glory of Ancient India: A Literary Overview; by Sures Chandra Banerji.
22. Kauṭilya's Arthaśāstra in the light of Modern Science & Technology; by Sunil Sen Sarma.
23. History of Jainism — With Special Reference to Mathurā; by V.K. Sharma.
24. Cultural Tourism in India: Museums, Monuments & Arts — Theory and Practice; by S.P. Gupta; Krishna Lal; Mahua Bhattacharya.
25. Ancient Indian Historiography — Sources and Interpretations; by G.P. Singh.
26. Republics, Kingdoms, Towns and Cities in Ancient India; by G.P. Singh.
27. Facets of Ancient Indian History and Culture — New Perception; by G.P. Singh.
28. Kamakhya — A Socio-cultural Study; by Nihar Ranjan Mishra.
29. History and Culture of Tamil Nadu as Gleaned from the Sanskrit Inscriptions Vol. 1 (up to c. AD 1310); by Chithra Madhavan.
30. Lifestyle of the Vedic People; by Pranati Ghosal.
31. History and Culture of Tamil Nadu as Gleaned from the Sanskrit Inscriptions Vol. 2 (up to c. AD 1310 - *c*. 1885 AD); by Chithra Madhavan.
32. Matrimonial Alliances and Ancient Indian Polity (*c*. 600 BCE to *c*. 650); by Preeti Prabhat.
33. Artisans and Craftsmen of Northern India; by Kuldeep Singh Thind.
34. The Evolution of Historiographical Tradition in Ancient and Medieval India; by G.P. Singh.
35. Warfare in Ancient India, Theory and Practice by Soma Basu.

Recontructing Indian History & Culture, no. 36

Sanskrit Education and Literature in Ancient and Medieval Tamil Nadu

— An Epigraphical Study —

Chithra Madhavan

With a foreword by
C.S. Radhakrishnan

DK PRINTWORLD
Publishers of Indian Traditions

Cataloging in Publication Data — DK
[Courtesy: D.K. Agencies (P) Ltd. <docinfo@dkagencies.com>]

Madhavan, Chithra, 1966-
Sanskrit education and literature in ancient and medieval Tamil Nadu : an epigraphical study, Chithra Madhavan; with a foreword by C.S. Radhakrishnan.
p. cm. (Reconstructing Indian history and culture ; no. 36).
Includes verses in Sanskrit (roman).
Includes bibliographical references (p.).
ISBN 9788124607008

1. Sanskrit language – Study and teaching – India – Tamil Nadu – History. 2. Inscriptions, Sanskrit – India – Tamil Nadu. 3. Sanskrit literature – India – Tamil Nadu – To 1500 – History and criticism. 4. Tamil Nadu (India) – Kings and rulers – Education – History. I. Title. II. Series: Reconstructing Indian history and culture ; no. 36.

DDC 491.2071095482 23

ISBN 13: 978-81-246-0700-8 (HB)
ISBN 13: 978-81-246-0705-3 (PB)
First published in India, 2013

Printed and published by:
D.K. Printworld (P) Ltd.
Regd. office : *'Vedaśrī,'* F-395, Sudarshan Park
(Metro Station: Ramesh Nagar)
New Delhi - 110 015
Phones: (011) 2545 3975, 2546 6019; *Fax*: (011) 2546 5926
E-mail:indology@dkprintworld.com
Web: www.dkprintworld.com

Dedicated

to

all the Great Sanskrit Scholars
of Ancient and Medieval
Tamil Nadu

Foreword

EPIGRAPHY is a subject not merely of great academic interest, but has been the backbone of history. It has helped scholars and governments in diving deep into the history of the past and fixing the dates of many a dynasty, kingdoms, besides shedding light on many land grants and what not! It is rather a cause for concern that the number of epigraphists is dwindling day-by-day and the situation is not very encouraging when a number of posts of epigraphists remaining vacant for several years.

The rock edicts are the best evidences when it comes to fixing the dates of several scholars, poets, philosophers in India, where there is a dearth of historical recordings and "where people believe more in the world to come than in the one they live in". "Hindu literature is remarkably deficient in works of history. But the value of inscriptions, has of late years, been more and more recognized as one of the chief sources from which trustworthy materials may be drawn for supplying that deficiency" thus said Lewis Rice who was commissioned in 1870 to translate the inscriptions photographed by Major Dixon under Governor-General Lord Canning. One verse of *Mukundamālā* of Kulaśekhara, who has been identified with the Śrīvaiṣṇava saint Kulasékhara Āḷvār, a king of Tiruvanchikulam in Kerala, is found in an inscription dated thirteenth century (*Epigraphia Indica*, VII: 197f) in Tamil characters in as far a place as Pagan in Burma. It indeed speaks volumes of the popularity of the work and its author. For, Kerala is in the southernmost tip of the Indian sub-continent and Burma is beyond the north-east. If the same verse is found in a palm-leaf manuscript or a copper plate, it could be construed that it was carried to that place by some traveller or scribe. But when it is found on a rock edict, it is a sure sign of its popularity. The historicity attached to it can never be wiped off or altered. That is the value of the inscriptions.

Under the inspiration and guidance of His Holiness, the Paramācārya of Kāñcī, the Uttankita Vidya Aranya Trust brought out the first volume, in 1985, of the inscriptions, sixteen of them, pertaining to Vidyāraṇya who was a philosopher–statesman responsible for the establishment of the Vijayanagara empire at Hampī. The further editions of volumes II (ed. K.G. Krishnan, Chief Epigraphist), vol. III (eds. K.G. Krishnan and J. Sundaram) furthered the noble cause of preserving for posterity the Sanskrit inscriptions (with English translation), belonging to the period 257 BCE – CE 320 and CE 320–600, respectively. Such editions are to be viewed as priceless possessions since they play a significant role as milestones for the journey on the sands of time.

Epigraphical studies may be classified under three categories. The first one is the publication of all inscriptions of a particular region, or of a particular period, or of a particular dynasty of rulers like the Pallavas and Coḷas. Such a study helps in preserving for posterity such inscriptions which have weathered the vagaries of time, which are most likely to be lost due to neglect or even with white-washing, painting, etc. The second category comprises such attempts, like that of Lewis Rice, which bring out English translations too, thereby opening the scope of the inscriptions to a wide circle of scholars, who, in the absence of the knowledge of the script, will have an authentic translation to study. The third category envisages not merely a study but an analysis of the contents of the inscriptions belonging to several centuries. Its task is all the more difficult.

The book *Sanskrit Education and Literature in Ancient and Medieval Tamil Nadu* by Chithra Madhavan belongs to the third category mentioned above, inasmuch as it is a study of the contents of the inscriptions so far as Sanskrit education is concerned in Tamil Nadu in the ancient and medieval period. Chithra Madhavan, undertook this study as a Post-Doctoral Fellow under the Indian Council of Historical Research. I have known Chithra Madhavan for the past twenty-five years. She is not merely a distinguished historian but is also very keen in taking these historical facts to the common man by reaching out to society. I have seen her delivering lectures to the general public with a sole motive of arousing their interest in knowing and preserving our rich archaeological heritage. This book, I am sure, is yet another feather on her cap. The topic itself is such that it will remove many misgivings about the understanding of the education scenario in Tamil Nadu in the ancient and medieval period. "Vedam niranda Tamil Nadu" proclaims Subramania Bharatiar, the celebrated patriot-poet of India, in one of his songs. This book provides ample testimony, as it were, to Bharatiar's statement. If the "Contribution of Tamil Nadu to Sanskrit Literature" by C.S. Sundaram studies the literary works, this book goes deep into the inscriptional evidences to shed more light on Sanskrit education in this part of the country. Chithra has systematically arranged her findings under headings such as Pallava, Pāṇḍya, Ay, Coḷa, Hoysaḷa, Vijayanagara, Nāyakas and later Pāṇḍyas.

I am privileged to write the Foreword for this edition. I am sure this book will a useful possession of not only the general readers but in particular of the research scholars in history, Sanskrit, epigraphy, archaeology and social science.

If this book enthuses the present generation of research scholars to take to epigraphic studies seriously, then the hard labour of Chithra Madhavan will be amply rewarded.

C.S. Radhakrishnan
Professor & Head
Department of Sanskrit
Pondicherry University

Preface

I HAD selected the topic *Sanskrit Education and Literature in Ancient and Medieval Tamil Nadu: An Epigraphical Study* for which the Indian Council of Historical Research (ICHR), New Delhi, had granted me a General Post-doctoral Fellowship. I would like to thank ICHR for selecting me for this fellowship which enabled me to take up a detailed study of this topic that covers the period from the time of the Pallava dynasty starting from *c.* fifth century CE to the time of the Marāṭhā rulers of the eighteenth century CE.

I thank Dr. K.V. Raman, Professor and Head (retd.), Department of Ancient History and Archaeology, University of Madras, for all his help and encouragement at every stage of my research. I am very fortunate to have had the benefit of his scholarly advice.

My very sincere thanks to my parents for their sustained support over the years. I specially thank my mother Smt. Charu Madhavan for translating many of the Sanskrit inscriptions for me. I am lucky to have had the support of my sincere well-wishers Shri L.J. Krishnamurthi, Smt. Shobha Jayaraman and Dr Padma Seshadri and my heartfelt gratitude to them for the same.

I am extremely grateful to Dr C.S. Radhakrishnan, Professor and Head, Department of Sanskrit, Pondicherry University, Puducherry, for writing the foreword to this book. To have a scholar of his eminence contribute the foreword is truly an honour for me.

I wish to thank Shri M.N. Srinivasan for the rare photographs of the Ūnamañjerī copper-plate inscription of the sixteenth century CE.

Particular thanks are due to Shri Susheel K. Mittal, Director, D.K. Printworld, New Delhi, for the interest and enthusiasm with which he has brought out this book.

Chithra Madhavan

Contents

Abbreviations

ARE	*Annual Reports on Epigraphy*
ASIAR	*Archaeological Survey of India — Annual Report*
ASLP	*Administrative and Social Life under the Pallavas*
ASLV	*Administrative and Social Life under Vijayanagara*
DCPV	*Dalavaypuram Copper Plates of Parantaka Vīra Narayana*
EC	*Epigraphia Carnatica*
EI	*Epigraphia Indica*
ECPR	*Esālam Copper Plates of Rajendra Coḷa I,* by R. Nagaswamy
IA	*Indian Antiquary*
JOR	*Journal of Oriental Research*
PJCG	*Paḷḷankovil Jaina Copper Plate Grant of Early Pallava Period,* by T.N. Subramaniam
SII	*South Indian Inscriptions*
SITI	*South Indian Temple Inscriptions*
SCVP	*Śivakāśī Copper Plates of Vīra Pāṇḍya*
TAS	*Travancore Archaeological Series*
TPC	*Thirty Pallava Copper Plates*
TVCP	*Tiruttani and Velanjeri Copper Plates,* by R. Nagaswamy
USVAE	*Uttankita Sanskrit Vidya Aranya Epigraphs*

Introduction

The literary and epigraphical wealth of Tamil Nadu are the most authentic and important sources of information about various spheres of activity in the ancient and medieval times. This is true of the field of learning and literature also. A study of the literature of the earliest historical period of the Tamil country known as the Sangam age — *c.* third century BCE to *c.* third century CE — clearly reveals that a lot of focus was given to learning and literature. Education, which must be at the bottom of any secular or aesthetic achievement of any people, was not merely known and encouraged but was a widespread social activity.[1] The importance given to education in the Sangam age is seen from the *Tirukkuraḷ* which states "the wealth which never declines is not riches but learning".[2]

In the subsequent ages, during the times of the Pallavas, Pāṇḍyas, Coḷas, Vijayanagara and Nāyaka, and also of the rule of the lesser chieftains, the encouragement given to education was one of the major duties of the kings. This study focuses on the Sanskrit education and literature from the Pallava times, mainly Vedic and Vedāntic in nature, besed on the information gleaned from epigraphs. The lithic epigraphs etched on the walls and pillars of temples as well as the copper-plate grants provide plenty of data on the subjects taught and works written in Sanskrit during times bygone. In addition

[1] N. Subrahmanian, *Sangam Polity*, Madurai, 1980, p. 337.

[2] P.S. Sundaram (tr.), *Tiruvalluvar The Kural*, New Delhi, 1990, p. 60.

to these important inscriptions, there are many Sanskrit texts which have come down to the present day, clearly showing the high standard of Sanskrit of those times. Many of the kings of the important dynasties as well as some of the lesser chieftains were extremely erudite and composed poems and dramas in Sanskrit themselves. While many of these texts are still studied by Sanskritists, many unfortunately have been lost in the tide of time and only the names of some of these works, by way of inscriptional evidence, survive till today to remind us of their copious literary output.

Whether they were by themselves scholars or not, it was an important duty of these rulers to patronize the learned of their land by giving them grants of land and money so that they could continue with their work of studying and teaching without hindrance. Such royal donations to promote individual learning are seen from many an epigraph in Tamil Nadu. The land given to the learned brāhmaṇas were called *bhaṭṭa-vṛtti*s. One of the earliest inscriptions (*c.* fifth century CE), the Oṁgoḍu grant of Pallava Vijayaskandavarman is a clear example of a *bhaṭṭa-vṛtti*; although the technical phrase *bhaṭṭa-vṛtti* is not used in this grant, it is however a gift to a brāhmaṇa in recognition of his learning.[3] The practice of endowing such *bhaṭṭa-vṛttis* is continued from the Pallava times, down the centuries including the Vijayanagara period. The inscriptions which give the details of the *bhaṭṭa-vṛtti* also provide a lot of information about the qualifications of the *bhaṭṭa*s who were found worthy enough to receive a piece of land or sometimes a whole village. The inscriptions repeatedly mention that the brāhmaṇa donees of the grants were extremely well-read. They are described as masters in the Vedas, Vedāṅgas (consisting of Chandakalpa, Vyākaraṇa, Jyotiṣa, Nirukta, Śikṣā and Chandoviciti), Itihāsa, Purāṇa, Sāṁkhya, Yama and Niyama.

---

[3] C. Minakshi, *ASLP*, p. 199.

The titles borne by these Sanskrit scholars like Caturvedin, Trivedin, Somayājin, Vasantayājin, Bhaṭṭa, Sarvakratuyājin, Agnicit Ṣaḍaṅgavid and Kramavid reveal their scholarship in their chosen fields of study. Incidentally, the inscriptions of Tamil Nadu, starting from the time of the Pallavas, reveal that many such learned *bhaṭṭa*s migrated from different parts of India to the Tamil country, settled down here and received munificent grants from the local rulers.

While an endowment to one or a few brāhmaṇa scholars was known as a *bhaṭṭa-vṛtti*, settlements of a whole village by a large number of brāhmaṇas was known as an *agrahāra*.[4] The *brahmadeya* (villages given to scholarly brāhmaṇa) is also variously known by other names — *agrahāra*, *agara*, *caturvedimaṅgalam* and *brahmapurī* — each having its own meaning and significance which ultimately goes to prove that they mainly contained brāhmaṇa population.[5] It is interesting to note that many of the *agrahāra*s and *caturvedimaṅgalam*s were named after the rulers or their consorts or other members of their families and that over time, the same villages had their names changed, when other dynasties came to power in subsequent times, to that of the then ruling monarch or members of his family. Among the *agrahāra*s too, it is known that some, when endowed to individual brāhmaṇa scholars, are called by the name *ekabhoga*. Regarding the *ekabhoga* village, the *Mayamata*, one of the authoritative textbooks on the Śilpaśāstra, gives the following description: "A plot of land granted to a single brāhmaṇa for his sole enjoyment and having on it his mansion and the houses of his dependents and farmers is called an *ekabhogam*."[6] Similarly, grants of land to two or to three scholars only are also known from the

[4] C. Minakshi, *ASLP*, p. 233.

[5] S. Gurumurthy, *Education in South India: Ancient and Medieval Periods*, Madras, 1979, p. 25.

[6] *EI*, vol. XV no. 5, p. 55.

inscriptions. Land which is thus enjoyed by two or more parties goes by the name *gaṇa-bhogya* and *tri-bhogya*. In some cases, two or more villages were clubbed together to form a *brahmadeya* or *agrahāra*. These villages, granted to the learned people, were usually very fertile lands, located near a main water source such as a large tank or river.

The boundaries of the *brahmadeyas* or *agrahāras*, thus donated, were very carefully demarcated. It is interesting to note that the ceremony of letting loose a she-elephant to go around a plot of land intended to be granted to anyone is an ancient institution: it is referred to in the Leiden grant also as *kāriṇī-parikramaṇa vispaṣṭa sīma catuṣṭayam*; a she- elephant is let loose, her wandering path is carefully marked and after she returns to the place from which she started, the plot of land enclosed by the path of the elephant is granted to the donee.[7] In most cases, the villages were given in perpetuity as *sarvamānya*, to be enjoyed by the donee and his descendants; with the grant of the village go the rights over the property and therein, with the king reserving no right over the village granted.

All these grants of lands to the learned were made for the dissemination of the Vedas and allied branches of learning; at the same time the kings also considered it a meritorious deed which would secure for them good health, strength, wealth and victory. Phrases like *asmad-āyur-bala-vijay-ābhivṛddhaye* (increase of the king's life, strength and victory), *asmad āyur ārogyābhivṛddhaye* (augmentation of the king's longevity and health) and *āyur-bala-vijaya-aiśvaryābhivṛddhaye* (increasing the king's life, strength, wealth and victory) are commonly seen in the Pallava grants in connection with the donation to brāhmaṇas.

---

[7] *EI*, vol. XV no. 5, p. 55.

In the Pallava times, other than the *agrahāras*, the inscriptions mention the educational institution called the *ghaṭika* or *ghaṭikasthāna*, the best known of which was situated in the Pallava capital Kāñcīpuram. The yeoman service to Vedic education rendered by the *ghaṭika* and its connection with royalty is also seen. The famous *vidyāsthāna* at Bāhūr (near present-day Pondicherry) was also a great educational centre of the Pallava times.

Subsequently, in the period of the Coḷas, the large "temple-colleges" served as important centres of learning. The Vaiṣṇava temples at Eṇṇāyiram (of the time of Rājendra Coḷa I), Tribhuvanam (of the reign of Rājādhirāja Coḷa I) and Tirumukkūḍal (of Vīra-Rājendra's time) were excellent centres that promoted Vedic education along with other subjects.

The *maṭha*s too played a prominent role in the spread of learning and it is surprising to see that even veterinary science was encouraged and practised. The *Amarakośa*, the Sanskrit lexicon, defines a *maṭha* as "a place where pupils (and their teachers) reside" (*maṭhaścchātrādi nilayaḥ*).[8] According to P.V. Kane, "The *maṭha*s were primarily intended for the instruction of pupils or the laity by some great teacher in the tenets of a sect or in the doctrines of some philosophy or in some branch of learning such as grammar, Mīmāṁsā, astronomy and the like."[9]

---

[8] Satyadeva Mishra (ed.), *Amarakośa*, Varanasi, 1972, II.2.8.

[9] P.V. Kane, *History of Dharmaśāstra*, vol. II pt. 2, Poona, 1941, p. 907.

1

Pallavas

THE glorious era of the Pallavas, which began in *c.* fifth century CE, ushered in a great age in the political, economic, social and cultural spheres. The Pallava rulers, with their capital at Kāñcīpuram and port-city at Māmallapuram, gave much impetus to the spread of Sanskrit language and literature during this time as seen from their numerous inscriptions and also the literary texts that have come down to the present age. Some of the earliest Sanskrit inscriptions of Tamil Nadu belong to this time. This empire came to an end in *c.* ninth century CE when the Coḷas under Vijayālaya Coḷa and his son Āditya Coḷa overthrew the last Pallava monarch, Aparājita.

Early Pallava Inscriptions

The inscriptions of the Pallavas, especially their copper-plate charters, provide some information regarding the education and scholarship of some of the early Pallava rulers. The Kaśākuḍi copper-plate inscription of the reign of Nandivarman II Pallavamalla, dated CE 753-54, mentions that all the kings born in the race of the Pallavas were "full of learning" (*ghanāgama*).[1] The early Pallava kings are described in this inscription as "those who are learned" (*paṇḍita-matayaḥ*).[2] The Hosakoṭṭai plates describe the Pallava king Siṁhaviṣṇu as "having attained eminence by the study of Vedic and Āgamic traditions" (*sakala mantra tantrāntarggatasya vividhāgama prakṣālita*

---

[1] *SII*, vol. II no. 73, l. 44, p. 348 (Kaśākuḍi plates).

[2] Ibid., l. 47.

viśuddha buddheḥ).[3] Vijayaskandavarman has been eulogized in the Oṁgoḍu (I) grant of *c.* fifth century CE as "one who ably understood the purport of all the Śāstras" (*sarva-śāstrārtha-nirṇaya-tattvajñaḥ*).[4] The Mangaḷūr inscription of *c.* fifth century CE describes Skandavarman as "one who grew old in respect of his learning" (*vidyāvṛddhaḥ*).[5] The same inscription describes Yuvamahārāja Viṣṇugopa as "one who was refined due to his learning" (*vidyāvinītātmanaḥ*).[6] The fact that the early Pallava rulers were also patrons of scholars is brought out by the Vesanta copper-plate epigraph (*c.* fifth century CE) which mentions that Vijayaskandavarman, the father of Siṁhavarman, the donor of this grant was a "tree of refuge to all learned men" (*vāsa-vṛkṣo vidvad janasya*).[7]

As mentioned earlier, the kings of south India donated a large number of villages as *agrahāra*s to learned brāhmaṇas for the spread of the Vedas and allied subjects. The inscriptions of the early Pallava rulers mention many such donations thus made. The Oṁgoḍu (II) copper-plate record of *c.* fifth century CE mentions that Siṁhavarman granted the village of Oṁgoḍu to Devaśarman who was "well-versed in all the Śāstras" (*sarva-śāstra-kuśalayaḥ*) for the "increase of the king's life, strength and victory" (*asmad-āyur-bala-vijaya-abhivardhaye*).[8] The Cura copper-plate inscription of *c.* fifth century CE registers that Viṣṇugopavarman made a grant of land in the village of Cura to a scholarly brāhmaṇa named Cesāmiśarman for the increase of this ruler's life, strength and success in exactly the same words as the Oṁgoḍu (II) grant.[9] Many other early Pallava

[3] *TPC*, p. 378.

[4] *EI*, vol. XV no. 11.

[5] *Ind. Ant.*, vol. V (May 1876) — Maṅgaḷūr plates.

[6] *Ind. Ant.*, vol. V (May 1876) — Maṅgaḷūr plates.

[7] N. Ramesan, *VGPS*, l. 14, p. 95.

[8] *EI*, vol. XV no. 11, p. 255 (Oṁgoḍu (II) plates).

[9] *EI*, vol. XXIV no. 18, p. 142 (Cura plates).

copper-plate charters record similar donations of land to scholars.

Ghaṭika

During the Pallava period, the most important Brāhmanical institution was the *ghaṭika*. Several Pallava Sanskrit inscriptions mention the *ghaṭika* and the importance given to it by the Pallava kings. The Sanskrit word *ghaṭika* has been explained by different scholars in various ways. According to Kielhorn, the *ghaṭika* is the same as the *goṣṭhi* and it was an establishment which comprised groups of holy and learned brāhmaṇas probably in each case founded by the king.[10] S.K. Aiyangar has suggested that it was a settlement of brāhmaṇas.[11] K.A. Nilakanta Sastri has described the *ghaṭika* as a corporate college.[12] C. Minakshi has stated that the word originates from the root *ghaṭ* which in Sanskrit means "to strive after" and that the *ghaṭika* was an institution where students strove after higher knowledge.[13] According to Bhaṭṭa Someśvara (*c.* CE 1200), the commentator of the *vārttika* of Kumārila Bhaṭṭa (seventh century CE), when candidates appeared for examinations in the Vedas, they were asked questions based on different symbols, denoting different portions of the Vedas, written on bits of palm-leaves and placed inside a *ghaṭika* otherwise known as *kuṁbha* or pot.[14] It appears that the educational institution *ghaṭika* derived its name from the vessel *ghaṭika* by means of which arrangements were made to test the proficiency of the successful candidates in the Vedic examinations.

---

[10] *EI*, vol. VIII, p. 26, fn. 1.

[11] S.K. Aiyangar, *Evolution of Hindu Administrative Institutions in India*, Madras, 1931, p. 105.

[12] K.A. Nilakanta Sastri, *History of South India*, Madras, 1988, p. 154.

[13] C. Minakshi, *ASLP*, p. 224.

[14] S. Sankaranarayanan, *The Viṣṇukuṇḍins and Their Times*, Delhi, 1977, pp. 236-38.

The most important *ghaṭika* of the period of the Pallavas was at Kāñcīpuram. The earliest inscriptional evidence referring to this *ghaṭika* is the Tāḷaguṇḍa pillar inscription of the Kadamba king Kākusthavarman which states that his ancestor, Mayūraśarman came to Kāñcī to study at this *ghaṭika*.[15] Moreas[16] has stated the date of Mayūraśarman to be CE 345-70. The *ghaṭika* in Kāñcīpuram to which Mayūraśarman sought admission must have been in existence for many years before the middle of the fourth century as it attained the prominence for pupils outside the Pallava kingdom to seek admission to it for higher learning.[17]

It seems that, in Kāñcīpuram, the examination system controlled by the king's officials was so tough that Mayūraśarman became angry because even after sincerely learning the Vedas, etc. under competent preceptors, a brāhmaṇa like him had to depend on the king for recognition of his own scholarship (*śākhām adhītyāpi yatnataḥ, brahmasiddhiḥ nṛpādhīnā*).[18] Hence, he quarrelled with the king's officials who were obviously in-charge of the examinations. His quarrel soon assumed a very significant political dimension and it ended with the foundation of the dynasty of the Kadambas of Banavāsī, a consequence which the Pallava had to acquiesce in for buying peace.[19]

Many Pallava inscriptions point to the connection between the Pallava kings and the functioning of the *ghaṭika*. Among the Pallava rulers, Skandaśiṣya, Mahendravarman II, Rājasiṁha and Nandivarman Pallavamalla were closely associated with

---

[15] *EI*, vol. VIII no. 5, pp. 24-26.

[16] G.K. Mores, *The Kadamba Kula*, Bombay, 1931, p. 14.

[17] C. Minakshi, *ASLP*, p. 224.

[18] S. Sankaranarayanan, "Sanskrit Education in Ancient Tamil Country (An Epigraphical Survey)", *ALB*, vol. 57, 1993, p. 8.

[19] Ibid.

this institution. The Velūrpāḷayam inscription records that the early Pallava king Skandaśiṣya seized the *ghaṭika* from Satyasena (*skandaśiṣya tato-bhavat dvijānām ghaṭikām rājñaḥ satyasenāj jahāra yaḥ*).[20] Although there is no unanimity among scholars as to who exactly this Satyasena was, it is obvious that he was an enemy of the Pallavas as the word seized (*jahāra*) in the verse implies. According to S. Sankaranarayanan, Satyasena was a Vākāṭaka king and had been managing the institution of the *ghaṭika*.[21]

The Kaśākuḍi plates record that Mahendravarman II founded a *ghaṭika* that housed some deities and brāhmaṇas and that his example was followed by his successors (*yasmāt prabhṛty alam avardhata dharma-karma devadvijanmaviṣayām ghaṭikām ca dātuḥ*)[22] and adds that Rājasiṁha founded a *ghaṭika* of the *caturvaidyaśālā* type (*cāturvaidyam avīviśat svaghaṭikām bhudevatā-bhaktitaḥ*).[23] The Velūrpāḷayam plates mention that this ruler reorganized the *ghaṭika* of the twice-born (brāhmaṇas) and built a temple made of stone for Śiva.[24]

Meeting Place of the Ghaṭika

The information supplied by the Velūrpāḷayam plates that Rājasiṁha reorganized the *ghaṭika* and also built a temple for Śiva is found in one and the same verse. According to Minakshi, the construction of the Kailāsanātha temple and the reorganization of the *ghaṭika* by Narasiṁhavarman II (Rājasiṁha), connecting the *ghaṭika* with the Kailāsanātha temple indicates that the location of the *ghaṭika* may be in that temple.[25]

---

[20] *SII*, vol. II no. 98, v. 7, p. 508 (Velūrpāḷayam plates).

[21] S. Sankaranarayanan, op. cit., p. 8.

[22] *SII*, vol. II no. 73, v. 23, p. 349 (Kaśākuḍi plates).

[23] Ibid., v. 25, p. 345; S. Sankaranarayanan, op. cit., pp. 8-9.

[24] Velūrpāḷayam plates, op. cit., v. 13, p. 508.

[25] C. Minakshi, *ASLP*, p. 227.

It may be presumed that Rājasiṁha constructed the *mahāmaṇḍapa* (big hall) in front of the Kailāsanātha temple to enable the members of the *ghaṭika* at Kāñcīpuram to meet there to study.[26] It appears that this *ghaṭika* continued to function even during the Coḷa period and was located to the east of the Kailāsanātha temple as seen from a Tamil epigraph in this shrine belonging to the period of Rājendra I (CE 1012-44).[27]

Members of the Ghaṭika

Some information about the members who constituted the *ghaṭika* is forthcoming from the inscriptions. This educational institution seems to have been composed of brāhmaṇas well-versed in Vedic and Vedāntic scriptures. The Kaśākuḍi plates refer to this institution as *ghaṭikām bhūdevatām,* i.e. "the *ghaṭika* of the *deva*s of the earth" (brāhmaṇas).[28] The Velūrpāḷayam grant refers to the *ghaṭika* as *dvijānām ghaṭikām,* i.e. the *ghaṭika* of the twice-born (brāhmaṇas).

The members of the *ghaṭika* seem to have played a crucial role in the political sphere also. A Tamil inscription found in the Vaikuṇṭha Perumāḷ temple in Kāñcīpuram records that the *ghaṭikaiyār*s (members of the *ghaṭika*) were instrumental in bringing about the accession of Nandivarman Pallavamalla along with other officials when there was chaos in the Pallava kingdom following the death of Parameśvaravarman II.[29] Minakshi has opined that the *ghaṭikaiyār*s are shown as participating in the coronation ceremony of Nandivarman Pallavamalla in the series of historical sculptures found in the Vaikuṇṭha Perumāḷ temple. The esteem in which the *ghaṭika* and its members were held is brought out by an epigraph of the Cāḷukyan ruler Vikramāditya

---

[26] C. Minakshi, *ASLP*, pp. 227-28.

[27] *ARE*, 240 of 1930/31.

[28] Kaśākuḍi plates, op. cit.

[29] *SII*, vol. IV no. 35, pp. 10-12.

II (CE 734-44) in the Kailāsanātha temple.[30] It states that this ruler, after his conquest of Kāñcī, did not confiscate the property of the temple but returned it to the god. It adds that "those who destroy these letters and the stability of the king's charity which was thus given shall enter into the world of those who had killed the great group of men (*mahājana*) of this *ghaṭika*".

Subjects Taught at the Ghaṭika

There is no direct epigraphical evidence pinpointing to the subjects taught at the *ghaṭika*. However, since the brāhmaṇas in the Pallava, Pāṇḍya and the Coḷa periods were famous as teachers mainly of the Vedas, Vedāṅgas and other religious texts, and since the epigraphical evidence indicates that the *ghaṭika* was composed of brāhmaṇas, it may be safely assumed that these were the subjects taught in this educational institution.

The Tāḷaguṇḍa Pillar Inscription also gives some information on the nature of study in the *ghaṭika*. This record mentions that Mayūraśarman, a brāhmaṇa (*dvijottama*), the founder of the Kadamba dynasty came to Kāñcīpuram with his *guru* Vīraśarman to study the whole of the scriptures (*pravacanam nikhilam*) and entered the *ghaṭika* directly (*āśu*) as an inquirer (*tārkika*). Since Mayūraśarman came to Kāñcī along with his *guru* not as a beginner, but as one who was well-versed in the Vedas, it appears that the *ghaṭika* must have been a centre of higher studies.

T.N. Subrahmanian has opined that military science was also taught at the *ghaṭika* at Kāñcī, stating that when Mayūraśarman quarrelled with a Pallava horseman, he was able to wield the flashing weapons of warfare with the hand accustomed to handling the *kuśa* grass and other sacrificial oblations and carve out a kingdom of his own.[31] Some Tamil

---

[30] *EI*, vol. III no. 48, pp. 359-60.

[31] *SITI*, vol. III pt. II, p. 9.

epigraphs such as the Pārthivaśekharapuram inscription of the Ay ruler Karunandaḍakkan reveal that military science was taught at educational institutions called *śālais*.[32] It is therefore possible that military science was one of the subjects of study at the *ghaṭika* also.

Other than the famous *ghaṭika* at Kāñcīpuram, there existed *ghaṭika*s at other places in the Pallava kingdom as seen from numerous Tamil inscriptions.[33] One of these was probably located at Śoḷingūr in erstwhile North Arcot district. The hill atop which is situated the famous Narasiṁha temple is known as Ghaṭikācala and it is thus possible that this educational institution functioned here. The famous Vaiṣṇava saint, Tirumaṅgai Āḻvar has mentioned this hill in his *Siriya Tirumaḍal*[34] and hence this place is as old as the eighth century CE since this saint was a contemporary of the Pallava ruler Nandivarman II Pallavamalla (CE 731-96).

Many inscriptions of the Coḷa times also mention the existence of *ghaṭika*s at various places in the Coḷa empire. A Tamil epigraph found on the wall of the central shrine of the Vedapurīśvara temple at Tirukaḷittaṭṭai states that there was a *ghaṭikai*.[35] The signatories of this record and in two more similar inscriptions[36] found here were highly learned brāhmaṇas (*kramivits*, *somayājins* and *bhaṭṭas*), living in various places in the town to Vembaṟṟūr (also called Śoḷamārtaṇḍa-caturvedimaṅgalam) of which Tirukaḷittaṭṭai was a hamlet. They are known as *ghaṭika madhyastara* and their appearance as signatories of official transactions of the village shows that these scholars also held positions of importance. The word

---

[32] *PCP*, pp. A-1 to A-4 (Pārthivaśekharapuram plates).

[33] C. Minakshi, *ASLP*, p. 23.

[34] S. Gurumurthy, *Education in South India*, Madras, 1979, p. 10.

[35] *ARE*, 293 of 1908.

[36] *ARE*, 292 and 294 of 1908.

ghaṭika madhyastara, appearing as the prefix to the name of a person, reveals that he was an arbitrator of the *ghaṭika* of the village or a member who acted as an intermediary officer of the *ghaṭika*.[37]

It may be mentioned in passing that similar *ghaṭika*s also existed in the ancient Karnataka area. A copper-plate inscription of Trailokyamalla, the Western Cāḷukyan king dated CE 1058, gives details about a grant of land for the maintenance of brāhmaṇas in the Nāgavāvi *agrahāra*.[38] This village, now called Nagai (Gulbarga district), was once known as Nāgavāpi or Nāgavāvi and it was a well-known educational centre. Provision was made for the maintenance of a *ghaṭikasthāna* and 200 scholars studying the Vedas and fifty-two scholars studying other Śāstras. This institution had a library too and the record mentions six librarians (*sarasvatī bhaṇḍārigas*) of the place indicating that this must have been a very large library.[39]

It appears that the *ghaṭika*s played an important role in fostering Tamil language and literature also. The Tamil inscriptions belonging to the Pāṇḍya period of the end of the thirteenth century CE, from Tirukkaciyūr (Chengalpet district) reveal the existence of a Tamil college in the village of Kāvanūr in the same district in this period and mention the name of this institution as *ghaṭika*.[40] A study of these epigraphs reveals that the *ghaṭika* at Kāvanūr was an educational institution or an academy of learned scholars who were all proficient in Tamil language and literature.[41]

---

[37] S. Gurumurthy, op. cit., p. 11.

[38] *HAS*, no. 8, p. 7.

[39] S. Leela Shantakumari, *History of Agrahāras* (*Karnataka, 400-1300*), Madras, 1986, pp. 106-07.

[40] *ARE*, 51 of 1932-33 and *ARE* 333 of 1917.

[41] S. Gurumurthy, op. cit., p. 68.

Simhavarman

Many of the inscriptions of the early Pallava kings, as seen earlier, record the donation of land to scholars of the Vedas. Interestingly, there is an inscription of *c.* CE 550, datable to the reign of Simhavarman, called the Paḷḷaṇkovil copper-plate epigraph, which provides important information about the Jain settlements at Tiruparuttikuṉṟam near Kāñcīpuram.[42] According to the Sanskrit part of this bi-lingual record, there existed a Jain monastery called Nandisaṁgha at the holy place (*dharmatīrtha*) of Śrī Vardhamāna, consisting of many virtuous teachers, among whom Vajranandi, a scholar in all sacred literature, was one. The village of Śramaṇāśrama (hermitage of the Śramaṇas) was donated to this ascetic for the worship of the *jinendras*, *jainendras* and *munindras* by Siṁhavarman.

The Tamil portion of this inscription records that in his sixth regnal year, Siṁhavarman gave the village of Amaṇśerkkai in Perunagara-nāḍu as *paḷḷicandam* to the religious teacher, Vajranandi of Paruttikuṉṟil (Tiruparuttikuṉṟam). It also registers the grant of another $16^1/_2$ *paṭṭī*s of land in Dāmar village to this Jain teacher.

Siṁhaviṣṇu (sixth century CE)

Siṁhaviṣṇu (Avanisiṁha), the son of Siṁhavarman and father of Mahendravarman I, other than being one of the greatest conquerors of the early Pallava times, was also a patron of Sanskrit learning. Bhāravi, the famous composer of the Sanskrit poem *Kirātārjunīyam* lived in his court.[43] Bhāravi was invited by Siṁhaviṣṇu and stayed in the Pallava capital Kāñcīpuram, having married locally and set up a family.[44]

---

[42] *PJCG*, pp. 41-83.

[43] C. Minakshi, *ASLP*, pp. 14-15.

[44] Ibid., pp. 336-37.

Incidentally, the Gaṅga king Durvinīta (*c*. CE 540–600), the son of the scholar-king Avinīta (*c*. CE 500-40), was the author of a commentary on fifteen cantos of the *Kirātārjunīyam* of Bhāravi (*kirātārjunīya-pañcadaśa-sarga-ṭīkā-kāraḥ*).[45] It is also believed that poet Bhāravi himself adorned the Gaṅga court for some time and that, on that poet's recommendation, his young poet-friend Dāmodara, the great-grandfather of Daṇḍin (of *Kāvyādarśa-Daśakumāracarita* fame), lived in the Gaṅga court for a short period before he finally moved to and settled in the Pallava court at Kāñcīpuram.[46] Thus, the kings of the western Gaṅga dynasty, who ruled over Gaṅgavāḍī (southern Karnataka) with Talakkāḍ (Tālavanapura) on the banks of the river Kāverī (near Śivasamudram) as their capital, were, at the same time as the other powers of south India, great patrons of Sanskrit education and literature.

Daṇḍin, the well-known Sanskrit poet who flourished in the reign of Rājasiṁha Pallava (*c*. CE 691–728), refers to his ancestry in the introductory portions of the *Avantīsundarīkathā*.[47] According to this account, Daṇḍin's great grandfather, Dāmodara, hailed from Acalapura in Gujarat and was a great friend of Bhāravi. Through the latter, he met the Cāḷukyan ruler Kubja Viṣṇuvardhana and later met the Gaṅga king Durvinīta and became attached to his court. Siṁhaviṣṇu, the Pallava ruler of Kāñcī, having heard about Dāmodara, invited him by giving him a *brahmadeya* village and several other gifts. Dāmodara was a great scholar and two of his works are *Gandhamādana* and a *lakṣaṇa grantha* for Sanskrit and Prākṛt *kāvyas*.[48]

---

[45] S. Sankaranarayanan, "Sanskrit Education in Ancient Karnataka", *ALB*, no. 58 (1994), pp. 104-05.

[46] S. Sathianathaier, *A Political and Cultural History of India*, vol. I (*Ancient India*), Madras, 1952; S. Sankaranarayanan, *Sanskrit Education in Ancient Karnataka*, op. cit., pp. 105-06.

[47] *Avantīsundarīkathā*, ed. G. Harihara Sastri, Madras, 1957.

[48] Ibid.; C.S. Sundaram, *Contribution of Tamil Nadu to Sanskrit*, Chennai, 1999, p. 165.

Mahendravarman I (c. CE 600-30)

Among the illustrious monarchs of the Pallava dynasty, Mahendravarman I occupies a unique place. This scholar-king was multi-faceted with interest in various fields such as literature, the fine-arts like music and painting, and temple art and architecture. Two inscriptions of this ruler which are in Sanskrit, one from Pallavaram[49] and another from Tirucirāpaḷḷi[50] record his title *Mattavilāsa*. This king composed the well-known farcical play in Sanskrit called *Mattavilāsaprahasana*, this name being derived from his title. His epigraph from Māmaṇḍūr mentions the *Mattavilāsaprahasana* (*Mattavilāsādipadam-prahasanottamam*) in line 6.[51] In this play, the king mentions explicitly that it is a composition of Mahendravikrama of the Pallava family and the son of Siṁhaviṣṇu.[52] Another Sanskrit play, *Bhagavadajjukam* has also been assigned to Mahendravarman I.[53] A fragment of line 6 mentioned earlier, *magavadajjuka* which is just before *mattavilāsadīpadam-prahasanottamam* is no doubt a reference to the work *Bhagavadajjukam* of this king.[54] It can also be seen from some of his inscriptions that this ruler was a lover of logic.[55] The epigraph in the cave-temple at Tirucirāpaḷḷi[56] and the Pallavaram[57] inscriptions mention *anumāna* (logician) as one of his *biruda*s. The Pallavaram epigraph also contains the title *upamānaḥ*, which once more reveals his interest in logic.

---

49 *SII*, vol. XII no. 13, p. 7.

50 *SII*, vol. XII no. 8, p. 6.

51 *SII*, vol. IV no. 136, p. 12.

52 *Mattavilāsaprahasana*, ed. N.P. Unni, Trivandrum, 1974, p. 41.

53 C. Minakshi, *ASLP*, p. 336.

54 T.V. Mahalingam, *Inscriptions of the Pallavas*, New Delhi, 1988, p. 115.

55 R. Nagaswamy, *Mahendra's Inscription from Tirucirāpaḷḷi*, from *Studies in Ancient Tamil Law and Society*, Madras, 1978, pp. 22-24.

56 *SII*, vol. XII no. 8, p. 5 (Tirucirāpaḷḷi inscription).

57 *SII*, vol. XII no. 13, p. 7 (Pallavaram inscription).

The Māmaṇḍūr inscription of this ruler gives a description of the interest he had in poetry.[58] According to T.N. Ramachandran:

> He was an admirer of poets like Vālmīki, Bharata and other *kavīs* and moving, as he did, in a galaxy of poetical stars, he has given us in his many inscriptions and in the two farces that have luckily been discovered, his achievements in the field of poetry.[59]

He was the royal poet-laureate of the day.[60] According to some scholars, Mahendravarman I was the composer of the Tirucirāpaḷḷi cave inscription.[61] Mahendravarman I also bore the *biruda citrakārapuli* (tiger among artists) which reveals his interest and proficiency in the art of painting.[62] His inscription in Māmaṇḍūr mentions that he caused to compile a commentary (*vṛtti*) called *Dakṣiṇacitrā* (south Indian art or painting), following the methods and rules laid down for such a work (*yathāvidhi*), after classifying the subject from an old work.[63] It is evident that he analysed the subject of painting that was laid down in an earlier work (*kalpa*) which was probably cumbrous or not clear or which had perhaps to be revised in the light of later inventions in the field.[64]

Parameśvaravarman I (CE 670-91)

The son of Mahendravarman II and grandson of Narasiṁhavarman I, Parameśvaravarman was a devotee of

---

[58] *SII*, vol. IV no. 136, p. 12.

[59] T.N. Ramachandran, "The Royal Artist, Mahendravarman", *IJOR*, vol. 7, p. 308.

[60] Ibid.

[61] P.R. Srinivasan, *Gaṅgādarāṣṭakam in Pallava Inscription from Tirucirāpaḷḷi* from *Śrīnidhiḥ (K.R. Srinivasan Felicitation Volume)*, Madras, 1983, p. 434.

[62] Pallavaram inscription, op. cit.

[63] Māmaṇḍūr inscription, op. cit., p. 12.

[64] T.N. Ramachandran, op. cit., p. 237

Śiva. Some of his inscriptions provide a glimpse into his contribution to the field of education. The Kūram copper-plate inscription of this king mention that he was fond of poetry (*kāvya*).[65] The Vuṇṇa Guruvapālem copper-plate charter of Parameśvaravarman I of his nineteenth regnal year, issued from Kāñcīpuram, granted a village to Devaśarman, son of Droṇaśarman, who was well-versed in the Śāstras, Yama, Niyama and an expert in the teachings of the Vedas, Vedāṅgas, Itihāsa, Purāṇa, as a *brahmadeya*, exempting it from all obligations.[66] This inscription also records a gift of this king of the village of Parameśvaramaṅgalam to the Vidyāvinīta-Pallava-Parameśvara temple at Kūram (near Kāñcīpuram) to provide for worship, bathing of the image, etc., and also for the *Bharatākhyāna*, which is the recitation of Bharata (*Mahābhārata*) in this temple.[67] Incidentally, this inscription states that the village of Kūram had 108 families that studied the four Vedas. The Tamil portion of the Kūram inscription states that the village of Parameśvaramaṅgalam was granted with the condition that the village should be divided into twenty-five shares, of which three shares were to be used for worship and repairs in the temple, one for reciting the *Bhāratam* in the same place and the remaining twenty shares as *brahmadeya* to twenty Caturvedins.

Narasiṁhavarman II (c. CE 691–728)

Better known by his title Rājasiṁha, Narasiṁhavarman II, the son of Parameśvaravarman I, is best known for his contribution to temple art and architecture. However, from his many inscriptions, it is clearly seen that this king was a scholar and also a patron of the learned. The Kailāsanātha (Rājasiṁheśvara) temple in Kāñcīpuram, constructed during the reign of this

---

65 *SII*, vol. I no. 151, p. 148 (Kūram plates).

66 *EI*, XXXII no. 9, pp. 96-98.

67 Kūram plates, op. cit.

monarch has, etched on its walls, approximately 300 titles (*biruda*s) of this king which offer a glimpse of this royal personage. A number of these titles such as *Śrī Itihāsa Priyaḥ* (one who is fond of Itihāsas) and *Śrī Kāvya Prabodhaḥ* (the reviver of poetry) reveal his scholarly bent of mind.[68] Another inscription in this temple describes Rājasiṁha as *vidita bahunayaḥ* (having mastered many sciences).[69] The Kandasvāmi temple in Tirupporūr (near Chennai) has an inscription of this king enumerating many of his titles, one of them being *Jñāna Sāgaraḥ* (the ocean of knowledge).[70] This king's interest and proficiency in music are clearly seen in his titles like *Śrī Vādya Vidyādharaḥ* (a *vidyādhara* on the instrument), *Śrī Ātodya Tuṁburu* (he who resembles Tuṁburu on the knowledge of musical instruments) and *Śrī Vīṇā Nāradaḥ* (he who resembles Nārada in the playing of the *vīṇā*).[71]

Rājasiṁha's knowledge of elephant-science (Gajaśāstra) and his fondness for elephants are very evident from his titles *Śrī Ibha Vatsarājaḥ* (he who resembles the king of Vatsa in the knowledge of elephants), *Śrī Ibha Vidyādharaḥ* (one who possesses the knowledge of elephants) and *Śrī Vāraṇa Bhāgadattaḥ* (he who resembles Bhāgadatta in the knowledge of elephants).[72] The reference to the king of the Vatsa country made above is to Udayana, the husband of Vāsavadattā, who is well known in Sanskrit literature as one greatly proficient in elephant craft and the comparison of Rājasiṁha to Udayana is but appropriate.[73] The reference to Bhāgadatta made above is to a king of Prāgjyotiṣa about whom frequent references

[68] *SII*, vol. I no. 25, pp. 17-18.

[69] *SII*, vol. I no. 1, p. 12.

[70] *SII*, vol. XII no. 27, p. 12

[71] *SII*, vol. I no. 25, pp. 14-18.

[72] Ibid.

[73] C. Minakshi, "Elephant Lore in Pallava History", *QJMS*, vol. 28, 1937, p. 291.

occur in the *Mahābhārata* associating him always with elephants and describing him as one who "fought riding on his elephant Supratīkā".[74]

It would not be out of context to mention that the Gajaśāstra or elephantology, dealing with different aspects of elephants, their capture, taming, training, etc. has been of great interest to kings in India. The *Hastyāyurveda*, an ancient work ascribed to Pālakāpya; *Mataṅga-Līlā* of Nīlakaṇṭha and *Mṛgapakṣī Śāstra* by a Jain author named Haṁsadeva are three authoritative treatises on this subject.[75] The term *ibha* given in one of the titles of Rājasiṁha refers to one of thirteen types of elephants described in the *Mṛgapakṣī Śāstra*.[76]

Incidentally, the Reyūru copper-plate grant of this king, which was issued from Kāñcīpuram and which is composed in Sanskrit and written in the Telugu–Kannaḍa script, records the gift of the village of Reyūru (identified with the village of the same name in Ātmakūr village, Nellore district) as a *brahmadeya* to a brāhmaṇa named Kumāramaṇḍaśarman.[77] This donee, referred to in this charter as *somayājin*, belonged to a learned family. Both his father Kumāraśarman and grandfather Kulaśarman were proficient in two Vedas. The latter is said to have known the essence of the Vedas, Vedāṅgas, Itihāsa and Purāṇas. The donee belonged to the Rathitara *gotra* and was a student of the *Āpastamba-Sūtra*. It is interesting to note the occurrence of the term *dvedapāraga*, qualifying all the three members of the family; evidently it is an abbreviation of *dvi-veda-pāraga* and may be taken to be equivalent of *divedin*, i.e. *dvivedin*.[78] This royal order was addressed to the inhabitants

[74] C. Minakshi, "Elephant Lore in Pallava History", *QJMS*, vol. 28, 1937, p. 291.

[75] Ibid., p. 290.

[76] Ibid.; *Mṛgapakṣīśāstra*, tr. M. Sundaracharya, Kalahasti, 1927.

[77] *EI*, vol. XXIX no. 11, p. 96.

[78] Ibid., p. 93.

of Reyūru and it was enjoined on pain of corporal punishment upon all ministers along with their subordinate officials, all officers of the state and all the courtiers that they should collect no dues whatsoever from the village.

It is the opinion of some scholars that Daṇḍin, who composed the famous Sanskrit works *Daśakumāracarita*, *Kāvyādarśa* and *Avantīsundarīkathā*, lived in Kāñcīpuram during the reign of Rājasiṁha. In his *Kāvyādarśa*, Daṇḍin mentions a Śaiva king Rājavarman, who judging from the manner in which he is introduced, should have been a contemporary of the author and was probably Rājasiṁha, whose inscriptions reveal that he was a devotee of Śiva.[79] M. Rangachariar has mentioned a tradition with reference to chapter five of the *Kāvyādarśa* that it was composed by Daṇḍin for giving lessons in rhetoric to a prince in Kāñcīpuram who was possibly Rājasiṁha's son.[80] According to other scholars, it was probably Rājasiṁha himself who was Daṇḍin's student.[81] From his works, it appears that Daṇḍin who was well-acquainted with life in royal courts and that he lived a happy life in affluent circumstances.[82] It was at Kāñcīpuram that Daṇḍin is believed to have composed the *Avantīsundarīkathā* and *Daśakumāracarita* during his long stay at the Pallava court.[83]

According to Minakshi, the series of dramas published in Travancore as those of Bhāsa are presumed to have been composed in the Pallava court.[84] Some scholars are of the view that *Svapnavāsavadattā* and certain other works of the series were special abridged versions of Bhāsa's works, prepared

---

[79] R. Narasimhachar, "Bhāmaha and Daṇḍi," *Ind. Ant.*, 1912, p. 92.

[80] Ibid.

[81] R. Gopalan, *History of the Pallavas of Kāñcī*, Madras, 1928, pp. 110-11.

[82] M.R. Kale, *Daśakumarācarita of Daṇḍin*, Delhi, 1977, Introd., p. xxi; D.K. Gupta, *A Critical Study of Daṇḍin and His Works*, Delhi, 1970, pp. 96-97.

[83] C. Minakshi, *ASLP*, p. 337.

[84] Ibid.

for staging them before a Pallava king at Kāñcī. These plays bear a close resemblance to *Mattavilāsaprahasana* of Mahendravarman I, but from their colophons, the Pallava king has been identified with Rājasiṁha.[85]

Nandivarman II Pallavamalla (CE 731-96)

Nandivarman II Pallavamalla (who till his accession was called Parameśvara), belonged to a collateral branch of the Pallava family (i.e. the descendants of Siṁhavarman, through Bhīmavarman, the brother of Siṁhaviṣṇu). Nandivarman II was the son of Hiraṇyavarman and the details of the events leading to his accession are given in a Tamil inscription of his reign on the walls of the Vaikuṇṭha Perumāḷ temple.

A few of the copper-plate inscriptions issued during his reign give some information to show that this king too was of a scholarly bent of mind. The Kaśākuḍi copper-plate grant, in the *praśasti* part, eulogizes the emperor by comparing him with various great heroes of epic and Purāṇic literature. The poet of this inscription, Trivikrama, compares him with Bṛhaspati, the preceptor of the *devas* (*tantrālāpa-vidhau-svayam nayabharaḥ*),[86] adding that he was like Vālmīki in composing poetry (*kavitā-bandhe sa ādyaḥ kaviḥ*).[87] The Udayendiram copper-plate grant of this king mentions that Nandivarman II was well-versed in poems, dramas and stories (*kāvya nāṭakākhyāyikāśu pravīṇaḥ*).[88] This epigraph also mentions that this king was skilled in metres such as *bindumatī*, *gūḍacaturthapāda*, *praheḷika*, *akṣaracyutaka*, *mātrācyutaka* and similar verses.[89] The Kaśākuḍi copper-plate grant states that he was "like the king of Vatsa with respect to the science of elephants and music" (*vāraṇa tantra-vādya viṣaye*

[85] C. Minakshi, *ASLP*, p. 338.

[86] Kaśākuḍi plates, op. cit., v. 29, p. 350.

[87] Ibid.

[88] *SII*, vol. II no. 74, l. 27, p. 365 (Udayendiram plates).

[89] Ibid.

vatseśvaraḥ).[90] Thus, he was like his predecessor Rājasiṁha, who evinced much interest both in the science of elephants (Gajaśāstra) and also in music.

The Udayendiram copper plates also mention that he resembled the king of Vatsa in the knowledge and science of elephants (*vatsarāja iva kuñjareṣu*).[91] Nandivarman Pallavamalla's fondness for elephants is seen from information found in the Tandantoṭṭam copper-plate grant of his reign, which mentions that after his victory over a contemporary Gaṅga king, he captured an elephant called Paṭṭavardhana.[92] In fact, Gaṅga history is replete with references to the love of their monarchs for elephants. Śrīpuruṣa (CE 726–88), the Gaṅga king who was the contemporary of Nandivarman Pallavamalla was the author of an important work in Sanskrit on elephants known as *Gajaśāstra*[93] and Śrīmāra Śrīpuruṣa's son Śivamāra II (CE 788–816) wrote the *Gajāṣṭaka* in Sanskrit which was of great poetical merit.

Incidentally, the verse of the Kaśākuḍi inscription mentioned earlier, compares Nandivarman II with Karṇīsuta in acquaintance with the arts (*kālaparicaye karṇīsutaḥ*). This clearly refers to Mūladeva or Karṇīsuta, believed to be the first propounder of the science of thieving.[94] The *Hārāvaḷi* of Puruṣottama Deva mentions Karṇīsuta, Kharapaṭa, Mūladeva and Kalaṅkura as synonyms.[95] According to ancient Indian

[90] Kaśākuḍi plates, op. cit., p. 249.

[91] *SII*, vol. II no. 74, l. 19, p. 366.

[92] *SII*, vol. II no. 99, v. 7, p. 515.

[93] C. Minakshi, "Elephant Lore in Pallava History", *QJMS*, vol. 28, 1937, pp. 290-92.

[94] M. Bloomfield, "Character and Adventures of Mūladeva", *Proceedings of the American Philosophical Society*, LII: 616-50; K. Anantalakshmi, "*The Art of Stealing in Sankskrit Literature*" (MA dissertation, University of Madras).

[95] Pandit G. Harihara Sastri, "Kharapata and Mūladeva", *Asutosh Memorial Volume*, Patna, 1926-28, p. 225; K. Anantalakshmi, op. cit.

tradition, the art of thieving was one in the list of many fine arts in which a prince had to excel. Daṇḍin who lived in the Pallava times, mentions in the *pūrvapīṭhikā* of his Sanskrit drama *Daśakumāracarita* that princes had to be proficient in various arts, including the art of thieving and gambling.[96] *Kalvum karru mara* (thieving must be learnt and later forgotten) is an old Tamil proverb.

Karṇīsuta and his proficiency in the art of thieving are referred to in many Sanskrit works like *Harṣacarita*.[97] In some Sanskrit texts, Karṇīsuta is also described as the master of all the fine arts. The *Bhāṇa Padmaprābhṛtaka*, believed to have been written by Śūdraka, states that Karṇīsuta was the master of the arts.[98] The *Kalāvilāsa* mentions that Mūladeva was a teacher of the arts.[99]

Karṇīsuta was also well known in the ancient Tamil country. The famous Tamil work *Śilappadikāram* contains a reference to a work on the science of theft by Mūladeva.[100] In his *Daśakumāracarita*, Daṇḍin refers to Karṇīsuta[101] and the same author, in his *Avantīsundarīkathā*, describes Karṇīsuta as a teacher of the art of thieving.[102] A thieves' manual called *Cora Śāstra* (science of theft) or the *Steya Śāstra* is mentioned in many Sanskrit works. In the Sanskrit play, *Mattavilāsaprahasana*, its author, Mahendravarman I refers to Kharapaṭa as the author

---

96 M.R. Kale, *Daśakumāracarita of Daṇḍin*, Delhi, 1997, Purvapīṭhikā; K. Anantalakshmi, op. cit.

97 *Harṣacarita of Bhāṇabhaṭṭa*, ed. P.V. Kane, Delhi, 1965.

98 Pandit G. Harihara Sastri, op. cit., p. 226.

99 *Minor Works of Kṣemendra*, ed. Aryendra Sarma, Hyderabad, 1961, p. 200; Pandit G. Harihara Sastri, op. cit.; K. Anantalakshmi, op. cit.

100 V.R. Ramachandra Dikshitar, *Studies in Tamil Literature and History*, Madras, 1982, p. 76; K. Anantalakshmi, op. cit.

101 M.R. Kale, *Daśakumāracarita*, op. cit., pp. 76 and 102.

102 *Avantīsundarīkathā*, ed. K.S. Mahadeva Sastri Trivandrum, 1954; see also Pandit G. Harihara Sastri, op. cit., p. 225.

of the *Cora Śāstra*.[103] According to a commentator on the *Daśakumāracarita*, Karṇīsuta authored the *Steya Śāstra*.[104]

The talented poet of the *praśasti* section of the Kaśākuḍi epigraph, who being a Sanskrit scholar living in the Tamil country, must have been familiar with the references to Karṇīsuta found in the Sanskrit texts, including the Pallava king's *Mattavilāsaprahasana* as well as the Tamil *Śilappadikāram*. He, therefore, in his composition — the Kaśākuḍi plates — wished to compare his patron, Nandivarman Pallavamalla, who was well-versed in various arts, with Karṇīsuta. However, Karṇīsuta was best known in connection with the art of burglary since the texts of the Pallava age namely *Mattavilāsaprahasa*, *Daśakumāracarita* and *Avantīsundarīkathā* refer to him only in this context. Perhaps, this scholar-composer of the Kaśākuḍi plates, Trivikarama, wanted to compare this king with this arch-thief, as the art of thieving was, in any case, one of the many arts to be learnt by princes.

Some of the copper-plate grants of the reign of Nandivarman II record his gift of land to scholars and the creation of *caturvedimaṅgalam*s for them to reside in and propagate their knowledge. The Udayendiram copper-plate epigraph registers the grant of the village of Kumāramaṅgala-veḷḷaṭṭūr renamed as Udayacandramaṅgalam to 108 brāhmaṇas by this king at the request of a military officer named Udayacandra.[105] The names of sixty-four of the 108 donees, their *gotra*s and *sūtra*s and original place of residence are given at the end of this inscription. This grant has a Tamil endorsement at the end belonging to the reign of Parāntaka Coḷa I.

---

[103] *Mattavilāsaprahasana*, ed. N.P. Unni, Trivandrum, 1974; K. Anantalakshmi, op. cit., p. 41.

[104] M.R. Kale, *Daśakumāracarita*, p. 76; K. Anantalakshmi, op. cit.

[105] Udayendiram plates, op. cit., pp. 365-70.

The Kaśākuḍi plates of this ruler mention that Nandivarman Pallavamalla, at the instance of his chief minister Brahmaśrīrāja, granted the village of Koḍukoḷḷi, renamed as Ekadhīramaṅgalam (after Ekadhīra, one of the titles of Nandivarman Pallavamalla) after it became a *brahmadeya* and gave it to a learned brāhmaṇa named Jyeṣṭhapāda Somayājin, who belonged to the Bharadvāja *gotra* and followed the Chandoga *sūtra*.[106] The brāhmaṇa donee of the grant is praised in glowing terms as one who had "mastered the Vedas" (*chandapārāvārapāragāya*), "who chanted the *Sāman* (*Veda*) which are sweet because of their melody" (*svarasamadhura-sāmagāya*), "who had completed the study of the six auxiliary works, namely, the Vedic ritual, grammar, astronomy, etymology, phonetics and metrics" (*chandakalpa-vyākaraṇa-jyotiṣa-nirukta-śikṣā-chandovicitti-ṣaḍaṅga-saṁśita-svādhyāyanāya*), "who knows the properties of the words and their sentences" (*pada-dharma vākya-dharma vastu-dharma vidhāya*), "who has studied the Śruti and Smṛti" (*śruti-smṛti-rasāyana-pānaya*), "who is proficient in rites and knowledge" (*karmakāṇḍa-jñānakāṇḍa paṇḍitāya*), "who is skilled in the ways of the world" (*lokāyukti*), "skilled in the arts" (*kāla-kauśala-peśalāya*), "who is proficient in poems, dramas, stories, epics and legends" (*kāvya-naṭakhākyāyiketihasapūraṇaya*), "learned in all branches of holy and profane knowledge" (*kiṁbahuna sarvajñāna-vijñāna-tiṣṇātāya*), "accomplished in the performance of all rites" (*sarvakarmānuṣṭhāṇa-niṣṭitāya*), "of good conduct" (*suvṛtaya*) and "who is ranked the first among the brāhmaṇas" (*dvijanmāgragaṇyāya*).

Yet another epigraph of this king, the Pullūr copper-plate grant states that at the request of Avanicandra Yuvarāja, the lord of Vilvalapura, who was devoted to the Pallavas, this king made a grant of four villages — Nelli, Pullūr, Kuḍiyūr and

---

106 *SII*, vol. II no. 73, ll. 71-103, pp. 350-51.

Takkāṟu — situated on the south bank of river Ceyyār, clubbed together into one unit, and renamed Nayadhīramaṅgalam (after the king's surname Nayadhīra) to 108 learned brāhmaṇas (*bappa-bhaṭṭārakas*).[107] The names of the donees, and their *gotras*, *sūtras* and place of origin are enumerated in this inscription.

The Tandantoṭṭam plates of Nandivarman II registers that a person named Dayāmukha entitled Kumāra, the treasurer of this king, with the permission of Nandivarman II, granted a village to 308 brāhmaṇas and called it Dayāmukhamaṅgalam after his own name.[108] These brāhmaṇa donees are described as being very learned, having studied the three Vedas and the Smṛtis.[109]

The enumeration of the names and titles of the donees who belonged to various *gotras* and *sūtras* occupies more than eleven plates of this copper-plate record. However, only 244 names out of 308 are registered and it can be presumed that a few plates of the grant portion are lost.[110] The titles of the donees such as Caturvedin, Trivedin, Somayājin, Vasantayājin, Ṣaḍaṅgavid, Bhaṭṭa, Kramavid, Sarvakratuyājin, Daśapurīya, Agnicit and Vājapeyin reveal that most of them were learned men as stated above.

The names of the villages to which the donees belonged indicate that many of them must have been originally residents of the Telugu country.[111] The donees whose native villages may be presumed to have been situated in the Telugu country need not necessarily have immigrated at the time of the grant; they might have settled there some time before.[112] However, it is clear that there was a large colony of Telugu brāhmaṇas

[107] *EI*, vol. XXXVI no. 20, pp. 152-53.

[108] *SII*, vol. II no. 99, vv. 9-10, p. 520.

[109] Ibid., v. 9.

[110] Ibid., p. 517.

[111] *SII*, vol. II no. 99, v. 9, p. 519.

[112] Ibid.

in the heart of the Coḷa country during this time. It is also interesting to note that a large number of the village names mentioned here are held now as family names by Śrīvaiṣṇava families — Dvedaikomapuram (Vedagomapuram), Vaṅgipaṟṟu (Vaṅgipuram), Urupiṭṭūr (Urupuṭṭūr), Kārambicceḍu (Karambicceṭṭu), Śrīmalai (Tirumalai), Pattaṅgi, Vīravaḷḷi (Vīravalli), Muḍumbe, Taṇukkil, Kamāṇḍūr, Puttūr, Śeṭṭalūr and Kuṇḍūr, being some.[113] There are also many villages which have distinctly Tamil names. One of these, Maṇaṟkkāl, has evidently lent its name to one of the later Śrīvaiṣṇava *ācārya*s of the twelfth century, Maṇakkāl Nambi.[114]

Some of the donees seem to have belonged to other parts of the country. The name Daśapurīya, enumerated as the surname of one of the donees means "belonging to or an emigrant from Daśapura", a village identified with Maṇḍasor in Mālwā.[115] Two grants of the Gurjara chief Dadda IV Praśāntarāga, which are referred to about the middle of the seventh century CE, mention a donee who was an emigrant from Daśapura.[116] The spurious grant of Dharasena II, dated Śāka Saṁvat 400 also mentions a corporation of the Caturvedins of Daśapura.[117]

Incidentally, one share of the land donated was allotted to "the reciter of the *Bhārata* (*Mahābhārata*)".[118] It can thus be seen that the tradition of expounding the epics was well in place during the Pallava period, an earlier example being found in the Kūram plates of Parameśvaravarman I. The Tandantoṭṭam plates of Nandivarman II states that one share

---

[113] *SII*, vol. II no. 99, v. 9, p. 519.

[114] Ibid.

[115] Ibid., fn. 1.

[116] *SII*, vol. II no. 99, v. 9, p. 519; *EI*, vol. V, pp. 38f.

[117] Ibid.

[118] Ibid., p. 534.

of land was assigned for "pouring water" and for "lighting fire" in the hall (*ambalam*); perhaps this was the hall where the village assembly used to meet and where the *Bhārata* was recited.[119]

The Paṭṭātaḷmaṅgalam copper-plate grant, also of Nandivarman II's reign, states that a chief officer of this king, ruling over the province of Maṅgaḷarāṣṭra and known as Maṅgaḷarāṣṭra-bhartṛ (the Lord of Maṅgaḷarāṣṭra) also called (in the Tamil portion of this charter as Maṅgaḷanāḍaḻvān) gave a *brahmadeya* to a number of learned brāhmaṇas after petitioning the king.[120] The *brahmadeya* comprised forty *velis* of land, which included an old *brahmadeya* of twenty-four *velis*, another *brahmadeya* of twelve *velis*, granted in the fifty-ninth year of the king's reign and the remaining four *velis* now assigned.[121] Like the Tandantoṭṭam plates, the titles of some of the brāhmaṇa donees are given in the Paṭṭātaḷmaṅgaḷam copper-plate epigraph too, like Trivedi, Ṣaḍangavid and Kramavid.[122]

Nandivarman III (CE 847-62)

Nandivarman III was the son of Dantivarman and the grandson of Nandivarman II. He was a patron of Tamil literature and the *Bhāratavenba* by Perundevanār was composed during his times, but unfortunately it survives only in parts.[123] The anonymous *Nandikkaḷambakam,* that has come down with many interpolations, is a quasi-historical poem of about eighty stanzas, dealing in various metres, with events of the reign of the last great Pallava monarch.[124] This book, which has Pallava

[119] *SII*, vol. II no. 99, v. 9, p. 519.

[120] *EI*, XVIII no. 14, v. 10, p. 121.

[121] Ibid., ll. 22-23.

[122] Ibid., p. 124.

[123] K.A. Nilakanta Sastri, *A History of South India*, Madras, 1988, p. 374.

[124] Ibid., p. 22.

Nandivarman III as hero, is trustworthy and of real value on the history of the time.[125]

This monarch, as seen from his inscriptions, also contributed to the spread of Sanskrit education in his land. The Kumaraḍimaṅgalam copper-plate grant of Nandivarman III states that this ruler gave the name of Kumaraḍimaṅgalam to the land (*brahmadeya*) in Nilanūru village which was given to twenty-four brāhmaṇas, well-versed in the Vedas on the request of Nayabhara Maṅgaḷamahārāja who was his minister. The names of the donees, their *gotra*s and *sūtra*s are given.[126]

The Veḷūrpāḷayam copper-plate inscription of Nandivarman III states that this king, at the instance of his minister Coḷa-mahārāja Kumārāṅkuśa, granted the village of Tirukkāṭṭupaḷḷi as *devadāna* to the temple of Yajñeśvara-Mahādeva at the village constructed by Caṇṇakuṟi Yajñabhaṭṭa. The latter, surnamed Bhaṭṭa-bhaṭṭāraka, was a profound scholar in the Śāstras, Vedas and *Sāṁkhya*.[127] The gift village, Tirukkāṭṭupaḷḷi, situated in Nāyaṟu-nāḍu, a sub-division of Pular-koṭṭam, has been identified with the place Kāṭupaḷḷi in Ponneri taluk of erstwhile Chengalpet district.[128]

Nṛpatuṅgavarman (ninth century CE)

Nandivarman III was one of the last few rulers of the line of the Pallavas. That he had two sons named Kaṁpavarman and Nṛpatuṅga was acknowledged by early scholars of south Indian history.[129] However, their relation to another Pallava

---

125 K.A. Nilakanta Sastri, *A History of South India*, Madras, 1988, p. 22.

126 N. Ramesan, "The Kumāraḍimaṅgalam Plates of the Pallava King Nandivarma III" from *Sri Mallampalli Somasekhara Sarma Commemoration Volume*, Hyderabad, 1976.

127 *SII*, vol. II no. 98, v. 22, p. 509 (Velūrpāḷayam plates).

128 T.V. Mahalingam, op. cit., p. 378, fn. 5.

129 T.V. Mahalingam, *Kanchipuram in Early South Indian History*, Madras, 1969, p. 221; R. Nagaswamy, *TVCP*, pp. 5-7.

king Aparājita was not clear. The discovery of a copper-plate inscription from Velāñjeri of Aparājita's ninth regnal year, is very important from the point of view of political history as it specifically mentions Apārajita as the son of Kaṁpavarman through Vijayā, a Gaṅga princess.[130] This inscription further shows that Kaṁpavarman and Aparājita had the support of the Gaṅga chieftains and that Kaṁpavarman captured the Pallava throne forcibly from Nṛpatuṅga.[131] According to R. Nagaswamy, when Kaṁpavarman the elder was alive, the younger, Nṛpatuṅga, though a boy, ascended the throne which obviously led to enmity between the two.[132] Nṛpatuṅga should have been chosen by Nandivarman III in preference to Kaṁpa, probably because of Rāṣṭrakūṭa influence; Nṛpatuṅga's mother Śaṅkhā being a Rāṣṭrakūṭa princess.[133] It is not known whether Nṛpatuṅga ascended the throne even when his father was alive or after his demise; but probably in his last years, Nandivarman installed Nṛpatuṅga.[134] Kaṁpavarman immediately after the demise of his father dislodged his brother, but treated him with moderately and even allowed him to issue charters. He also installed his son Aparājita very early as his co-regent.[135]

Some data about an educational institution of the Pallava times is available in the Bāhūr copper-plate inscription of Nṛpatuṅgavarman.[136] This important inscription records a land grant to a *vidyāsthāna* (seat of learning) at Vāgūr (present-day Bāhūr near Pondicherry). This centre of learning appears to

---

[130] R. Nagaswamy, op. cit.

[131] Ibid.

[132] Ibid., p. 7.

[133] Ibid.

[134] Ibid.

[135] Ibid.

[136] *EI*, vol. XVIII, pp. 9-12.

have been a well-established institution even before the time of their grant.[137] This bi-lingual record states that three villages called Ceṭṭupākkam, Viḷāṅgāṭṭaṅkaḍuvaṉūr and Iṟaippuṇaicceri were donated to this centre of learning by a chieftain called Mārtaṇḍa of the family of Veśālī, whose surname was Nilaitāṅgi, who in turn had received them from his king, Nṛpatuṅga. These villages were granted to the *vidyāsthāna* as a *brahmadeya* gift and the residents were to receive the revenues of the villages. The former residents of the three villages were dispossessed and the earlier charities and *brahmadeyas* were excluded. All the three villages had Vāgūr as a neighbour. The granted villages are attached to Vāgūr itself, thereby enjoying the *parihāra* and *vyavasthā* enjoyed by Vāgūr and these were made into a *brahmadeya*. This informative charter explicitly records that this grant was to be a *vidyā-bhoga* (source of revenue for the promotion of learning). This is perhaps the earliest case on record of a university scholarship or educational endowment.[138]

This inscription also gives some information on the subjects taught in this *vidyāsthāna*. According to H. Krishna Sastri, this educational organization in Bāhūr consisted of fourteen *gaṇa*s (*caturdaśa-gaṇakula*) and was controlled by the learned men of the village, being organized and maintained by them.[139] Minakshi has opined that this educational institution had a comprehensive curriculum consisting of fourteen *gaṇa*s (branches of learning which include the four Vedas, the six Vedāṅgas, the Purāṇas, the Mīmāṁsā system of philosophy, the Nyāya system and the Dharmaśāstras).[140] At the end of the Sanskrit *praśasti* portion of this epigraph is a verse which

---

[137] C. Minakshi, *ASLP*, p. 238.

[138] Bahur plates, op. cit., p. 8.

[139] C. Minakshi, *ASLP*, p. 206.

[140] Ibid., p. 207.

states that this part was composed by Nāgaya, who was a servant of the Vāgūr college.

Kopperuñjiṅga

Although this chapter deals mainly with the contribution of the dynasty of the imperial Pallavas to education, yet mention must be made of a Pallava chieftain named Kopperuñjiṅga. He was a petty chieftain of the thirteenth century CE who rose from near obscurity to the position of a ruler of a vast territory of south India. He claimed descent from the imperial Pallavas of Kāñcīpuram who were vanquished by the Coḷas in the ninth century CE, and it is indeed very ironical that this Pallava descendent should have been partly responsible for the fall of the great Coḷas.

His contribution to the religious and cultural spheres were many. He was a religious person and an ardent devotee of Śiva. This Kāḍava chieftain was also a great scholar. An inscription from Āṭṭur describes him as *Sāhityaratnākara* (ocean of literature).[141] In some of his inscriptions found at Tripurāntakam[142] and Drākṣārāma[143] in Andhra Pradesh, he is described as *Sarasa-Sāhitya-Sāmyātrikaḥ* (navigator in the ocean of literature).[144] This later Pallava ruler was also a poet as seen from an inscription from Tirupati which describes him as *Kavi Sārvabhauma* (emperor of poetry).[145] His love for the Tamil language is seen from a Tamil inscription in which is he called *peṇu sentamiḻ vaḻappiranda kāḍava* (the Kadava born to foster and protect Sentamiḻ).[146]

---

[141] *SII*, vol. II, p. 516.

[142] *SII*, vol. XII no. 120, pp. 58-59.

[143] *SII*, vol. XII no. 247, p. 155.

[144] *SII*, vol. IV no. 1352-B; p. 472; 491-C of 1893.

[145] *TTD Inscriptions*, vol. I no. 10, p. 18.

[146] *EI*, vol. XXIII no. 27, ll. 3-7, p. 180.

Epigraphical Poets

As with many of the other imperial dynasties of ancient India, the Pallava kings too must have patronized a number of poets. Most unfortunately, none of their works have survived to the present day. However, a study of the epigraphs of this age, especially the copper-plate charters and to a lesser extent the lithic inscriptions, reveals that these records are themselves works of poetry composed by poets of no ordinary calibre. At the end of the Sanskrit *praśasti* portion or at the end of the Tamil portion are one or a few verses giving the name of the poet who composed the Sanskrit *praśasti* and some details such as the family background and his educational qualifications.

An in-depth study of the copper-plate charters of the ancient and medieval periods in Tamil Nadu, which can be termed as *rāja-śāsana* (royal charter), *tāmra-śāsana* (royal order engraved on plates of copper) and *dāna-śāsana* (recording gifts) reveals that they follow a certain convention with regard to their composition. Beginning with a few verses in praise of various deities, they go on to describe the lineage, ancestry and achievements of the kings of the dynasty to which the donor of the charter belonged. They subsequently praise the qualities and achievements of the donor-king and then proceed to give the details of the grant or benefaction which was usually to one or many scholars or to a temple. The actual operative portion of the inscription, mentioning the various details of the gift and the officials in charge of carrying out the transactions, is usually in Tamil. The scholars who composed the Sanskrit portions of these copper-plate inscriptions were well-versed in Vaiṣṇavite and Śaivite lore as evident from the verses which are in praise of various deities and also in the places where they compare their patron-kings with various gods.

The Paḷḷankovil copper-plate inscription (CE 550) of the reign of Pallava Siṁhavarman is the earliest record in which mentions the name of the poet who composed the Sanskrit *praśasti* portion of this bi-lingual inscription.[147] The name of this poet was Medhāvi and the very last verse of this small poem consisting of nine verses which he composed provides some information about him as follows:

> *samasta śāstra niṣṇāta dhiṣano dhiṣanopamaḥ* |
> *mānyo nāmapi medhāvi praśastiṁ kr̥tavān imām* | |

> This eulogy (*praśasti*) was composed by Medhāvi who was immersed in all the sciences, who was very respectable and who was like Br̥haspati in intelligence.

These nine verses have been composed in beautiful metres like *upajātī, śārdūlavikrīḍita, pr̥thvī, indravajra* and *anuṣṭubh*. His descriptions of the Coḷa country and the river Kāverī are worthy of special mention.

The Udayendiram copper-plate inscription dated CE 746 belongs to the time of the famous Pallava ruler Nandivarman II Pallavamalla as seen earlier in this chapter.[148] This record is almost wholly in Sanskrit and is a *caṁpū-kāvya* (written partially in prose and partially in verse). The eight verses found here and composed in four metres are delightful to read as also the prose sections which are interspersed between the verses. The section, which eulogizes Udayacandra, the faithful and brave general of Nandivarman II his many victorious wars, reveals the mastery of the composer. It is describing in the very last verse that the name and some details of this poet are given. The verse states:

> *putraḥ śrī candradevasya kavistu parameśvaraḥ* |
> *praśasteḥ kavitāncakre sa medhāvi kulodbhavaḥ* | |

> The poet Parameśvara, who was the son of the illustrious Candradeva and who was born from the race of Medhāvin, made the poetry of the (above) eulogy (*praśasti*).

---

[147] *PJCG*, v. 9, p. 76.

[148] Udayendiram plates, op. cit., pp. 365-79.

This inscription, as seen earlier in this chapter, mentions that at the request of Udayacandra, his king, Nandivarman II gave to 108 brāhmaṇas, the village named Kumāramaṅgaḷa Veḷḷaṭṭūr and renamed it as Udayacandramaṅgalam to honour his great general. The poet Parameśvara was allotted one share in this village probably as a reward for composing this fine poem.[149]

The next poet-composer of a Pallava inscription whom we come across was the author of the Kaśākuḍi copper plates (CE 753-54) also of the reign of Nandivarman II Pallavamalla.[150] The Sanskrit part of this epigraph is again, like the Udayendiram plates, a beautiful *campū-kāvya* (written partially in prose and partially in verse). There are thirty-one stanzas altogether in various metres, deployed with great sensitivity, bearing in mind the import of the verses and the rest is in prose. The scholar-poet who composed this *campū-kāvya* was Trivikrama and he mentions in the last Sanskrit verse:

> *akr̥timas trayī vidhi krama kratu pravartakaḥ* |
> *samasta śāstra tatvavid praśastikr̥t trivikramaḥ* | |
>
> The author of the (above) *praśasti* was the honest Trivikrama, who knew the truth of all sciences (and) who performed sacrifices according to the rules of the three Vedas.[151]

Yet another copper-plate grant of Nandivarman II Pallavamalla is the Tandantoṭṭam inscription dated CE 789.[152] This too is a bi-lingual inscription, but here the Tamil portion is much longer than the Sanskrit *praśasti* which comprises fourteen verses set in seven different metres. These stanzas eulogize this ruler and mention the gift of a village named Dayāmukhamaṅgalam to 108 brāhmaṇas along with many other interesting details.

---

[149] Udayendiram plates, op. cit., p. 373.

[150] Kaśākuḍi plates, op. cit., pp. 346-53.

[151] Ibid., v. 31, p. 351.

[152] Tandantoṭṭam plates, op. cit., pp. 517-35.

The poet of these stanzas was Parameśvara surnamed Uttarakāraṇika.

> *paramottara kāraṇikasyākṛta kavitāsvayamvṛtavarasya* |
> *uttarakāraṇikākhyastanayaḥ parameśvaraḥ praśastimimām* | |

> This eulogy (*praśasti*) was drawn up by Parameśvara, surnamed Uttarakāraṇika, son of Paramottarakāraṇika, the self-chosen lord of poetry.[153]

Minakshi has opined that since the Udayendiram and the Tandantoṭṭam copper-plate inscriptions record gifts made in the period of Nandivarman II Pallavamalla and since the number of years separating the two inscriptions is only seven, it is possible that the poet Parameśvara who composed the *praśasti* of the Udayendiram inscription is the same as Parameśvara who had the surname Uttarakāraṇika who wrote the *praśasti* of the Tandantoṭṭam plates and that Candradeva the father of the poet can be identified with Paramottarakāraṇika.[154]

It is also worth mentioning that in the Udayendiram plates, Parameśvara is described as "one whose residence was in Uttarakākula".[155] The learned editor of this inscription has stated that Uttarakākula or northern Kākula could refer to the place Chicacole in the Gañjam district of Andhra Pradesh as distinguished from southern Śrīkākulam.[156]

The Udayendiram epigraph states very clearly that Parameśvara was born in the family of Medhāvi (*medhāvi kulodbhavaḥ*) and it seems clear that this Medhāvi was an ancestor of the family of Parameśvara and that he was a famous poet, perhaps one who composed similar *praśasti*s. It is very likely that Medhāvi who composed the Sanskrit portion of

---

[153] Tandantoṭṭam plates, op. cit., v. 14, p. 521.

[154] C. Minakshi, *ASLP*, p. 78.

[155] Udayendiram plates, op. cit., p. 373.

[156] Ibid., p. 373, n. 6.

the Paḷḷankovil grant was the ancestor of the composer of the Udayendiram charter.[157]

It is interesting to note that a very short and damaged stone inscription in Sanskrit found around the *garbha-gṛha* of the Vaikuṇṭha Perumāḷ temple in Kāñcīpuram which was built in the reign of Nandivarman II Pallavamalla, a great devotee of Viṣṇu in the eighth century CE, carries the name of the poet who composed it. This record in Grantha characters, datable to the second half of the eighth century CE has only two verses and mentions a gift to the Parameśvara Viṣṇugṛha (Vaikuṇṭha Perumāḷ temple). It clearly records the name of the poet as Manodhīra.[158] This epigraph could belong to the time of either Nandivarman II Pallavamalla or his son and successor Dantivarman who also donated to this temple as seen from a Tamil inscription in the same place in this temple.[159]

The Velūrpāḷayam copper plates (CE 852) consisting of thirty-one *śloka*s which form the major portion of this record interspersed with a short Tamil portion belongs to the reign of Nandivarman III.[160] The *praśasti* of this charter, the objective of which was the gift of the village of Śrīkāṭṭupaḷḷi or Tirukāṭṭupaḷḷi to a Śiva temple at the village constructed by one Yajñabhaṭṭa was composed by a poet named Maheśvara Manodhīra. The fourth-last verse of this inscription states:

vagma kāya karmāṇi parārthānyeva yasya saḥ |
maheśvara manodhīraḥ praśastim kṛtavānimām | |

Maheśvara Manodhīra, the act of whose words, thoughts and body were (all) for the benefit of others, composed this *praśasti*.[161]

It is therefore likely that poet Manodhīra of the short Sanskrit

---

157 T.N. Subrahmaniam, *PJCG*, p. 74.

158 *ARE*, 32 of 1888; *SII*, vol. IV no. 130.

159 *ARE*, 34 of 1888; *SII*, vol. IV no. 132A.

160 *SII*, vol. II no. 98, pp. 507-10.

161 *SII*, vol. II, v. 28, p. 509.

epigraph of the Vaikuṇṭha Perumāḷ temple, datable to the second half of the eighth century CE, was the very same poet-composer of the beautiful *praśasti* of the Velūrpaḷaiyam plates of the time of Nandivarman III dated CE 852. Since the Sanskrit record at the Vaikuṇṭha Perumāḷ temple does not mention the exact name of the ruler, Manodhīra could have been a poet in the royal court during the last few years of Nandivarman II Pallavamalla and continued to be so in the reigns of his son Dantivarman and grandson Nandivarman III.

During the Pallava and Coḷa times, it was a common practice for officials and other employees of the king to bear the name of their ruler. For example, the Bāhūr copper-plate grant of Nṛpatuṅgavarman mentions that this inscription was incised by a person named Nṛpatuṅga who was "a hereditary servant of the Pallava family" (*pallava kula mūla bhṛtyaḥ*).[162] According to Minakshi, this person was perhaps named after his sovereign Nṛpatuṅgavarman.[163] Similarly, it is perhaps likely that Maheśvara, the poet had the suffix Manodhīra which may have been a title of one of the Pallava emperors whom he served with distinction as court-poet and composed the royal charters.

Of the later Pallava rulers like Nṛpatuṅga and Aparājita, there are some copper-plate epigraphs which provide the names of the poets of the ninth century CE. Although the Pallava empire was by then on the wane, these kings encouraged and supported poets and scholars as per the tradition of their ancestors and their names were recorded for posterity in these documents. There are two bi-lingual copper-plate epigraphs of the time of Nṛpatuṅgavarman. The first of these is the Cirrur inscription dated CE 875 consisting of seventeen verses in as many as nine metres.[164] These stanzas were composed by a poet named Kumāra who is described thus:

---

[162] *EI*, vol. XVIII no. 2, v. 32, p. 12.

[163] C. Minakshi, *ASLP*, p. 75.

[164] T.V. Mahalingam, *Inscriptions of the Pallavas*, pp. 439-46.

kṛtavān nakṛtaka hṛdayaḥ kṛtīkṛtagñyaḥ ।
kaviḥ kumārākyaḥ vidyānadhyāmbhu nidhiḥ ।
praśasta-śilāḥ praśastim imām ।।[165]

The Bāhūr copper-plate record of the same king written two years after the Ciṟṟūr record in CE 877 consists of thirty-two verses in four metres.[166] It contains very important data about a seat of learning (*vidyāsthāna*), already mentioned in this chapter. The poet who composed this charter was Nāgaya and a verse in this grant describes him thus:

dāsaḥ sthānasya vidyāya vāgūr grāmajuṣam imām ।
kṛtavān śāstra tattvajñaḥ praśastiṁ nāgayas sukṛt ।।

The servant of the seat of learning of the residents of the village of Vāgūr, the pious Nāgaya, who knew the truth of sciences, composed this *praśasti*.[167]

The very last inscription of the Pallavas which provides the name of the *praśasti* composer is the Velāñjēri copper-plate epigraph of Aparājita Pallava, the last ruler of this illustrious dynasty who was defeated by Āditya Coḷa I, son of Vijayālaya Coḷa.[168] This record, dated CE 878 is in twenty verses in six metres. The poet who wrote the Sanskrit portion was Mahādeva who is described as the son of a brāhmaṇa of the Kāśyapa family named Śrī Kumāra "who set aside the eloquence of his rivals and was the composer of *mahākāvyas*". It is also stated poetically that this "Śrī Kumāra, the foremost of the learned, was born of Keśava, just as Subrahmaṇya (Kumāra) of Śiva".[169]

śambhu saṁbhava kambajabhūt keśajvat kṛtadhiyam purasaraḥ
srīkumāra iti viśrutaḥvayaḥ kaśyapāṇvaya bhavāt mahīsurāt ।

165 T.V. Mahalingam, *Inscriptions of the Pallavas*, v. 17, p. 442.

166 *EI*, vol. XVIII no. 2, pp. 9-12.

167 Ibid., v. 30, p. 11.

168 *TVCP*, *Velāñjēri Plates of Aparājita Pallava*, v. 19, plate V, p. 1.

169 Ibid., vv. 18-19.

vipaksavādi pratibhāvahartuḥ kartuḥ mahākāvya nibandhanānām kṛta mahādeva samaḥvayena praśastireṣā tanayena tasya | |

This poet, Śrī Kumāra, was obviously a very great poet as he is mentioned as the composer of *mahākāvyas*. It is unfortunate that none of the poems of Śrī Kumāra has survived till the present day. It is only through this copper-plate document that the name of this poet and his ability to compose *mahākāvyas* are known.

It is interesting to note that the Sanskrit verses of the Ciṟṟūr plates of Nṛpatuṅgavarman were composed by one poet Kumāra and the *ślokas* of the Velāñjēri plates of Aparājita were composed by Mahādeva, son of Śrī Kumāra. As seen earlier, Kaṁpavarman had installed his son Aparājita very early as his co-regent as the latter was known for his valour. Aparājita had become a ruler by the sixth regnal year of Nṛpatuṅga and thus the two were contemporaries.[170] It is thus certain that Mahādeva of the Velāñjēri plates was the son of Śrī Kumāra of the Ciṟṟūr copper-plate inscription. It is thus not surprising that Śrī Kumāra composed Nṛpatuṅga's charter and Śrī Kumāra's son Mahādeva composed Aparājita's plates, both father and son obviously serving in the royal court.[171]

Inscriptions as a Mirror to Sanskrit Literature

The poets who composed the Sanskrit inscriptions and the Sanskrit portions of the bilingual records of the Pallavas were familiar with the works of Sanskrit literature of ancient India, in particular, with the *Vālmīki Rāmāyaṇa* and the *Raghuvaṁśa* of Kālidāsa.

A line from the *Raghuvaṁśam: saṅgrāma nirviṣṭa sahasrabāhur aṣṭādaśa dvīpa nikhāta yūpaḥ* has been incorporated in describing

---

[170] R. Nagaswamy, *Studies in Ancient Tamil Law and Society*, Madras, 1978, pp. 36-37.

[171] Ibid., p. 37.

the valorous deeds of Narasiṁhavarman I in the Kūram copper-plate inscription of the time of Parameśvaravarman thus: *sahasrabāhōr iva samara śata nirviṣta sahasrabāhu karmaṇaḥ*.[172]

Incidentally, one of the inscriptions of Narasiṁhavarman I found on the monolithic monument called Dharmarāja Ratha in Māmallapuram, the seaport of the Pallavas, records one of his titles (*birudas*) *satyaparākramaḥ* and this very same epithet is found in the *Vālmīki Rāmāyaṇa* to praise Rāma.

Another inscription of the Pallava times which as a stanza resembling a work of Bhāsa is seen from an eighth-century Sanskrit inscription of the reign of Narasiṁhavarman II (Rājasiṁha) found in the Kailāsanātha temple in Kāñcīpuram.[173] This inscription, which is in the form of an eulogy (*praśasti*), comprises twelve *ślokas*, with the eighth verse of this poem being a benediction for Rājasiṁha's continued victory.[174] However, the last stanza also contains a benediction for the long reign of this king and it would seem that there is no necessity for this verse as the benediction is already there in the poem earlier. Yet, the poet who composed this inscriptions seems to have thought it essential to conclude his composition with another benediction, just as all Sanskrit dramas conclude with one, technically known as *bharatakāvya*.[175] It is significant to note that the main part *rājasiṁha ciram pātu mahim* in this last verse bears a remarkable resemblance to the sentence *rājasiṁhaḥ praśastu mahim* contained in the *bharatakāvya* found in the Sanskrit plays of the famous dramatist Bhāsa.[176] The

---

172 C. Sivaramamurti, *Epigraphical Echoes of Kālidāsa*, Madras, 1944, p. 29.

173 Ibid.

174 S. Sankaranarayanan, "A Pallava Inscriptional Poem from Kāñchī: An Evaluation", from *Rare Facets of Ancient History and Culture*, New Delhi, 2009, p. 92.

175 Ibid.

176 Ibid.

second half of Bhāsa's *bharatakāvya* runs as *imām api mahim kṛtsnām* (or *mahim ekatapatrañkam*) *rājasimhaḥ praśastu naḥ*. This occurs with slight variations in many of the known plays of Bhāsa and one may therefore be right in concluding that the last benedictory verse in this poem betrays a strong influence of Bhāsa's *bharatakāvya*.[177]

Incidentally, the famous Aihoḷe inscription of the reign of the Cāḷukya king Pulakeśin II dated CE 634 (who was a contemporary of the Pallava rulers Mahendravarman I and Narasiṁhavarman I) was composed by a talented poet called Ravikīrti.[178] This inscription is a historical document but is also an excellent Sanskrit poem. In it, the composer equates himself with greats like Kālidāsa and Bhāravi.[179] This inscription too, like some Pallava epigraphs seen earlier, clearly shows the influence of the *Raghuvaṁśa* of Kālidāsa.[180] According to F. Kielhorn, the *kāvya* of Kālidāsa was well known in widely different parts of India and even beyond the confines of Indian proper.[181] This inscription of Ravikīrti also reveals a number of parallel passages from the *Kirātārjunīyam* of Bhāravi.[182] Thus, the work of Bhāravi who flourished in the court of Pallava Siṁhaviṣṇu in the sixth century CE had obviously become so popular in south India by the seventh century CE that it was emulated in epigraphic poetry also.

---

177 S. Sankaranarayanan, "A Pallava Inscriptional Poem from Kāñchī: An Evaluation", from *Rare Facets of Ancient History and Culture*, New Delhi, 2009, p. 92.

178 *EI*, vol. VI no. 1, pp. 4-7.

179 Ibid.

180 Ibid., v. 37, p. 7.

181 Ibid.

182 Ibid.

2

Pāṇḍyas

THE Pāṇḍyas, who were the contemporary of the Pallavas, ruled from Madurai, their traditional capital over a vast portion of south Tamil Nadu. Like the Pallavas, their era too is remembered for the contribution to various spheres of governance. They too issued many inscriptions, both in Sanskrit and in Tamil. Their copper-plate records are, in particular, very important as they reveal the high level of Sanskrit language and literature of that time.

Māravarman Rājasiṁha I (c. CE 730-65)

Māravarman Rājasiṁha I was the contemporary of the Pallava ruler Nandivarman II Pallavamalla (CE 731-96). He was the father of the well-known Pāṇḍyan king Jaṭila Parāntaka Neḍuñjaḍaiyaṉ who issued the famous inscription called the Veḷvikuḍi copper-plate grant in CE 770, i.e. in his third regnal year. This inscription provides a glimpse into the scholarly mindset of Māravarman Rājasiṁha I describing him as "an ornament of learning" (*vidyācāra-vibhūṣanaḥ*) and a "depository of sacred knowledge" (*śruta-dhāraḥ*).[1] The Larger Siṉṉamaṉūr copper-plate epigraph of the tenth century CE of the reign of Rājasiṁha II describe a certain Sundara Pāṇḍya as "a helmsman in the ocean of all Śāstras" (*samasta śāstrārṇava karṇadhāro yadudbhavaḥ sundara pāṇḍya nāmaḥ*).[2]

---

[1] *EI*, vol. XVII no. 16, v. 10, p. 229 (Veḷvikuḍi plates).

[2] *EI*, vol. III no. 206, v. 8, p. 451 (Larger Siṉṉamaṉūr plates).

Jaṭila Parāntaka Neḍuñjaḍaiyaṉ (eighth century CE)

Neḍuñjaḍaiyaṉ (Varaguṇa I), the son of Māravarman Rājasiṁha I, is well known from many of the inscriptions datable to his reign including the Veḷvikuḍi and the Madras Museum copper-plate grants. The Veḷvikuḍi copper-plate record (CE 770) described him as *paṇḍita-vatsalaḥ* (lover of the learned) in the Tamil portion.[3] Interestingly, the Veḷvikuḍi inscription in the Tamil portion relates an incident which happened in the reign of one of this Pāṇḍyan ruler's ancestors. The *keḷvi-brāhmaṇas* (which could either mean learned brāhmaṇas or, when used in a technical sense, to a class of administrative officers whose business was to carry the applications of petitions to the "hearing" of the king) of Pāganūr-Kūṟṟam, seeing that one of their own community, namely Naṟkoṟṟan, the headman of Koṟkai, who had contemplated the performance of a Vedic sacrifice with the help of the ruling Pāṇḍyan king, Palyāgaśālaimuḍukuḍumi Peruvaḻudi, placed his petition before the king and themselves standing in front of the sacrificial hall, blessed that spot to be henceforth called Veḷvikuḍi (the village of the sacrifice).[4] The king granted the village to Naṟkoṟṟan and it was that the village came to be enjoyed by the latter for a long time. Later, in the third year of Neḍuñjaḍaiyaṉ, a person named Kāmakkāṇi Naṟciṅgaṉ, the headman of Koṟkai, complained to the king that his village, Veḷvikuḍi originally granted under that name by his ancestor Palyagamuḍukuḍumi Peruvaḻudi was taken over by the Kalabhras and since then remained even after the resumption of government by the Pāṇḍyas. The king requested him to produce the necessary evidence and when this was done, the ruler renewed the grant to the applicant. The donee, who owned the *brahmadeya* (Veḷvikuḍi),

[3] *EI*, vol. III no. 206, p. 302.

[4] *EI*, p. 293, fn. 2.

reserved one-third of this village for himself and gave the remaining two parts to fifty learned brāhmaṇas.

The Madras Museum plates of Neḍuñjaḍaiyaṇ, also called the Śrīvaramaṅgalam plates, registers a grant of land to a learned brāhmaṇa.[5] It records that this king *paṇḍita vatsalaḥ*[6] gave the village of Velānguḍi, having deleted its name from former times and having given it the new name Śrīvaramaṅgalam as a *brahmadeya* with all exemptions (*parihāra*) to Sujja Bhaṭṭa, son of Sihu Miśra, who had thoroughly studied all the Śāstras along with a knowledge of sacrifices, who was born in Bhārgava *gotra*, followed Āśvalāyana *sūtra* and was a Bahvṛca and who resided in the village called Sabdāḷi which had been apportioned to the brāhmaṇas from the country known as Magadha.[7] The name Magadha is evidently the place of the same name in north India. The fact that there was a colony of Magadha brāhmaṇas settled in the Pāṇḍyan country shows that communication between north and south India was not infrequent.[8]

Parāntaka Vīra Nārāyaṇa (tenth century CE)

Parāntaka Vīra Nārāyaṇa was the second son of Śrīmāra Śrīvallabha and the younger brother of Varaguṇa II and issued the Daḷavāypuram copper-plate grant which describes him as *viprāgre śarata juṣām* (patron of the learned).[9]

This inscription mentions that Parāntaka Vīra Nārāyaṇa gave learned brāhmaṇas many villages as *ekabhoga* gifts. This king gave the village of Śrīvallabhamaṅgalam to very scholarly brāhmaṇas (*viprāgre*), who had reached the highest level of education (*vidyāpāradṛṣām*), were humble (*vinītamanasām*), had

[5] *Ind. Ant.*, vol. 22, pp. 57-75.

[6] Ibid. l. 50, p. 71.

[7] Ibid., ll. 53ff, p. 71.

[8] Ibid., fn. 91, p. 74.

[9] T.N. Subramaniam, *DCPV*, v. 18, p. 15.

character and fame (*vṛttapratiṣṭhāvatām*), and had concentrated on reciting and expounding the scriptures (*pravacana-vyākhyāna niṣṭātmanām*).[10]

The previous history of this gift village is also given in this epigraph. In former times, a king called Mānam-pertta-Kaṭuṁkon gave the village of Śrīmaṅgalam to twelve brāhmaṇas and gave them a copper-plate charter. These twelve brāhmaṇas have been praised in this charter as great Vedic scholars who performed oblations twice a day, tending the three fires (*dakṣiṇāgni, gārhapatya* and *āhavanīya*), preserving in their memory the four Vedas, performing the five sacrifices (*pañca mahā-yajña*, i.e. for *brahma, deva, pitṛ, mānuṣya* and *bhūta*) and adopting the six professions (recite and teach, performing sacrifices and making others do it, receive and grant gifts).

Another village called Somāśikuṟucci was given by another king as an *ekabhoga* gift to Kāṭhaka Somāyaji in a similar manner. The copper-plate records of these two villages were lost in turbulent times. Subsequently, another person fixed the boundaries of Śomasikuṟucci, appropriating it for himself and converted the remaining land as *kuḍiniḷam* (farming by tenents) under the name Maduratarana llūr. At this stage, a person named Keśava, a great expert in *Baudhāyana-kalpa* and a resident of Śrīmaṅgalam (*brahmadeya*), who was the son of Nārāyaṇa and belonged to the Vana *gotra*, petitioned the king to remove the status of *kuḍinilam*, making the *puravu* (land-tax) payable to Śomasikuṟucci, club the two villages into one and issue a fresh charter. The king accordingly gave it with a copper-plate grant.

Sundara Pāṇḍya (tenth century CE)

The fact that Sundara Pāṇḍya was also a patron of scholars is seen from the Śivakāśī copper-plate inscription datable to the

[10] T.N. Subramaniam, *DCPV*, v. 18, pp. 15-16.

tenth century CE which describes Sundara Pāṇḍya, the elder brother of Vīra Pāṇḍya as *vibhudāśrayaḥ* (the refuge of the learned).[11]

Rājasiṁha II (tenth century CE)

Rājasiṁha II, the son of Parāntaka Vīranārāyaṇa, is mainly known from an inscription of his reign, namely the Larger Siṉṉamaṉūr copper-plate grant which provides considerable historical material.[12] This inscription records that a brāhmaṇa named Parāntaka Śarmā, the son of Śreṣṭhiśarman and grandson of the Vedic scholar Bhāskara and the grandson of Śreṣṭhin was a favourite of king Rājasiṁha. The ancestors of Parāntaka were followers of *Āgniveśya-kalpa* (evidently the science of medicine). To Śreṣṭhiśarman, king Parāntaka Vīra-Nārāyaṇa had given the village of Maṇiyāci surnamed Tiśaiccuḍarmaṅgaḷa. His son, king Rājasiṁha gave to brāhmaṇa Parāntaka, the *agrahāra* Nārceygai-Puttūr surnamed Maṇḍaragaurava-maṅgaḷam. Parāntaka has been eulogized in this epigraph as a very learned scholar.

Vīra Pāṇḍya (tenth century CE)

Vīra Pāṇḍya was the son and successor of Rājasiṁha II. His father had been defeated by the Coḷas during the reign of Parāntaka I, but the Coḷa ruler did not appoint a local viceroy to rule over Madurai, the capital of the Pāṇḍyas. Moreover, Parāntaka Coḷa I was preoccupied with the Rāṣṭrakūṭa threat to the Coḷa land. Due to all these factors, Vīra Pāṇḍya became the king at Madurai like his ancestors, but was ultimately defeated during the reign of Sundara Coḷa (Parāntaka Coḷa II).

The Śivakāśī copper-plate inscription of the reign of Vīra Pāṇḍya states that when this king was residing at

[11] T.N. Subramaniam and P.R. Srinivasan, *SCVP*, v. 7, p. 44.

[12] *SII*, vol. III no. 206, pp. 452-56.

Vīrapāṇḍyapura, he wanted a poet to draft the verses (*ślokas*) in the Sanskrit portions of his orders (*śāsana*) and directed that Vāsudeva Pītāmbara Bhaṭṭa, belonging to the family of Govindasvāmī Bhaṭṭa Somayājī of the Rathitara *gotra* and Āśvalāyana *sūtra* should be the person for the same.[13] Being pleased with the *anuṣṭubh* verses composed by him, the king gave him 3 *velis* of land as his fee and a plot of land for his residence, renaming the area as Śāsanamaṅgaḷam in the form of *ekabhoga* gift. The poet Pītāmbara is praised as a great Vedic scholar and one who learnt the Vedāṅgas (Śikṣā, Vyākaraṇa, Chandas, Nirukta, Jyotiṣa and Kalpa) thoroughly.

Epigraphical Poets of the Pāṇḍyas

The first copper-plate inscription of the early Pāṇḍyas which mentions the name of the composer of the *praśasti* section of the record is the Veḷvikuḍi epigraph dated *c.* CE 770 of the reign of Neḍuñjaḍaiyaṉ (Varaguṇa I).[14] This *praśasti* which is in twenty-three verses composed in eight metres is a beautiful poem which gives the genealogy of the ancestors of Neḍuñjaḍaiyaṉ and their achievements. The poet of this inscription was Varodaya Bhaṭṭa and a Tamil line at the end of the Sanskrit portion and at the beginning of the Tamil section states:

> *i praśasti sarvakratu yāji āgiya* |
> *varodaya bhaṭṭanār ceyappaṭṭadu* | |

> This *praśasti* was composed by Vārodaya Bhaṭṭa who was a performer of all sacrifices.[15]

The Daḷavāipuram copper-plate grant dated CE 910 which belongs to the reign of Parāntaka Vīra Nārāyaṇa is in thirty-

[13] T.N. Subramaniam and P.R. Srinivasan, *SCVP*, pp. 43-52.

[14] *EI*, vol. XVII no.16, pp. 298-301.

[15] Ibid., l. 30, p. 300.

nine verses and is composed in thirteen metres.[16] The poet of this *praśasti* was Mādhava Kavi who is described in verse 34 thus:

yam yogeśvara bhaṭṭam aṣṭadharaṇī deveśvara bhrātaram vidya vṛtta nidhim
vidhur guṇa nidheḥ putram gaṇasvāminaḥ |
tat putrasya mukhāt praśastir uditā tīrtthasya śāstrevyam yas
śrīvallabha maṅgaḷe vasatimān vagmi kaviḥ mādhavaḥ | |

> This eulogy (*praśasti*) came from Mādhava Kavi of (good) speech, living at Śrīvallabhamaṅgaḷam, an adept in scriptures, son of Yogeśvara Bhaṭṭa (who was) the brother of Aṣṭadharaṇi Deveśvara and son of Gaṇasvāmin, a repository of (good) traits.[17]

Poet Mādhava, is referred to as Mādhava Bhaṭṭa in verse 36 of this charter which mentions that the two wells Mahaviḷal and Paruṭṭivayakkāl along with the lands irrigable by them were granted to Mādhava Bhaṭṭa, the author of the eulogy.[18]

The next copper-plate grant of the Pāṇḍyas which gives the name of the composer of the *praśasti*s is the Larger Siṉṉamaṉūr charter dated *c.* CE 926-27 of the reign of Rājasiṁha II Pāṇḍya.[19] The *praśasti* of this epigraph is a long poem consisting of thirty-eight verses and employing as many as twelve metres. Brimming with historical facts relished by historians, this poem is a delight to the lover of Sanskrit literature as well. The talented poet of these stanzas was Vāsudeva who is described in the last verse of the *praśasti*:

vidhita sakala vāṅgmayasya viṣṇor vinaya naya prabhāsya pūrvajo yaḥ |

---

[16] T.N. Subramaniam, *DCPV*, pp. 13-131.

[17] Ibid., v. 34, p. 18.

[18] Ibid., v. 36.

[19] *SII*, vol. III pt. IV no. XVII, pp. 450-56.

aracayad atulām imām praśastiṁ madhuraguṇasya sakhā sa vāsudevaḥ | |

Vāsudeva, the friend of Madhuraguṇa and the elder brother of Viṣṇu, who had studied the whole science of literature and was the birth-place of modesty and intelligence, composed this matchless *praśasti*.[20]

The very last copper-plate charter of the early Pāṇḍyas is the Śivakāśī copper plate dated CE 940-41 of the reign of Vīra Pāṇḍya. This record has a nice Sanskrit *praśasti* of twenty-eight verses in five metres.[21] Some information about the poet who composed the Sanskrit part of this inscription is available in the last verse of this section. This *śloka* in *śārḍulavikrīḍita* metre states:

pautra sat kavitāspadasya dhīṣaṇa prakhyasya
yoyam raver viṣṇutrāta samāhvayaḥ |

śruta nidhir yasyorukīrttiḥ pitā nṛpated |
dharmmopadeṣṭā guru śravyam pārthivakesari
sa kṛtavān enam praśastim kaviḥ | |[22]

This pleasant eulogy was composed by Pārthivakesari, hailing from Antagrāma, adviser to the king on *dharma*, son of the greatly famous Viṣṇutrāta, a treasure-house of learning and grandson of Ravi, a repository of good poetry and an equal of Bṛhaspati.

An earlier verse in this inscription provides the name and qualifications of another poet who was patronized by Vīra Pāṇḍya. It poetically states:

govindasvāmināmnaḥ tulitaśatadhṛteḥ pītasomasya pautraḥ
patyurvvācāmaśeṣāgama saridudadher vāsudevasya putraḥ |

[20] *SII*, vol. III pt. IV, v. 38, p. 454.

[21] T.N. Subramaniam and P.R. Srinivasan, *SCVP*, pp. 43-52.

[22] Ibid., v. 26, pp. 46-47.

prajñasya vyāsadhāmnaḥ śrutavinayanidheḥ |
śrīdharasyāgrajanma tasya premaikapātram kaviramalamatērasti
pitāmbarākhyaḥ | |

There is poet Pītāmbara, grandson of Govindasāmi, who is equal to Indra and who has drunk the juice of the *soma* (plant), son of Vāsudeva, who is like the ocean to the rivers of all scriptures and who is the master of Śāstras and elder brother of the wise Śrīdhara who is a repository of discourses on Vyāsa and a treasure of learning and humility.[23]

There are a few more verses about this poet, giving the names of his erudite brother and mother and adding that this Pītāmbara "had studied the *sūtra* of Āśvalāyana (*āśvalāyana kṛtam sūtram*) and that he of great intelligence composed these verses for the copper-plates of Vīra Pāṇḍya".[24]

This king gave to Pītāmbara of the Rathitara *gotra*, 3 *veli*s of land in the village of Nalapura in Mel Vemba Rāṣṭra and the area called Valaikoṭṭa along with 10 *mā* of house site with both the rights of cultivation and proprietorship demarcated by a female elephant, created separately as a *brahmadeya* and an ideal *agrahāra* and named it Śāsanamaṅgaḷam.[25]

The Tamil portion of this same grant while mentioning this gift to poet Pītāmbara, adds more details. This part of the grant mentions that Vīra Pāṇḍya honoured and asked the Vedic scholar Vāsudeva Pītāmbara Bhaṭṭa, born in the lineage of Govindasvāmī-Bhaṭṭach-Comāśi, capable of composing verses for royal orders according to rules, belonging to Ten Vīrataramaṅgalam in Muḷḷināḍu, of Rathitara *gotra* and immeasurably good conduct, of Āśvalāyana *sūtra*, a brāhmaṇa, consistently unique, tending the three fires (*dākṣiṇāgni*, *āhvanīya* and *gārhapatya*) in the tradition of the four Vedas, performing

[23] T.N. Subramaniam and P.R. Srinivasan, *SCVP*, v. 10, p. 44.

[24] Ibid., vv. 11-12.

[25] Ibid., vv. 13-18, pp. 45-46.

the five oblations (to God, Brahmā, creatures, men and manes); having learnt the six parts of the Vedas (Śikṣā, Vyākaraṇa, Chandas, Nirukta, Jyotiṣa and Kalpa) to compose poems.

This inscription also mentions that this king, seeing the excellence of the poems in *anuṣṭubh* (metre) happily composed by him (Pītāmbara), ordered from his camp the land-grant to this scholar-poet. Thus, this inscription is unique in that it was a royal document which described the gift to a Pītāmbara, a poet *par excellence* and the Sanskrit portion consisting of a string of delectable verses composed by another fine poet, namely Pārthivakesari.

Other than the names of the poets who composed these beautiful Sanskrit verses for the *praśasti*s of the royal epigraphs, there is available to us, the name of a poet of the eighth century CE from some of the inscriptions of Pāṇḍyan Neḍuñjaḍaiyaṉ. A Sanskrit inscription from Āṉaimalai, near Madurai,[26] dated CE 770, which consists of three verses, the first two in *āryā* metre and the third in *vaṁśastha* metre, records that a minister (*mantrī*) of this Pāṇḍyan king, who was apparently an expert in the art of composing poetry mentions his name as Madhurakavi, who hailed from a village named Karavandapura. He is also described as a learned and illustrious member of the *vaidya* family (*śrīman vaidyaḥ*). This record also states that he was the son of Māra (*māra-sūnuḥ*) and very wise (*matimān*).[27]

The second inscription in Tamil, at the same place, states that he bore the title Muvendamaṅgaḷapperaṟaiyaṉ and the village of Karavandapura is called Kaḷakkuḍi. This record states that he was the prime minister (*uttara-mantrī*) and caused the stone-temple (i.e. the cave temple for Narasiṁha) to be made, but died without consecrating it. Subsequently, his younger brother Māṟaṉ Eyiṉaṉ alias Pāṇḍimaṅgaḷaviśaiyaraiyaṉ, who became the prime minister, completed it.

[26] *EI*, vol. XVIII no. 33, pp. 319-20.

[27] Ibid., p. 320.

The Veḷvikkuḍi copper-plate inscription, also belonging to the time of Pāṇḍyan Neḍuñjaḍaiyaṉ, mentioned earlier in this chapter, again mentions this poet in a Sanskrit verse stating that "the *ājñapti* of this document was Maṅgaḷarāja, the very sweet (*madhuratara*) poet (*kavi*), well-versed in the Śāstras, a *vaidya* and a resident of Karavandapura".[28]

āsīt maṅgalarājo madhurataraḥ śāstravit kavir-vvāgmi |
ājñaptir asya vaidyaḥ karavandapurivāstavyaḥ | |

The Tamil portion of the same copper-plate charter states that the *ājñapti* (*āṇatti*) of this grant was Madaviklaṉ Māraṅgāri, alias Muvendamaṅgaḷa Peraraiyaṉ, the crest-jewel of the *vaidyaka*s and a native of Karavandapura, who was a favourite of the Pāṇḍya king Neḍuñjaḍaiyaṉ. He is also mentioned in this section as being a brave warrior who participated in the battles of his king. It is evident that the members of the family of this poet were well-versed in sacred literature as revealed by the term *vaidyaka*.[29] This place Karavandapura, alias Kaḷakkuḍi has been identified with Uggirankottai in Tirunelveli district.[30]

The poet named Madhurakavi alias Māraṉgāri, minister to Pāṇḍyan Neḍuñjaḍaiyaṉ and who excavated the cave-temple at Āṇaimalai, has been identified by some scholars with Madhurakavi Āḻvar, one of the twelve Āḻvars (Vaiṣṇava saints) who hailed from Pāṇḍya Nāḍu and who was a disciple of Nammāḻvār.[31] It has also been supposed that Nammāḻvār (Kāri Māraṇ) was the son of this minister and that he may have given his own father's surname, Madhurakavi to his disciple as *dāsyanāma*.[32]

---

[28] *EI*, vol. XVII no. 16, v. 18, p. 303.

[29] *EI*, vol. VIII no. 33, p. 318.

[30] *EI*, vol. XXIII no. 45, p. 284.

[31] K.A. Nilakanta Sastri, *The Pāṇḍyan Kingdom*, Madras, 1972, p. 86.

[32] T.A. Gopinatha Rao, *History of the Śrī Vaiṣṇavas*, Madras, 1923, p. 19.

3

Āys

The Āys were the earliest ruling dynasty in South Kerala. Ptolemy (second century CE) refers to the region from the Baris (Pamba) to Cape Comorin (Kanyākumārī) as Āioi, where the chieftains of the Āy clan ruled.[1] They were the dominant power up to the tenth century CE. At its height, the Āy kingdom extended from Tiruvaḷḷa in the north to Nāgarkoil in the south including the Western Ghāṭs which comprised its most important portion.[2] That the Āy kings did much to promote education is seen from the sources that have come down over the centuries. This area, particularly in the ninth century CE, was famous for the institutions called the *śālai*s which encouraged Sanskrit studies of an advanced nature.[3] The word *śālai* has many meanings, but in most inscriptions, it refers to a feeding house either attached to a temple[4] or as an independent one[5] for feeding brāhmaṇas, students and the servants of the temple. However, there existed many *śālai*s where feeding brāhmaṇas was not the main focus, but where literary activity of the students was.

Karunandaḍakkaṉ (CE 857-85)

Karunandaḍakkaṉ, also called Śrī Vallabha, was one of the important kings of the Āy dynasty. His keen interest in the

[1] A. Sreedhara Menon, *A Survey of Kerala History*, Madras, 1998, p. 71.

[2] Ibid., p. 113.

[3] S. Gurumurthy, *Education in South India; Ancient and Medieval Periods*, Madras, 1979, p. 2.

[4] *ARE* 323 of 1917; 134 of 1919; 43 of 1925.

[5] *ARE* 266 of 1913; 343 of 1917; 354 of 1954-55.

promotion of learning is seen from a copper-plate record which gives plenty of details about a *śālai*. The most important *śālai* known is the one which existed at Pārthivaśekharapuram (Pārthivapuram, Kanyākumārī district), established at this place by Karunandaḍakkaṉ according to a copper-plate inscription dated CE 866.[6] This copper-plate grant consists only of five plates, with some inbetween, unfortunately, missing. However, the existing plates supply enough information to show the importance of this great educational institution of the ancient times.

This ninth-century charter records that this king acquired some cultivable land in exchange for other lands from the *sabhā* of Mincirai, fixed its boundaries, constructed a temple for Viṣṇu (Viṣṇu Bhaṭṭāraka) there and installed the deity. This village was named Pārthivaśekhara-puram and a *śālai* (*śālā* in Sanskrit) was also established for ninety-five scholars (*caṭṭar*s), on the scale of the one at Kāndaḷūr. All this was done by the king himself.

The charter provides very interesting details regarding this *śālai*. The fellowships (*kaḷam*) for the *caṭṭar*, including mainly food, were allotted on the following scale: Paviḻiya (Bahvr̥ca) *caraṇam* 45 *kaḷam*; Taittirīya *caraṇam* — 36 *kaḷam*; Talavakāra *caraṇam* — 14 *kaḷam* and the rest provided in future for all the three *caraṇa*s.

It is interesting to note that the students admitted into this institution were called *caṭṭar*s which suggests that they were all learned scholars probably pursuing higher studies or imparting lessons to advanced students.[7] Moreover, the members of the institutions, both teachers and students were all called by the same word *caṭṭar*.[8]

---

[6] *TAS*, vol. I, pp. 1-14.

[7] S. Gurumurthy, op. cit.

[8] Ibid.

There were very strict rules for entering the *śālai*s as given in this inscription. The applicants for admission into this institution were required to have a knowledge of Vyākaraṇa (grammar), Mīmāṁsā and Paurohitya, and the learning necessary to conduct the affairs of the "three kingdoms" (*trairājya vyavahāra*). According to K.G. Krishnan, if this term is applied to the contemporary sense, it must refer to the kingdom of the Pallavas, the Pāṇḍyas and the Keralas. If, on the other hand, it should refer to the traditional practice, it may refer to the Ceras, the Coḷas and the Pāṇḍyas. The second stipulation for admission into this centre of learning was that the student wanting to join must be duly certified on oath by five *caṭṭar*s that the former was proficient in Vyākaraṇa, Mīmāṁsā and Paurohitya. It was also stressed that the student must be free from the fault of forgetfulness. The next portion of this epigraph prescribes the mode of recitation of the Vedas.

The subsequent section contains many rules and regulations prescribed for the *caṭṭar*s with regard to their conduct:

1. A *caṭṭar* should not speak in abusive language of another *caṭṭar* within the precincts of the temple; otherwise he could eat in the *śālai* only after paying a fine of 5 *kanam* of gold to the *perumakkaḷ* (elderly professors).
2. If a *caṭṭar* strikes (*kuttu*) or is struck by another he must pay a fine of 1 *kāśu* and 5 *kanam* of gold, respectively.
3. The *caṭṭar*s should not attend the gathering (*kūṭṭam*) with weapons of warfare (*padaikkaḷam*) and should not fight within the precincts of the temple in default of which they would have to forgo a day's food. Making wounds with a weapon was not considered an act of *dharma* or *aram*.

4. The *caṭṭars* should not practise any kind of deceit.
5. The *caṭṭars* should not alienate the lands of the *śālabhoga* and the *devadāna;* otherwise he should pay a fine of 5 *kaḷañju* of gold.
6. They should not keep *veḷḷaittigaḷ* in the *maḍham*. *Veḷḷaitigaḷ* refers to ladies of a particular community, but in the context here obviously refers to "concubines" as translated by the late Gopinatha Rao.[9] The use of the word *maḍam* is very significant, though the entire establishment, as already explained, is called *śālai*.[10] The servants of the establishment were to be fined 1 *kāśu* if they insulted a *caṭṭar*.

The long list of rules and regulations shows that a high level of discipline was maintained in the *śālai* at Pārthivaśekharapuram. Since the *caṭṭars* were not permitted to appoint maid-servants, it may be inferred that they were all unmarried and living in a *maṭha* which was probably an adjunct to the temple and the *śālai*.[11] It is stated in the inscription that the students were not permitted the use of weapons of warfare on certain occasions. However, T.N. Subramaniam has opined that the *caṭṭars* were instructed in military science.[12] M.G.S. Narayanan has also suggested that the *caṭṭars* were arms-bearing brāhmaṇa scholars.[13]

The *caṭṭars* were designated duties of different types. They were to collect *mudal* (amount) from tenants of the *śālabhoga* and *devadāna* without the use of force. Those who owed taxes to the *sabhā* should be bound by the decision of the *caṭṭars*.

---

[9] K.G. Krishnan, "Caṭṭānam Maḍham" from *Studies in South Indian History and Epigraphy*, Madras, 1981, p. 33.

[10] Ibid.

[11] S. Gurumurthy, op. cit., p. 62.

[12] *SITI*, vol. III pt. II, p. 8.

[13] *IHC*, 1970, vol. I, pp. 125-36.

They were also in charge of the everyday routine of both the temple and the *śālai,* and also participated in the administration of the village assembly. It is therefore evident that the entire control of both the *śālai* and the temple was vested in the hands of the *caṭṭar*s who composed the institution.[14]

Therefore, it seems that this *śālai* was an important institution offering advanced studies in Vyākaraṇa, Mīmāṁsā, Paurohitya and the three Vedas. It is also likely that since it is stated that the *caṭṭar*s should be well-versed in the *trairājya-vyavahāra,* they must have been trained in the art of administration as well.[15] Sanskrit could have been the medium of communication.

Kāndaḷūr Śālai

The copper-plate inscription of Karunandaḍakkaṉ dated CE 866 mentioned above records that this *śālai* at Pārthivaśekharapuram was modelled on the one at Kāndaḷūr (in ancient Kerala country). This clearly reveals that a *śālai* would have existed at Kāndaḷūr in the same period or even earlier and it enjoyed wide popularity and fame and that it was possible for it to serve as a model for the creation of a similar one at Pārthivaśekharapuram.[16] The Kāndaḷūr *śālai* was so powerful an institution that all the kings from the time of Rājarāja Coḷa I (CE 985–1014) claim to have limited it or regulated (*aṟattu*) it. Rājarāja Coḷa I assumed the title *kāndaḷūr śālai kaḷam aṟuttu aruḷiya* or as *kāndaḷūr śālai kaḷam aṟuttu* or as *śālai kaḷam aṟuttu aruḷiya.* Almost the first military achievement of Rājarāja's reign was the campaign in the Kerala country of which the result was summed up in the phrase *kāṇdaḷūr śālai kaḷamarutta* which precedes the name of this king in several of his inscriptions from the fourth year onwards.[17]

[14] S. Gurumurthy, op. cit., p. 62.

[15] Ibid., p. 63.

[16] Ibid., p. 64.

[17] K.A. Nilakanta Sastri, *Coḷas,* Madras, 1984, p. 169.

The Kāṇḍaḷūr *śālai* is referred to in later times till the reign of Rājarāja's grandson Rājādhirāja I (CE 1018-52).[18] Parākrama Pāṇḍya, a subordinate ally of Vikrama Coḷa (CE 1118-35) also claims to have done the same.[19]

Many explanations have been given as to the nature of this institution. K.K. Pillai has suggested that it was an institution of learning where free food was provided for the students. It appears that this may be the most plausible explanation.[20] However, the use of force in capturing this institution as recorded in a few inscription needs some explanation. The use of force and the capture of the *śālai* indicates that Rājarāja Coḷa I had some reason to come into conflict (the reasons of which are not known) with the members of the *śālai* and finally brought it under his control by applying force (the reasons for which are also not known).[21] It can be said that since the *caṭṭar*s at Pārthivaśekharapuram were said to be familiar with the use of weapons of warfare, the members of the *śālai* at Kāndaḷūr (which served as a model for the former) were possibly also trained in warfare and Rājarāja I was constrained to make use of his army to force them to surrender.[22]

K.G. Krishnan has identified the Kāndaḷūr *śālai* with the establishment known as *caṭṭānam maḍham* described in a Prākṛt work (*campu*) called *Kuvalayamāla* by Uddyotana Sūri (CE 728-78).[23] The *caṭṭar*s of that *caṭṭanam maḍham* are described as learning the Vedas, Vyākaraṇa, Mīmāṁsā and other branches of arts and sciences including archery and fighting with swords, daggers, lances, etc.[24] A classical work in Maḷayālam of the

[18] K.G. Krishnan, op. cit., p. 34.

[19] *TAS*, vol. I, pp. 19ff; K.G. Krishnan, op. cit., p. 34.

[20] *JORM*, XXIX, pp. 87-89.

[21] S. Gurumurthy, op. cit., p. 65.

[22] Ibid.

[23] K.G. Krishnan, op. cit., pp. 31-35.

[24] Ibid.

fourteenth century CE called *Anantapuravarṇanam* mentions the existence of a college of advanced Vedic studies at Kāndaḷūr and the proficiency of the scholars there in the use of weapons of warfare.[25] Kāndaḷūr has been identified with Valiya *śālai,* a locality in Trivendrum, the capital of Kerala, on the basis of a manuscript of recent date in the Mincarai-*maḍam* which still has the rights of Puṣpāñjali in the Śiva Temple at Valiya *śālai.*[26]

An inscription of Rājādhirāja I, dated in his thirtieth regnal year from the Guhanāthasvāmi temple in Kanyākumārī, mentions a *śālai.*[27] It was known as Śrīvallavapperunśālai and also as Rājarājapperuncālai and was situated in Kaḷikkuḍi in Purattayanāḍu.[28] From another inscription at the same place, it is known that Kaḷikkuḍi was part of Kumārī (Kanyākumārī) in Purattayanāḍu. According to K.G. Krishnan, this *śālai* was known as Śrīvallavapperuncālai, apparently after Śrīvallabha, a Pāṇḍya ruler (CE 810-62) or a ruler of the Āy family probably identical with King Karunandaḍakkaṉ (CE 866).[29] This *śālai* was known as Rājarājanpperuncālai, evidently named after Rājarāja I after his conquest of this area thus attesting to effective control of the institution by the Coḷas.[30] This institution was not destroyed but remodelled. According to T.N. Subramaniam, Rājarāja I remodelled it and placed it on a firm footing and issued a fresh order.[31] It is also believed that the *śālai* may be the same as Pārthivaśekharapuram because the Venāḍu chief who founded the *śālai* at Pārthivaśekharapuram seems to have had the surname Śrī Vallabha in token of his subordination to the then Pāṇḍyan ruler.[32]

---

[25] *SITI*, vol. III pt. II, p. 9; K.G. Krishnan, op. cit., p. 35.

[26] K.G. Krishnan, op. cit., p. 35.

[27] *TAS*, vol. I, pp. 240-42.

[28] Ibid., pp. 246-47.

[29] K.G. Krishnan, op. cit.

[30] Ibid.

[31] *SITI*, vol. III pt. II, p. 13 and n. 3.

[32] Ibid., p. 13.

4

Coḷas

THE glorious period of the imperial Coḷas started from the time of Vijayālaya Coḷa in the middle of the ninth century CE and finally came to an end in the third quarter of the thirteenth century CE after Rājendra Coḷa III. This was an unparalleled age as far as territorial aggrandizement, administration, temple art and architecture, and various other spheres of activities were concerned. It was also an age in which literature, both Tamil and Sanskrit, flourished. It is well known that the age of the Coḷas was the golden age of Tamil literature and that the courts of the Coḷa emperors and their vassals were adorned by poets of great magnitude like Jayankoṇḍar, Oṭṭakūṭṭar, Seikkiḻār and Kaṁban, but it is not so well known that the same age also witnessed the excellent works carried on in the realm of Sanskrit.[1]

Āditya Coḷa I (c. CE 871–907)

Āditya Coḷa I was the first king of the dynasty of the Imperial Coḷas to be praised for his learning. The Tiruvālaṅgāḍu copper-plate charter (dated CE 1018), of the reign of Rājendra Coḷa I describes Āditya I as being "equal to Bṛhaspati in learning" (*dhiṣaṇas tarasvi*).[2] This ruler has also been extolled for his patronage of scholars. The Tiruvālaṅgāḍu[3] and the Eśālam[4]

---

[1] K.A. Nilakanta Sastri, "Sanskrit Learning in the Coḷa Empire", *JOR*, vol. IX pt. I, 1937, p. 1.

[2] *SII*, vol. III no. 205, v. 47, p. 396.

[3] Ibid., v. 47, p. 396.

[4] R. Nagaswamy, *ECPR*, v. 9, p. 31.

copper-plate records (dated CE 1036) praise Āditya I as the "abode of scholars" (*budhāśrayaḥ*).

An epigraph, probably belonging to the reign of Āditya I of the ninth century CE, describes an *agrahāra* called Ratnāgrahāra or Ratnagrāma as a very famous and prosperous one and in which many scholars dwelt.[5] It is also interesting to note that the names of these *agrahāra*s underwent changes over time. The village now known as Maṇimaṅgaḷam, also known as Ratnāgrahāra and Ratnagrāma in some Coḷa inscriptions, was in the time of Rājakesarivarman surnamed Lokamahādevī-caturvedimaṅgalam, in the time of Rājādhirāja, Rājendra and Vīra-Rājendra as Rājacuḷāmaṇi-caturvedimaṅgalam and later as Pāṇḍiyanai-irumaḍi-veṅkaṇḍa-śoḷa-caturvedimaṅgalam. In the time of Rājarāja III, it had another name, Grāmaśikhāmaṇi-caturvedimaṅgalam.[6]

An inscription from the Viṣṇu Temple in Ukkal (North Arcot district) of the twenty-third regnal year of a Coḷa king Ko-Rājakesarivarman (possibly Āditya Coḷa I) records that a certain Brahmādhirāja deposited 200 *kalañju* of gold with the village assembly for feeding twelve learned brāhmaṇas who were scholars in the Vedas out of the interest. The donor was Trivikrama-Bhaṭṭar alias Brahmādhirāja who was one of the Āḷumgaṇattār of Uttaramallūr.[7]

Parāntaka Coḷa I (CE 907-55)

Parāntaka Coḷa I, son of Āditya I, was also fond of learning as seen from the Veḷāñjeri plates which record that "wise men considered him to be Bṛhaspati himself" (*dhiṣaṇam bhūdendrāḥ*).[8] This ruler also had the title *paṇḍitavatsalaḥ* (he who is fond of

---

[5] *SII*, vol. III no. 27, pp. 50-51.

[6] *SII*, vol. III, p. 49.

[7] *ARE*, 19 of 1893; *SII*, vol. III no. 1, pp. 2-3.

[8] R. Nagaswamy, *TVCP, Veḷāñjeri Plates of Parāntaka I*, pt. II, v. 13, p. 2.

scholars), testifying to his being a patron of scholars.[9] Parāntaka, also well known by his title *vīra-coḷa*, has been praised in many of the Coḷa copper-plate charters as having generously donated many *agrahāra*s with the purpose of spreading Vedic knowledge. The Veḷāñjeri copper-plate inscription (CE 932) of this king records that this ruler donated three villages called Tālaiveḍu, Mayangāṟu and Kilagal in their entirety with 3,000 *kāḍi* of paddy and 9 *niṣka*s (as tax) to the brāhmaṇas of Meliruñjeru village who were great scholars in the Vedas and Vedāṅgas including *Sāmaveda* with the 3,000 *śākhā*s (*sahasraśākalaṅkṛta sāmaveda sahita veda vedāṅga vidbhyaḥ*).[10] This gift was made by Parāntaka at the request of a person named Brahmavanavādhirāja. The epigraph records the boundaries of the villages gifted, the taxes exempted, and the rights and privileges attached to the same.[11]

The Karandai copper-plate inscription of Rājendra I (CE 1021) states that Parāntaka I established a village called Vīranārāyaṇa *agrahāra* (*caturvedimaṅgalam*) after his own name, which is described in this epigraph as being "of great wealth, immutable even at the end of the age" (*sa vīranārāyaṇam agrahāram rāja svanāmna tilakam pṛthivyāḥ, niveśayāmasa mahā-vibhūtim kalpavasaneśvapi nirvikāram*).[12] The same inscription poetically records that "this chief among kings (i.e. Parāntaka), himself prosperous, founded many prosperous and great villages (*agrahāra*s) in various places" (*śrīmato mahātmas śrīman agrahārān nyaviviśatat, atyānyān api sa rājendraḥ tatra tatra mahītale*).[13] Similarly, the Kanyākumarī inscription (CE 1069) of the reign of Vīra-Rājendra, the third son of Rājendra I (which

---

[9] *ASIAR*, 1904-05, p. 141.

[10] R. Nagawamy, *TVCP*, *Veḷāñjeri Plates of Parāntaka I*, Pl. III, p. 1.

[11] Ibid., p. 28.

[12] K.G. Krishnan, *KTPR*, v. 19, p. 70.

[13] Ibid., v. 20, p. 71.

is identical verse by verse with the Carāla copper-plate record of the same ruler found in Andhra Pradesh) mentions that he "satisfied the needs of learned men" (*jahāra tāpam budha-samhatinām*), thereby indicating that he generously gave them all that they needed including grants of land.[14] The same inscription registers that Parāntaka I "created many *agrahāras* commencing with the name Vīranārāyaṇa, fit to be enjoyed by learned brāhmaṇas, just as Brahmā created *svarga*" (*vidvad vipra bhogyān anupama vibhavān Vīranārāyaṇādhyaḥ*).[15] This is also probably indicated by a verse in the Larger Leiden plates (CE 1006), the Sanskrit portion of which was composed in the reign of Rājendra I. This verse mentions that Parāntaka I brought many large villages into existence (*grāman niveśya vividhān mahato*).[16] Similarly, the Udayendiram plates of Pṛthvīpati, the Gaṅga king who was a vassal of Parāntaka I states that his many meritorious acts and gifts included "gifts (of land) to brāhmaṇas" (*brahmadeya*).[17]

A great *bhāṣya* on the *Ṛgveda* was composed on the banks of the river Kāverī in the reign of Parāntaka I. This extensive and important work was authored by Mādhava, son of Veṅkaṭārya and Sundarī. This scholar clearly states that he lived happily in the Coḷa country when he wrote this work (*jagatāmekavīrasya coḷeśu nivasan sukham, tīram āśritya nivasan kāveryā dakṣiṇām sukham*).[18]

The existence of a Vedic school at a place known as Kamapullūr (Kapallūr in erstwhile North Arcot district) is known from an inscription of the reign of Parāntaka Coḷa I found in the Tirukkāmeśvara temple in Kapallūr.[19] This

[14] *EI*, vol. XVIII no. 4, v. 64, p. 44.

[15] Ibid., v. 60, p. 143.

[16] *EI*, vol. XXII no. 34, v. 16, p. 239 (Larger Leiden plates).

[17] *SII*, vol. II pt. 3, v. 7, p. 383.

[18] K.A. Nilakanta Sastri, op. cit., p. 2.

[19] *ARE*, 268 of 1938-39.

inscription, belonging to the time of Parakesarivarman (Parāntaka I) datable to his thirteenth regnal year, registers a sale of land by the assembly (*sabhā*) of Kamapullūr to Muḍumbai Iḻaiya Attindakramavittan, a member of the *ālum-gaṇam* (village executive) of the place for the maintenance of a Vedic school (*chāndoga-kiḍaippuram*) for teaching the *Chāndoga* to students. There is another inscription of the time of his descendant Parāntaka II (Sundara Coḷa) of this transaction.[20]

Incidentally, two more inscriptions from this temple in Kapallūr, belonging to the twenty-fifth regnal year of the Rāṣṭrakūṭa king, Kannaradeva "who took Kāñcī and Tañjai", i.e. Kṛṣṇa II, throw some light on educational activities. The first of these records registers a similar sale of land by the same assembly (as above) to four members of the *āḷum-gaṇam* for being utilized as *dānappuram* among scholars.[21] The second epigraph of this king mentions a gift of land by purchase as *bhaṭṭa-vṛtti* by four members of the *āḷum-gaṇam* of Kamapullūr.[22]

It is interesting to note that the Udayendiram copper-plate record of the eighth century CE of the reign of Nandivarman Pallavamalla (Chapter 1) which records the donation of the village Kumāramaṅgaḷa-Veḷḷattūr, renamed as Udayacandramaṅgalam to 108 brāhmaṇas, has, at the end, a Tamil endorsement dated in the twenty-sixth year of Maduraikoṇḍa Ko-Parakesarivarman, i.e. Parāntaka Coḷa I, recording that the *sabhā*s of the two villages of Udayacandramaṅgalam and Kāñcivāyil alias Iganmaraimaṅgalam decided to club both the villages into one and continue to live as such henceforth.[23] Thus, two *caturvedimaṅgalams*, both surely of scholarly people propagating education, were made into one.

[20] *ARE*, 270 of 1938-39.

[21] *ARE*, 269 of 1938-39.

[22] *ARE*, 272 of 1938-39.

[23] *SII*, vol. II no. 74, p. 370.

A number of *maṭhas* flourished during the Coḷa times, many being attached to temples. These religious institutions were also important centres of education and helped in the dissemination of the religious and philosophical works in ancient and medieval India. According to P.V. Kane, "the *maṭhas* were primarily intended for the instruction of pupils or the laity by some great teacher of the tenets of a sect or in the doctrines of some philosophy or in some branch of learning such as grammar, Mīmāṁsā, astronomy and the like".[24] Some of the Sanskrit inscriptions of the Coḷas provide information about an important *maṭha* which functioned in Tiruvoṟṟiyūr (near Chennai). One inscription from the Ādipurīśvarar temple in Tiruvoṟṟiyūr, belonging to the tenth century CE records the existence of a *maṭha* in this place.[25] According to this inscription, an army general of the Coḷa crown-prince Rājāditya (son of Parāntaka Coḷa I) called Vallabha who lost interest in worldly pleasures, renounced his worldly life and coming to Tiruvoṟṟiyūr, took his initiation in the cave of Nirañjanaguru. Vallabha, who took up the *dīkṣā* name Caturānana, established a *maṭha* at Tiruvoṟṟiyūr, whose successive heads came to be called Caturānana *paṇḍita* after the founder.[26]

The Caturānana *paṇḍitas* of Tiruvoṟṟiyūr are known from several other Coḷa inscriptions of the subsequent times. An inscription of the reign of Rājendra Coḷa I (CE 1043), from the Ādipurīśvara temple in Tiruvoṟṟiyūr, states that an architect named Vīra-Coḷa Ravi constructed the *vimāna* of this temple as directed by Caturānana.[27] Another inscription of the reign of Kulottuṅga Coḷa (CE 1077) also mentions the name of a Caturānana Paṇḍita.[28] An inscription of the time of Rājādhirāja

[24] P.V. Kane, *History of Dharmaśāstra*, vol. II pt. 2, Poona, 1941, p. 907.

[25] *EI*, vol. XXVII no. 47, pp. 292-303.

[26] Ibid., p. 297.

[27] *JOR*, vol. XXXII, pp. 11-15.

[28] *SII*, vol. V no. 1356.

II dated CE 1171-72 mentions that this monarch was present during a Paṅguni Uttiram festival in this temple and on the same occasion, Caturānana Paṇḍita, who owned a *maṭha* in the temple and Vāgīśvara Paṇḍita who expounded the *Soma Siddhānta* (doctrine of the Kāpālikas) were also there.[29]

Parāntaka II (CE 956-73)

The Anbil copper plates of Parāntaka II (Sundara Coḷa) record that he gave to his minister Aniruddha, who was a learned and respected brāhmaṇa, 10 *veli*s of land in the village of Nalviḷankuḍi, situated in Ālandūr-raṣṭra. It was renamed Karuṇakaramaṅgalam and was granted with its *karanmai* and *miyatchi*, all taxes on the land were abolished and the enjoyment of the new village with all its plants, trees, gardens, tanks and wells was bestowed on Aniruddha.[30]

The Tirukkameśvara temple in Kapallūr (called in the inscriptions as Kamapullūr) has two inscriptions referred to earlier, of the reigns of Parāntaka I and Sundara Coḷa, recording the existence of a Vedic school in this village. The first record of the time of Parāntaka I mentions the details of the endowment of this institution by a member of the village executive (*āḷum-gaṇam*).[31] The second record is dated in the sixth year of Maduraikoṇḍa Rājakesari (Sundara Coḷa) and it registers, as in the previous record, the sale of land by the same assembly to two members of the *āḷum-gaṇam* for endowment as *Chāndoga vṛtti*.[32]

It is very interesting to note that during the Coḷa period, competitions were held among students who recited the Vedas and prizes were presented to them. A bilingual record of the reign of Sundara Coḷa dated CE 971 from the Matsyapurīśvara

[29] *ARE*, 371 of 1911.

[30] *EI*, vol. XV no. 5, vv. 38-41, p. 63.

[31] *ARE*, 268 of 1938-39.

[32] *ARE*, 270 of 1938-39.

temple, Koil Tevarāyaṇpeṭṭai (Tañjāvūr district) mentions that a person named Baradayaṉ-Seṉda Nakkapiraṉbhaṭṭa Sarvakratu-yājiyar made an endowment of a certain sum of money to this temple with the provision that the annual interest from this sum would be given to the best reciters of some portions of the *Jaiminīya Sāmaveda* among all those who participated, excepting those who had been successful in this competition in the previous years. This was to be recited before the god on the night of Tiruvādirai in the month of Mārgaḻi.[33]

The temples, in the days of the Coḷas, played a very important role in education. Many centres of learning were situated in the premises of large and small temples. These "temple-colleges" received generous royal donations and played a vital part in the dissemination of knowledge. The copper-plate grants and the numerous inscriptions on the walls of the temples themselves speak of the educational activities which took place in the precincts of these sacred institutions. These "temple-colleges", which received numerous royal benefactions, served as great centres of learning and played a vital role in the spread of education. The inscriptions found etched on the walls of the temples where these educational centres functioned are a mine of information about the activities that took place herein.

An inscription discovered in the Agasteśvara temple in Poṉṉeri (near Chennai), which is unfortunately only a fragment, records in characters of about the ninth century CE, an endowment made for the maintenance of a person capable of teaching one Veda including the *Paviḻiyam* (*Bahvṛca*) and the *Āraṇa* (*Āraṇyaka*).[34] Another epigraph from the Nāgeśvarasvāmi temple in Kuṁbakoṇam (Tañjāvūr district) dated CE 959 of the reign of Sundara Coḷa mentions that a person purchased some land and

[33] *SII*, vol. XIII no. 250, p. 133.

[34] *ARE*, 15 of 1933-34.

gave it as a *bhaṭṭa-vṛtti* (land allotted for maintaining a learned brāhmaṇa) to a teacher who expounded the *Prābhākara Mīmāṁsā Śāstra* in that temple.[35] Another lithic record dated CE 959 mentions gifts of land by Bhadraṅkāḍu Vasudevabhaṭṭa Somāsiyār and others as *vyākhyā-vṛtti* for the maintenance of those who gave discourses on Vyākaraṇa-śāstram (grammar) in the village of Uttarameru-caturvedimaṅgalam, the *sabha* of the village being entrusted with the gift.[36]

Rājarāja Coḷa I (CE 985–1014)

Rājarāja Coḷa's contributions to the expansion of the Coḷa empire and its administration have been well-recorded. In addition, his contribution to the sphere of education is clearly seen from the Coḷa lithic and copper-plate records. The Tiruvālaṅgāḍu copper-plate grant of his son Rājendra Coḷa I, praises him as being of "matchless prosperity, majesty, learning, strength of arms, prowess, heroism and courage" (*anupama-vibhāva-prabhāva-vidyā-bhujabala-vikrama-śaurya-dhairya rāśiḥ*).[37] During his reign, numerous endowments were made for the teaching and recitation of many subjects in the temples. An inscription of the time of this ruler from the Bhairava temple, Tirukkoṣṭṭiyūr (Rāmanāthapuram district) mentions a gift of land by a person to the temple of Tirumayānadevar, i.e. Bhairava at Tirukkoṣṭṭiyūr for teaching the Prābhākara Mīmāṁsā in this temple.[38] Another interesting epigraphs of Rājarāja dated in his thirteenth regnal year is found in the Karkoṭakeśvara temple in Kamarāsavalli (Tirucirāpaḷḷi district).[39] It relates to the recitation of *Tāḷvakāra Sāmaveda*

---

[35] S. Sankaranarayanan, "Sanskrit Education in Ancient Tamil Country (An Epigraphical Survey)", *ALB*, vol. 57, 1993, p. 10 (hereafter "Sanskrit Education").

[36] *ARE*, 18 of 1898; *SII*, vol. III no. 161, p. 338.

[37] *SII*, vol. III no. 205, v. 76, p. 397 (Tiruvālaṅgāḍu plates).

[38] *ARE*, 333 of 1923; S. Sankaranarayanan, op. cit., pp. 10-11.

[39] *ARE*, 76 of 1914.

during the night preceding the day of Tiruvādirai festival in the month of Mārgaḻi before the god started for the sacred bath. The details of recitation specified in the record are very obscure. Each reciter was fed and paid 1 ¼ *kaḷañju* gold.[40]

A fragmentary inscription from the Vedanārāyaṇa Perumāḷ temple in the village of Āniyūr (now called Ānūr) in Chengalpet district on the banks of river Pālār belonging to the fourteenth regnal year of Rājarāja I (*c.* CE 999) records a gift of land by the *mahāsabhā* of the village (Āniyūr) as *bhaṭṭa-vṛtti* to a brāhmaṇa (name lost) of the village well-versed in one Veda, besides the *Sāmaveda*, in the Pāṇiṇi grammar (*Paṇiṇīya-Vyākaraṇa*), the *alaṁkāra* and twenty chapters of the Mīmāṁsā.[41] He was to teach these subjects to four pupils and also feed them everyday. A certain piece of land at Āniyūr, originally granted to the Subrahmaṇya temple at Tiruttani, was now endowed as *bhaṭṭa-vṛtti* to be enjoyed by the Bhaṭṭa while the money income accruing from the land was "as of old" to be paid to the temple by the *mahāsabhā*. The mention of twenty chapters of Mīmāṁsā is notable; we have now only sixteen, the rest are believed to have been lost, but were still available in the reign of Rājarāja I.[42] This inscription clearly mentions the qualifications to be acquired by a *bhaṭṭa* to receive this *bhaṭṭa-vṛtti*: he should be a person born of a Sāmavedin and should not be a native of the village but come from outside and settle down in the village in which he is to reach the required subjects.

A very interesting inscription from the Vaikuṇṭha Perumāḷ temple in Uttiramerūr (Chengalpet district) belonging to the Coḷa age of the tenth century CE deals with the establishment of an institution of higher learning and the qualifications prescribed for the professor, the method of appointment and

[40] *ARE*, 1915; pt. II, para 21, p. 97.

[41] *ARE*, 76 of 1932-33.

[42] K.A. Nilakanta Sastri, *Coḷas*, Madras, 1984, p. 630.

the duration of his service.[43] The inscription records the gift of land as *bhaṭṭa-vṛtti* by a lady called Sannaiccani alias Uttaramerunaṅgai. The following qualifications were prescribed on the recipients of the *bhaṭṭa-vṛtti*: the *bhaṭṭas* were not to own shares in the village lands; they should be learned either in one of the Vedas, the Vyākaraṇa, the Mīmāṁsā and two *darśanas*; or in one Veda and the *Nirukta Bhāṣya*; or in one Veda, the Vyākaraṇa, the *Nyāya Bhāṣya* along with the *Vārttika* and Vaiśeṣika along with the *ṭīkā* (commentary). The recipients, once selected, were to stay for three years in the *maṭha* constructed by the same lady on the bank of the tank dug on her sponsorship and expound their respective subjects. In the course of the succeeding terms also, the same selection was to be held for the *apūrvīs*. The *sabhā* of Uttaramerūr-caturvedimaṅgalam rendered the granted land tax-free. It can be seen from this inscription that a very high standard was expected from these *bhaṭṭas*. For three years, as prescribed in the rule, they would have imparted their knowledge to the students thus ensuring that they attained a high level of proficiency in their subjects of study.

Needless to say, many literary works of prose, poetry and drama would have been composed during the reign of Rājarāja I. That two works — one a drama (*nāṭaka*) known as *Rājarājeśvara-nāṭakam* and a poem (*kāvya*) called *Rājarāja-vijayam* were composed with the great emperor as the subject is certainly known.[44] The *Rājarājeśvara-nāṭakam* was probably not a drama based on Rājarāja's life, but rather a dramatic representation of the construction of the great temple in Tañjāvūr and it was to be enacted in the Tañjāvūr temple during festivals.[45] Endowments were created for the purpose of this enactment. This *nāṭaka* was enacted in the Bṛhadīśvara

[43] *SII*, vol. VI no. 322, p. 154; *ARE*, 39 of 1898.

[44] *ARE*, 120 of 1931; *ARE*, 1931, pt. II, para 12, p. 44; *SII*, vol. II no. 306.

[45] K.A. Nilakanta Sastri, *Coḷas*, p. 663.

(Rājarājeśvaram) temple in Tañjāvūr during the reign of Rājarāja II by the actor (*śantikūttan*) Tiruvalan Tirumudikunran, alias Vijaya-Rājendra-acāryaṉ and his troops.[46] It is not known whether this drama was in Tamil or in Sanskrit as it has not been traced.

The *kāvya, Rājarāja-vijayam* must have been a work composed probably during the time of Rājarāja I, glorifying his military achievements and was evidently different from the *Rājarājeśvara-nāṭakam*.[47] It should therefore have been a quasi-historical poem.[48] In the Puṣpavaneśvara temple in Tirupunturutti (Tañjāvūr district) is an inscription of Coḷa times, fragmentary in nature, which mentions a donation of land made to a *savarṇan* (doctor) named Naranan-Bhaṭṭādittaṉ for reading of the *Śrī Rājarāja-vijayam*.[49] This work too has not been traced and it is not known whether it was in Tamil or in Sanskrit. In any case, both these works must have contained several allusions, if not accurate description, of some of the most striking episodes in Rājarāja's life and the loss of these works is much to be regretted.[50]

In addition to the Sanskrit works, it would not be out of context to mention the pride of place with regard to the Tamil *Devāram* hymns in the reign of Rājarāja I. The recitation of *Devāram* hymns was made a regular feature in the time of this monarch. Tradition associates the discovery of the *Devāram* hymns in the Cidambaram temple to Rājarāja I.[51] The tradition of singing the *Devāram* hymns in Śiva temple in the ancient

---

[46] *SII*, vol. II, p. 306.

[47] *ARE*, 1930-31, pt. II, para 12, p. 44

[48] K.A. Nilakanta Sastri, *Coḷas*, p. 663.

[49] *ARE*, 1930-31, pt. II, para 12.

[50] K.A. Nilakanta Sastri, *Coḷas*, pp. 663-64.

[51] R. Nagaswamy, *Śaivism under Rājarāja: A Study from Rājarāja the Great* (*Seminar Proceedings*), Anantacharya Indological Research Institute, Bombay, 1987, p. 63.

Tamil country was there even in the eighth century CE as seen from the information provided by inscriptions in various places. However, there is an interesting tradition connecting Rājarāja I and the *Devāram* hymns.[52] One of Rājarāja's dreams was to recover all the *Devāram* hymns which remained hidden somewhere. He had heard about a great miracle that happened to a boy named Nambi Āṇḍār Nambi of a place called Tirunāṟaiyūr (in the ancient Coḷa country) and hastened to request the latter to help recover the *Devāram* hymns. Nambi, due to his divine prowess, revealed that all the *Devāram* verses were in a pile of cadjan leaves in a room in the western *prākāra* (circumambulatory passage) in the Naṭarāja Temple in Cidambaram. The king and Nambi then went to this temple and requested the Tillai three-thousand (group of brāhmaṇa priests of Tillai or Cidambaram) to open the room which was sealed. However, they replied that this could happen only if the great saints themselves were physically present on the occasion. Rājarāja then arranged for a celebration in honour of Tamil Nāyaṇmārs (Tamil Śaivite saints) and brought their images to the front of the room. The seals then broke and the room opened. The pile of cadjan leaves was there, but covered with termites. However, a large number of hymns were recovered.

Rājarāja I, thrilled with this monumental discovery, arranged for the recitation of these hymns in this great Śiva temple in Tañjāvūr. Forty-eight *Pidarar*s or *Tiruppadiyam-viṇṇapam sevars* were appointed by him for singing these hymns in front of Lord Śiva. Two musicians, who played on a small drum and a big drum to keep the beat when they sang, were also appointed. They were all paid generously and provision was also made for the appointment of their successors. The names of all the fifty musicians are found incised in this temple.

---

[52] B. Natarajan, *Tillai and Naṭarāja*, Madras, 1994, pp. 210-14.

This royal devotee of Śiva had an image of Candraśekhara (Śiva) made and practised the *Devāram* hymns in front of this deity, which in his inscriptions, is called Devāradevar. In many other temples of the Coḷa era and subsequent times too, the practice of singing the *Devāram* hymns continued.

Whenever there is an endowment of his reign giving a comprehensive *nibandha* for creating various services in the temple, reciters of *Devāram* are invariably mentioned. In the Rājarājeśvaram temple in Tañjāvūr, Rājarāja I appointed forty-eight *Devāram* singers.[53]

Rājendra Coḷa I (CE 1012-44)

Rājendra Coḷa I, the son and successor of Rājarāja Coḷa I, was a mighty conqueror who brought vast areas under Coḷa hegemony. His contribution to the sphere of education was also profound, this emperor himself being well-read and of a scholarly bent of mind. The Karandai copper-plate inscription (CE 1021) records the education and training given to Rājendra Coḷa I.[54] It states that even when he was a boy, Rājendra was well-versed in all the Vedas and Śāstras, well-trained in riding on horses, elephants and chariots, and also knew the use of arms and weapons very well. The Eśālam copper-plate inscription of the same king describes him poetically as "the ocean into which all the rivers of knowledge flow".[55] Among his many titles (*birudas*) was *Paṇḍita Coḷa*, as recorded in some Tamil inscriptions, revealing his scholarship.[56] It could also be understood that Rājendra Coḷa I encouraged learned Sanskrit scholars and helped them in propagating knowledge of the subjects like the Vedas and Śāstras to such an extent that he came to be called *Paṇḍita Coḷa*, signifying "a Coḷa who favoured

[53] *SII*, vol. II no. 65, pp. 253-55.

[54] K.G. Krishnan, *KTPR*, v. 42, p. 72.

[55] R. Nagaswamy, *ECPR*, v. 16, p. 32.

[56] *SII*, vol. II nos. 12 and 13, pp. 97-99; *SII*, vol. III, p. 127.

or was loved by the learned scholars" (*paṇḍita priyaḥ coḷaḥ*).[57] The contribution of this great emperor to the dissemination of learning in his land is seen from the information contained in many inscriptions, especially in the Karandai copper-plate grant.

This lengthy inscription records that this ruler gave to 1,080 brāhmaṇas, who were great masters of the Vedas, a whole *agrahāra* called Tribhuvana-Mahādevī (*caturvedimaṅgalam*) named after his mother by joining together fifty-one villages in Vīra-Coḷa-vaḷanāḍu, a sub-division of Nityavinod-vaḷanāḍu.[58] These plates state that "this monarch made this *agrahāra* the most beautiful place on earth by making it fertile with the waters of the Kāvērī and reverberating with the loud chants of the Vedas". This inscription also praises the brāhmaṇas (*bhūmidevāḥ*) of this *agrahāra* very eloquently as unequalled in courage (*dhairye*), stability (*sthairye*), penance (*tapasī*), greatness and humility (*mahasi praśraye*), who considered the Vedas a trifle on account of the greatness of their intellect (*sarvān-vedān sva-mativibhavāt-svalpam āmanyamānāḥ*), who were abodes where the wealth of the Śāstras sported (*śāstrārtha-śrī-viharaṇa-gr̥hāḥ*), who were the holiest of the holy (*pāvanaḥ pāvanānām*) and who daily displayed their extraordinary intellect (*nityam yatra sva-ati-mati-ratim kurvate*).

This inscription gives the names of a large number of *brahmadeyas* (*caturvedimaṅgalams*), most of them bearing the names of the Coḷa emperors or their queens. Malari or Śrīkaṇṭa-catruvedimaṅgalam is the earliest of such villages formed into an *agrahāra* in the Coḷa period since Śrīkaṇṭa was the name of Vijayālaya's father according to the Anbil plates.[59] There is

---

[57] S. Sankaranarayanana, *Sanskrit Education*, p. 16.

[58] K.G. Krishnan, *KTPR*, vv. 65-69, p. 61.

[59] Ibid., p. 56.

also mention of Vijayālaya-caturvedimaṅgalam in these plates, which was named after Vijayālaya. Śrī Parāntaka-caturvedimaṅgalam and Siṁhalāntaka-caturvedimaṅgalam were named after Parāntaka I; Kodandarāma-caturvedimaṅgalam, Gandarāditya-caturvedimaṅgalam, Aṟiñjaya-caturvedimaṅgalam, Uttamasili-caturvedimaṅgalam and Naṅgai Brahmadeyam alias Aṟiñjigai-caturvedimaṅgalam were all named after the sons of Parāntaka I; two bearing the name Uttamaśola-caturvedimaṅgalam were probably named after Uttama Coḷa (although Rājendra Coḷa also had this title); Vānavaṉ-mahādevī-caturvedimaṅgalam, Kundavai-caturvedimaṅgalam, Sembiyan-mahādevī-caturvedimaṅgalam, Loka mahādevī-caturvedimaṅgalam, Teṉṉavaṉ-mahādevī-caturvedimaṅgalam, Coḷa-mahādevī-caturvedimaṅgalam were names of some Coḷa queens and princesses; Coḷamartaṇḍa-caturvedimaṅgalam, Jayankoṇḍacoḷa-caturvedimaṅgalam, Mummuḍicoḷa-caturvedimaṅgalam and Rājāśraya-caturvedimaṅgalam were all named after the titles of Rājarāja I and Jananātha-caturvedimaṅgalam was the title of Rājendra I. Kaṟṟaliyeri alias Vikramakesari-caturvedimaṅgalam could be for Kaṟṟali a queen of Bhūti Vikramakesari, the famous chieftain of Koḍuṁbāḷūr.[60]

Other than these villages, which were called *caturvedimaṅgalams*, there were many *brahmadeyas*, without the suffix *caturvedimaṅgalam*, the brāhmaṇa residents of which received shares of land under the grant mentioned in the Karandai inscription.[61] This grant makes it very clear that the practice of establishing *brahmadeyas*, which started in the Pallava period was completely adopted by the Coḷas, resulting in such large numbers of *brahmadeyas*.[62] This phenomenal rise of *brahmadeyas* during this period is clear indication of the fact

[60] K.G. Krishnan, *KTPR*, pp. 64-68.

[61] Ibid., p. 57.

[62] Ibid., p. 57.

that the ruling kings patronized the brāhmaṇa settlers from the Andhra country almost continuously, for as seen from the Karandai record, no less than 775 brāhmaṇas among the 1,083 donees bore the names of villages in the Andhra country, while it is possible that in the case of the rest, they had arrived in the Tamil country much earlier and therefore had adopted a local village.[63] This distinction made between the two groups is supported by another factor — the brāhmaṇas who are stated in this record as hailing from places with Tamil names belong mostly to *sūtra*s other than Āpastamba, i.e. Āśvalāyana, Drahyāyana, Satyāsadha, Jaimini, etc.[64]

During the reign of Rājendra Coḷa, a number of educational centres functioned in the premises of the temples of the Coḷa empire. The *ghaṭika* at Kāñcīpuram which was a famous educational centre in the Pallava times (Chapter 1) seems to have continued to function even during the Coḷa era as recorded in a Tamil inscription of the period of Rājendra Coḷa I in the Kailāsanātha temple in Kāñcīpuram.[65] This lithic epigraph, the date of which is lost, mentions that an officer of the king named Śiṟijñār-Kiḻavar audited certain accounts of the *Peria-tirukkaṟṟali* (i.e. the Kailāsanātha temple) while he was camping in the college (*surrukalluri*) to the east of the Tiruvaṇukkavāśal in the temple (*kovil*) in Kāñcīpuram.[66] The *ghaṭika* (which was an establishment for learned men) is, in a sense, a word similar to *kallūri*.[67]

A very important inscription of the eleventh century CE of the reign of Rājendra Coḷa I (CE 1012-44) provides a lot of information about the cultural milieu of the Coḷa era, especially from the view-point of education and religion as it regards

---

[63] K.G. Krishnan, *KTPR*, p. 57.

[64] Ibid.

[65] *ARE*, 240 of 1930.

[66] *ARE*, 1930-31, pt. II, para 12, p. 43.

[67] Ibid.

the functioning of an educational institution attached to the Aḻagiya Narasiṁha Perumāḷ temple at Eṇṇayiram (South Arcot district).[68] This Tamil inscription, written in the Tamil script in characters of the eleventh century CE, is engraved on the north side of the central shrine of this Viṣṇu temple. The portion which records the details of the date of this epigraph is badly damaged, making the decipherment of the regnal year of the king difficult. However, since the introductory portions of the Coḷa epigraphs (*meykkritīs*) list the achievements of the monarchs in chronological order and since this inscription concludes with the conquest of Kaḍāram by Rājendra, usually found in the corresponding portion of his other inscriptions dated from the fourteenth year of his reign (CE 1025-26) only, this record can be safely assigned to the period CE 1025-44.[69]

This epigraph records a resolution passed by the *mahāsabhā* (the great administrative council) of the village Rājarāja-caturvedimaṅgalam (the present Eṇṇāyiram), made in the immediate presence of an officer of the king's administration and in accordance with the terms of the king's own order.[70] This resolution created four endowments. The first one provided for the expenses of worship and offerings to Lord Narasiṁha of the temple and for the recitation of the *Tiruvāymoḻi* hymns in the temple. The second made provisions for the daily feeding of twenty-five Vaiṣṇavas in the *maṭha* of the same temple. The third endowment was meant to meet the expenditure of some festival of the said God. The fourth endowment, which is very vital, was meant to arrange for feeding of the pupils and for the remuneration of the teachers of the college which was named Gaṅgaikoṇḍaśoḻan, and was instituted to commemorate Rājendra's success in bringing the

[68] *EI*, vol. XXXIX no. 34, pp. 223-36 (Eṇṇāyiram inscription).

[69] *EI*, vol. XXXIX no. 34, p. 224.

[70] S. Sankaranarayanan, op. cit., p. 11.

Gaṅgā (waters) after defeating the rulers of the Uttarapatha (north India). The details of this part of the resolution provide an accurate idea about the subjects offered for study by the college and about the strength of the students and of the teaching staff of the respective departments.[71] The average cost of maintaining students varied according to their grades, viz. the *brahmacārin* (the junior) and the *chātra* (the senior). Likewise, the remunerations of the teachers also differed from subject to subject. These indicate the then prevailing popularity of different courses and of the relative esteem in which the teachers of the different subjects were held.[72]

The subjects taught at this educational centre were R̥gveda, Yajurveda, Chāndoga Sāma, Tāḷavakāra Sāma, Vājasaneya (Śukla Yajurveda), Baudhāyanīya (Gr̥hya, Kalpa and Kāṭhaka), Atharvaveda, Vyākaraṇa, Prābhākara Mīmāṁsā, Rūpavatāra and Vedānta. This institution housed a total of fifteen teachers and 350 students. Of this, the majority of eleven teachers and 230 students belonged to the discipline of Vedic studies. The number of students and teachers for the four Vedic subjects were: seventy-five students and three teachers for R̥gveda; 105 students and five teachers for Yajurveda; forty students and two teachers for Sāmaveda and ten students and one teacher for Atharvaveda. It can therefore be said that this college was essentially a centre of Vedic studies (*pāṭhaśālā*) attached to the temple where all the four Vedas were taught.[73]

Although this lithic record does not specify the two branches of Yajurveda, viz. the Śukla (white) and Kr̥ṣṇa (black), the separate mention of Vājasaneya (in line 10 of the inscription) which is the well-known recension of the *Śukla Yajurveda* makes it clear that the word Yajurveda refers only to the *Kr̥ṣṇa*

---

[71] S. Sankaranarayanan, op. cit., p. 11.

[72] Ibid.

[73] Ibid.

Yajurveda.[74] The importance given to the study of the Kṛṣṇa Yajurveda is seen further from the mention of the study of the three well-known works of Bodhāyana — the *Baudhāyana, Gṛhya, Kalpa* and *Kāṭhaka* — which are the Sūtras belonging to the Taittirīya school of the *Kṛṣṇa Yajurveda*.[75] The inscription mentions the study of *Tāḷavakāra Sāman* and *Chāndoga Sāman* showing that each of the two important schools of the *Sāmaveda* — the Tāḷavakāras and the Taṇḍins — gained importance for study at the Eṇṇāyiram college.[76]

S. Sankaranarayanan has opined that while the Eṇṇāyiram college offered courses in all the four Vedas, it included in its syllabus the Baudhāyanīya Sūtra alone which belonged to the Taittirīya branch of the Kṛṣṇa Yajurveda, but why the other Kalpa and Gṛhya Sūtras were neglected is difficult to explain.[77] In the same manner, the college encouraged the study of Prābhākara Mīmāṁsā (less popular now) and totally neglected the Bhāṭṭa Mīmāṁsā (more popular now).[78] According to S. Sankaranarayanan, this phenomenon may be explained in the light of a tradition according to which, Prabhākara, the real founder of the Prābhākara School was a southerner, perhaps a Keralite, while Kumārila Bhaṭṭa, the founder of the Bhāṭṭa School was a southerner by birth, but became a northerner by domicile or vice versa.[79] *Prābhākaram* is the work of Prabhākara Miśra (*c*. CE 650–720) commenting on the *Mīmāṁsā-sūtra Bhāṣya* of Śabarasvāmin, one of the important systems of Pūrva-Mīmāṁsā. Two commentaries called *Laghvī* and *Bṛhatī* were written by Prabhākara Miśra and perhaps they were taught in the Eṇṇāyiram college.[80]

[74] S. Sankaranarayanan, op. cit., p. 11.

[75] Ibid.

[76] Ibid.

[77] Ibid.

[78] Ibid.

[79] Ibid.

[80] Eṇṇāyiram inscription, op. cit., fn. 2.

It is interesting to note that a lithic record from Gadag (Dharwad district, Karnataka), of the reign of the Kalyāṇī Cāḷukya ruler, Vikramāditya VI (CE 1076–1126), mentions that his minister Someśvara Bhaṭṭa established a Prābhākara-vyākhyāna-śālā, i.e. a *pāṭhaśālā* or school for teaching the Prābhākara Mīmāṁsā in the town of Lokkiguṇḍi (i.e. modern Lakkuṇḍi, near Gadag), a place which is praised as an abode of many learned pious brāhmaṇas, completely devoted to the study and teaching of the Vedas and allied subjects and to the continued performance of Vedic sacrifices.[81] The founder of this *śālā* made full provisions for the teacher who taught the above Mīmāṁsā there. Like the Tamil country, the Kannada region too seems to have been particularly in favour of the Prābhākara School of Mīmāṁsā, in preference to the Bhāṭṭa School.[82] This is very interesting as according to some traditions the founders of both the schools hailed from the south: Kumārila Bhaṭṭa hailed from the Andhra country and his pupil Prabhākara Miśra from Kerala.[83]

In addition to the Vedas, other subjects were also taught at this educational centre in Eṇṇāyiram. Among these was *Rūpāvatāra*, an elementary work on Sanskrit grammar, the authorship of which is attributed to Dharmakīrti, whose identity and date are not well settled.[84] *Rūpāvatāra* was also taught at several other institutions in the eleventh and twelfth centuries CE as indicated by epigraphical evidence from Tiruvavḍuturai (Tañjāvūr district)[85] and Tribhuvanai (Pondicherry).[86] M. Rangacharya has ascribed this work to

[81] *EI*, vol. XV, pp. 350ff; S. Sankaranarayanan, *Sanskrit Education*, pp. 114-16.

[82] Ibid., p. 116.

[83] K.A. Nilakanta Sastri, *A History of South India*, Madras, 1988, pp. 353-53; S. Sankaranarayanan, op. cit., p. 116.

[84] Eṇṇāyiram inscription, op. cit.

[85] *ARE*, 159 of 1925.

[86] *ARE*, 176 of 1919.

the twelfth century CE.[87] However, the fact that the *Rūpāvatāra* had already become so popular by the first quarter of the eleventh century CE as to be prescribed for study at the Eṇṇāyiram college, weighs against ascribing this work to the twelfth century CE.[88] M. Krishnamacharya refers to a tradition by which Bhaṭṭa Nārāyaṇa and Dharmakīrti jointly composed the *Rūpāvatāra* and assigns a date slightly later than the fifth or sixth centuries CE to Dharmakīrti.[89] There is a tradition that at the instance of Bāṇa, Bhaṭṭa Nārāyaṇa secretly studied under a Buddhist monk and after learning the secrets of their teaching, vanquished Dharmakīrti; they then became good friends and jointly composed the grammatical work, *Rūpāvatāra*. This would make Bāṇa, Bhaṭṭa Nārāyaṇa and Dharmakīrti contemporaries.[90]

This important inscription mentions the eight chapters of *vyākaraṇa* and it may be safely concluded that it was only the *Sūtrapāṭha* or *Aṣṭādhyāyī* of Pāṇini that was studied by the senior students of the Eṇṇāyiram college.[91] This epigraph mentions the teaching of Vedānta and by this perhaps the Āraṇyakas and the Upaniṣads, as constituting Uttara-Mīmāṁsā was meant.

The remuneration paid to the teachers and the allowance given to the students, both in cash and in kind are recorded in great detail in this epigraph. The paddy remuneration of the teachers of the first seven courses (Ṛgveda, Yajurveda, Chāndoga-Sāman, Tāḷavakāra-Sāman, Vājasaneya, Baudhāyana (Gṛhya, Kalpa and Kāṭhaka Sūtras) and Atharvaveda was exactly twice the maintenance allowance of the *chātras*.[92] The

87 M. Rangacharya (ed.), *Rūpāvatāram, Introduction;* Eṇṇāyiram inscription op. cit., p. 227.

88 Eṇṇāyiram inscription, op. cit.

89 M. Krishnamachariyar, *History of Classical Sanskrit Literature*, Delhi, 2009, p. 733, fn. 8; Eṇṇāyiram inscription, op. cit.

90 M. Krishnamachariyar, op. cit., p. 733, fn. 8.

91 Eṇṇāyiram inscription, p. 228.

92 S. Sankaranarayanan, *Sanskrit Education*, p. 14.

Rūpāvatāra teacher (subject number 8) alone received four *nāḷi* (or half a *kuruni*) more per day. The remuneration of the two teachers of Vyākaraṇa and the Prābhākara Mīmāṁsā (subject numbers 9 and 10) was four times that of the teacher of *Rūpāvatāra*. In addition to paddy, the teachers of Vyākaraṇa and Mīmāṁsā got 1 *kaḷañju* of gold per chapter (eight chapters for Vyākaraṇa and twelve chapters for Mīmāṁsā) they taught to students who studied the subjects under them for the first time (*apūrvam*) and it appears that they would not get the gold for teaching the chapters second time to the same *chātra*.[93] The teacher of Vedānta did not receive gold, but got daily remuneration of 1 *tuni* or one-third of a *kaḷam* more than the other two teachers of Vyākaraṇa and Mīmāṁsā got. The lower salary of the Vedic teachers and the higher remuneration of the *śāstrins* may have to be explained on the basis of lower and higher qualifications of these teachers.[94] The Vedic teachers had mastered the Vedas alone while the Śāstra teachers had got proficiency in one Śāstra or more after initially mastering their respective Vedic *śākhās* too, since a boy's education in ancient times started with the study of the Vedas.[95]

The Eṇṇāyiram inscription appears to stipulate that only those *brahmacārins* who studied their respective subjects for the first time (*apūrvam*) were eligible for the maintenance-allowance and it is possible to deduce that those who failed in their examinations and therefore had to study that subject again were not fed freely in the hostel.[96] Maybe they had to make their own arrangements such as the *bhikṣācāraṇa* or other means for their food. It may also be seen that the allowance of a *chātra* was nearly twice as much as that which a *brahmacārin* received. This difference was there because as young boys,

---

93 S. Sankaranarayanan, *Sanskrit Education*, p. 14.

94 Ibid.

95 Ibid.

96 Ibid.

the *brahmacārins* entered the college and started their education first by learning the Vedas and after completing their Vedic study in about eight or ten years, they themselves, as youthful *chātras*, joined the classes of different Śāstras. That is why the maintenance of a *chātra* was to cost much more than that of a *brahmacārin*. All this indicates, as mentioned above, that in ancient times, a study of any Śāstra was generally preceded by the study of a Vedic *śākhā*.

It appears from the data gleaned from another Tamil inscription at Eṇṇāyiram that there was a hostel attached to this "temple college" at the Narasiṁha temple here.[97] Unfortunately, this record is much damaged and has neither beginning nor end. However, it refers to the maintenance of a hostel in which provision was made for feeding 506 brāhmaṇas, among whom were scholars well-versed in the Vedas and brāhmaṇas in general.[98] This number must have included the 350 students who were attached to the college. The record also stated that on Jayantyāṣṭamī, the birthday of Veṇṇai-kūttar (Kṛṣṇa), those scholars who studied to the end, the Ṛg, Yajus and Sāma Vedas would receive a gold-flower and a gold ring.[99]

The Eṇṇāyiram lithic epigraph also states that four people were appointed to recite the *Tiruvāymoḻi* (the hymns of the Tamil Vaiṣṇava saint Nammāḻvār) which forms part of the *Nalāyira Divya Prabandham* before the deity. This is probably the earliest reference to the practice of recitation of *Tiruvāymoḻi*.[100] It is perhaps likely that it was included in the curriculum. It can be clearly seen from plenty of epigraphs of the Coḷa times that the recitation of the *Tiruvāymoḻī* hymns of

---

97 *ARE*, 343 of 1917.

98 *ARE*, 1918, pt. II, para 29, p. 147.

99 Ibid.

100 Eṇṇāyiram inscription, op. cit., p. 225.

Nammāḻvār gained prominence in Viṣṇu temples. Interestingly, an earlier inscription of Rājarāja I from Ukkal (near Kāñcīpuram) mentions the name of the deity as *Tiruvāymoḻidevar.*[101] Although the record from Eṇṇāyiram, a strong centre of Vaiṣṇavism, might possibly be the earliest reference to the practice of the recitation of *Tiruvāymoḻī*, it appears to have become a regular feature in Vaiṣṇava temples in the succeeding periods as seen from epigraphical evidence.[102] For example, an inscription from a ruined Viṣṇu temple at Tirumālpuram (North Arcot district) belonging to a certain Rājakesarivarman of the Coḷa times (date unfortunately lost) mentions the provision made for the recitation of *Tiruvāymoḻī.*[103] Two inscriptions of the reign of Rājendra Coḷa I from the Sundaravarada Perumāḷ temple in Uttaramerūr (near Chengalput) mention the recitation of *Tiruvāymoḻī* in this temple.[104]

There were several other temples where classes for teaching the Vedas were active in the reign of Rājendra Coḷa I as revealed by inscriptions. One of these is found on two door-jambs of the shrine of Goddess Sudhāvalli Thāyār in the Śrī Bhaktavatsala Perumāḷ temple in Tiruninravūr near Chennai. This highly damaged inscription unfortunately does not have the exact regnal year, but registers a gift of land for conducting the Śrībali service in the temple and for feeding students studying the Vedas.[105] A similar epigraph is etched in the Kadambeśvara temple in Tuṟaiyūr (Tirucirāpaḷḷī district) dated in the eighth regnal year of Rājendra Coḷa I and registers a gift of land to a brāhmaṇa for reciting the *Śrī Rudra* during the

[101] Eṇṇāyiram inscription, op. cit., p. 225.

[102] Ibid.

[103] *ARE*, 326 of 1906.

[104] *ARE*, 176 of 1923.

[105] *ARE*, 176 of 1937-38.

morning service in the temple at Tuḍaiyūr (Tuṟaiyūr) and for teaching the Vedas to the students therein.[106]

Another epigraph of this ruler from the Vaikuṇṭha Perumāḷ temple in Uttaramerūr records grants of land by the assembly (*sabhā*) of the village for teaching the Bahvṛca *Paviḻiya-kiḍaippuram* and stipulates that the men who enjoyed the income from it should live in the village and teach the Veda.[107] Another record also of the same king from the same place mentions a similar gift of land as *Taittirīya-kiḍaippuram*, obviously for the study of the Kṛṣṇa Yajurveda as well as the *Vājasaneya-kiḍaippuram* for studying the Śukla Yajurveda.[108] Yet another inscription of the same king from the same place though not an educational grant, lays stress on Vedic scholarship. It mentions a gift of land to the temple for various services which were to be conducted by an honest brāhmaṇa well-versed in the Vedas.[109] These inscriptions, as all others from the Coḷa times from this town dealing with many educational grants, reveal that this *caturvedimaṅgalam* had a number of special schools for higher studies, which must necessarily have attracted students not only from this village, but from places far and wide.

Two more Tamil inscriptions of Rājendra Coḷa's time offer glimpses to new settlements of brāhmaṇas ostensibly to promote dissemination of the Vedas and ancilliary subjects. The Kailāsanātha temple in Agaram (Chengalpet district) has, on the *maṇṭapa*, an inscription of the eighth regnal year of this emperor recording the founding of the village of Vaṉamaṅgai (or Vaṉavaṉmādevī), probably identical with the village of Agaram, where he settled 4,000 brāhmaṇas.[110] Another lithic

---

[106] *ARE*, 157 of 1937-38.

[107] *SII*, vol. VI no. 312; *ARE*, 29 of 1898.

[108] *ARE* 33 of 1898; *SII*, vol. VI no. 316; K.A. Nilakanta Sastri, *Studies in Coḷa History and Administration*, Madras, 1932, p. 116.

[109] *ARE*, 30 of 1898; *SII*, vol. VI no. 313.

[110] *ARE* 232 of 1930-31; ibid., pt. II, para 12, p. 43.

record of this emperor from the Nāganāthasvāmi temple in Tirunāgeśvaram (near Kuṁbakoṇam) records a grant made for expounding the *Śaiva dharma* in the assembly hall called Tiruccirrambalamuḍaiyan in this temple.[111] Other Coḷa inscriptions mention that works such as the *Śrīpurāṇa* of Aḷuḍaiyanambi and the *Somasiddhānta* were also recited.[112] These instances of recitations, popular in character, were intended for the instruction and edification of the devotees.[113] The nature of these works is unclear, but the *Somasiddhānta* appears, from a reference to it in the *Prabodhacandrodaya* to have propounded the doctrine of the Kāpālika school of Śaivism.[114]

A damaged epigraph of the seventh regnal year of Rājendra I from the Airāvateśvara temple at Niyamam (Tañjāvūr district) registers that he established an institution of learning at Niyamam and named it Rājendra-Coḷan-Śālai.[115] The institution is referred to in this inscription as tirupaḷḷi which would definitely mean "a school", because it is named Rājendra Coḷan-Śālai.[116] It is known that in the ancient times, *śālai* meant a school as indicated by an inscription from Hottal (Nanded district) dated CE 1101 and a late Tamil work *Kuśalopākhyānam* which refers to *śālai* as an institution of learning.[117] If the word *tirupaḷḷi* had been taken to mean a temple, then the inscription would certainly not have referred to it as *śālai*. Therefore the *śālai* here meant a *pāṭaśālai*, the composition of which is unclear.[118]

---

111 *ARE* 214 of 1911.

112 *ARE* 403 of 1896 and 321 of 1917.

113 K.A. Nilakanta Sastri, *Coḷas*, p. 640.

114 *ARE*, 1912, pt. II, para 29; K.A. Nilakanta Sastri, op. cit., pp. 640-41.

115 *ARE* 405 of 1961-62.

116 S. Gurumurthy, p. 66.

117 Ibid.

118 Ibid.

There must have been many literary works composed in the reign of Rājendra Coḷa I, but unfortunately very little is known about them. Śaiva works of the type of *Siddhāntasārāvaḷī* must have been largely patronized by the king who was himself a devout Śaiva.[119] It is stated in the *Siddhāntasārāvaḷī* of Trailocanaśivācārya that Rājendra Coḷa, on the occasion of his visit to the Gaṅgā saw there the best of Śaivas and brought them with him and settled them at Kāñcī and other places in the Coḷa country.[120] The *Siddhāntasārāvaḷī* is a compendium of the esoteric ritual of the Śaiva School. Jaina and Buddhist literature also had their share of patronage. From the *Upāsakajanalavikāra* of the Mahāthera Ānanda, it may be inferred that the king lent his patronage to Buddhist literature.[121]

Rājādhirāja Coḷa I (CE 1018-54)

Rājādhirāja Coḷa was probably the eldest of the three sons of Rājendra Coḷa I who succeeded their father one after the other. An able conqueror and administrator, he was co-ruler with his illustrious father for ten years before he ascended the throne at Gaṅgaikoṇḍacoḷapuram. His contributions to the sphere of education are known particularly from one famous Tamil inscription from the Varadarāja Svāmi temple in Tribhuvanai (Pondicherry). This epigraph is similar to the Eṇṇāyiram inscription and is found on the east wall of the Varadarāja Svāmi temple in this town which was originally called Tribhuvana-mahādevī-caturvedimaṅgalam. This inscription which records the lands gifted for running a Vedic college, is dated in the thirtieth regnal year of Rājādhirāja Coḷa I.[122] The details of the date given

---

[119] *SII*, vol. III pt. I, p. 22.

[120] Ibid.

[121] *SII*, vol. III pt. I, p. 22.

[122] *ARE* 176 of 1919.

in the record work out correctly for Wednesday, 2 March 1048.[123] On this day, the great assembly of the village met together in the *maṇḍapa* built by Sembiyaṉ Imbalanattuvelar and purchased lands in the name of God Vīranārāyaṇa-Viṇṇagar-Āḻvār to meet all the requirements of a charity known as Rājendraśolan-uttamāgram established in the temple by the general (*senāpati*) Rājendraśoḷa-Māvali Vāṇarāja, in order to secure the health of King Rājendra Coḷa. Evidently, the charity was instituted while the king was living and was named after him.[124] This inscription was most likely etched on the wall of this temple only in the reign of his son Rājādhirāja Coḷa I. Land was purchased for various offerings, worship, etc., on a large scale and for conducting festivals, for feeding Śrīvaiṣṇavas and for reciting the *Tiruvāymoḻī* and for running a Vedic college.

The subjects in this educational institution included the Ṛgveda, Yajurveda, Chāndoga Sāma, Tāḷavakāra Sāma, Apūrva, Vājasaneya, Baudhāyanīya, Satyasadhasūtra, Mahābhārata, Rāmāyaṇa, Vedānta, Vyākaraṇa, Rūpāvatāra, Manuśāstra and Vaikhānasa Śāstra. The number of teachers and students for these subjects as well as their respective allowances are given in detail in this record.

The Tribhuvanai college had 260 students and 12 teachers and the curriculam was almost the same as the educational centre at Eṇṇāyiram. There were three teachers of Ṛgveda, three of the Yajurveda and one each of Chāndoga Sāma, Tāḷavakāra Sāma, Apūrva, Vājasaneya, Baudhāyanīya and Satyasadhasūtra, thus making a total of twelve teachers. There was one person each for expounding the Vedānta, Vyākaraṇa, Rūpāvatāra, Śrī Bhārata (Mahābhārata), Rāmāyaṇa, Manuśāstra and Vaikhānasa Śāstra. The college had sixty students each of the Ṛgveda and Yajurveda, twenty of Chāndoga Sāma and

123 *ARE*, 1919, pt. II, para 18, p. 96.

124 Ibid.

fifty of other Śāstras; there were seventy other students of the Vedānta, Vyākaraṇa and Rūpāvatāra.[125]

While the Prābhākara Mīmāṁsā was not taught at Tribhuvanai, some other subjects such as the Satyasadhasūtra, Mahābhārata, Rāmāyaṇa, Manuśāstra and the Vaikhānasa Śāstra were taught. It seems that works like the *Mahābhārata* and *Rāmāyaṇa* were being expounded to the general audience rather than taught as a regular subject in classes.[126] Another probability is that the college gave regular training to a set of its own capable students in the art of making public and popular discourses on these epics for propagating *dharma*.[127]

Like the Eṇṇāyiram record, the Tribhuvanai epigraph also gives detailed information about the payment made to the teachers and the daily allowances to the students of this educational institution. The payment to the teachers and the students was in the form of paddy. The amount given to the teachers differed according to the subjects which they taught. The teacher of Vedānta received one and one-sixth *kaḷam* of paddy per day and was the highest paid, while the other teachers were paid amounts varying from 1 *kaḷam* to one fourth of a *kaḷam*. With regard to the daily allowances of the students, the junior pupils were given 6 *naḷi* of paddy per day and the senior pupils received 8 *naḷi* each. The inscription also records that the *mahāsabhā* had passed a resolution that the teachers and students of the college were exempted from active services on the different committees of the village administrative assembly. This was perhaps to serve two purposes — the first to free the college from local politics and administration and the second to enable the community of teachers and students to concentrate fully on their respective fields.[128] Although this

[125] *ARE*, 1919, pt. II, para 18, p. 96.

[126] S. Sankaranarayanan, *Sanskrit Education*, p. 17.

[127] Ibid.

[128] Ibid.

long record is much damaged, it gives a lot of information that reveals that temple charities were not exclusively meant for ceremonials in the temple, but for scientific (śāstric) and religious (Vedic) education.[129]

Similarly, an inscription from the Trivikrama temple in Tirukoyilūr (South Arcot district) of the reign of Tribhuvanacakravartin Rājādhirājadeva records that a lady of Singaḷava-nāḍu made a gift of 7 *kaḻañju* of gold to the assembly of Candraśoḷa-caturvedimaṅgalam for conducting the festivals of Arpāśi and Vaigāśi and for the daily recitations of *Tiruvāymoḻī* and for offerings to the gods.[130] Another epigraph from the Gopālasvāmi temple at Mannārkoyil (Tirunelveli district) of the time of Tribhuvanacakravarti Koṉeriṉmaikoṇḍaṉ, which is unfortunately unfinished, refers to land given to twelve *bhaṭṭa*s of Kulaśekhara-caturvedimaṅgalam and to the temple of Nalāyira-Viṇṇagar-Emberumāṉ for the recitation of *Tiruvāymoḻī*.[131] There are many other instances of the recitation of *Tiruvāymoḻī* in temples in the Coḷa era and in subsequent times as well.

Vīra-Rājendra (CE 1062/63–1070)

Vīra-Rājendra was the third son of Rājendra Coḷa I and ascended the throne upon the death of his brother Rājendra II (who was the successor of his elder brother Rājādhirāja I). Although he reigned only for a short period, he kept the empire of his predecessors virtually intact and made important contributions towards the cause of education. The most important inscription of the time of this emperor with regard to education is found in the Appan Veṅkaṭeśa Perumāḷ temple in the village of Tirumukkūḍal (Chengalpet district).[132] This

---

[129] *ARE* 1919, pt. II, para 18, p. 97.

[130] *ARE* 343 of 1921.

[131] *ARE* 393 of 1916.

[132] *EI*, vol. XXI no. 38 (Tirumukkūḍal inscription).

temple, over many centuries, was known by various names like Viṣṇu Bhaṭāra, Tirumukkūḍal Āḻvār, Mahā Viṣṇu and Veṅkaṭeśvara Svāmin. The village Tirumukkūḍal means the "confluence of three sacred (streams)". This temple is situated where three rivers — the Pālār, the Cheyyār and the Vegavatī — meet is an ideal place to set up a Vedic college. This eleventh century inscription is one more in the list of Coḷa epigraphs giving details of a large "temple college". It consists of fifty-five lines and is engraved in two sections on the east wall of the first *prākāra* of this temple. It is one of the lengthiest epigraphs of the world and registers a royal order donating lands as *devadāna* to this temple for meeting various expenses such as conducting various festivals, daily worship of the deity, for feeding Śrīvaiṣṇavas on various festive occasions and for the payment of people attached to this temple such as the person reciting the *Tiruvāymoḻī*, hymns, the cultivators who looked after the flower-gardens, accountants and others.

However, the most important portion of this inscription is with regard to the maintenance of a Vedic college in this temple housed in a building called the Jananātha-maṇṭapa (named after one of the titles of Rājarāja Coḷa I). Just like the Eṇṇāyiram and the Tribhuvanai inscriptions, here too information is given about the number of teachers and students of this Vedic college, the payment made and other such interesting and valuable details. Eight subjects were taught in this college, i.e. Ṛgveda, Yajurveda, Vyākaraṇa, Rūpāvatāra, Mahā-Pāñcarātra, Śaivāgama, Vaikhānasa and one more subject (the name of which is lost in the inscription). This Vedic college in Tirumukkūḍal had three teachers and sixty students. There was one teacher of the Ṛgveda who received annually 60 *kaḷam* of paddy and 4 *kāśu*; another taught the Yajurveda and was paid similarly. A *bhaṭṭa* expounded the Vyākaraṇa and Rūpāvatāra and was annually paid 120 *kaḷam* of paddy and 10 *kāśu*, i.e. a little more than the combined honorarium paid to the two Vedic teachers.[133] Among the sixty students in this college, ten were for Ṛgveda, ten for Yajurveda, twenty for Vyākaraṇa and Rūpāvatāra, ten for Mahā-Pāñcarātra, three Śiva brāhmaṇas (perhaps studying Śaivāgama) and five Vaikhānasas (studying Vaikhānasāgama) and two for another subject (name lost in the inscription). The word Śiva brāhmaṇa occurs very frequently in south Indian inscriptions and it has generally been taken to mean those belonging to the Śaiva religion; but this inscription seems to indicate that it has the special significance of one studying the Śaivāgama, referring as it does to a class of students in this school.[134]

Interestingly, there was a hostel attached to this temple where the sixty students (namely ten for the Ṛgveda, ten for the Yajurveda, twenty for Vyākaraṇa and the Rūpāvatāra, ten Mahā Pāñcarātras, three Śiva brāhmaṇas, five Vaikhānasas and two of another subject (not mentioned) were fed. The feeding expenses, inclusive of the cost of the mats and oil for lamps and for bathing for fifty-one Saturdays of the year and wages of cooks and maid-servants who served the students and the teachers came to 1,642 *kaḷam* and 6 *kuruṇi* of paddy and 37 $^5/_8$ *kāśu*. It is interesting to find that the students in the hostel were provided with mats to lie on and lights for studying at night and were given oil for a bath once a week throughout the year. The appointment of maid-servants was to keep the premises clean.[135] From the fact the hostel fed not only the students studying the Ṛgveda, Yajurveda, Vyākaraṇa and Rūpāvatāra, but also a certain number of Mahā-Pāñcarātras, Śiva brāhmaṇas and Vaikhānasas, it may be inferred that the Āgamas and Tantras such as the Pāñcarātra, Śaiva and Vaikhānasa were also taught.[136]

---

[133] *EI*, vol. XXI no. 38 (Tirumukkūḍal inscription).

[134] Tirumukkūḍal inscription, p. 223.

[135] Ibid.

[136] Ibid.

It may be seen that no separate teachers are mentioned in the record for teaching the Pañcarātra, Śaiva and Vaikhānasa Āgamas to the students, all totalling twenty.[137] Maybe, they studied their respective Āgamic subjects under some different scholar-servants attached to some of the local temples. Or, perhaps, these twenty were themselves servants in some local temples and were simply fed along with the students in the hostel.[138] It may be noted that though the college was a Vaiṣṇava dominated one, it had among its *chātras*, some Śiva brāhmaṇas.[139]

This royal record mentions as the last item of expenditure, the maintenance of a hospital where the students living in the hostel and temple servants who fell ill were treated. This hospital, called Vīraśoḷan, had fifteen beds and was in-charge of a physician named Savarṇṇa Kodaṇḍarāman Aśvatthāma Bhaṭṭan who was annually paid 90 *kaḷam* of paddy and 8 *kāśu* in addition to land to be enjoyed by himself and his descendants, for prescribing medicines to the patients in the hospital. Besides the physician, there was a surgeon who received 30 *kaḷam* of paddy, two persons for fetching medicinal herbs, supplying firewood and attending to the preparation of medicines who received 60 *kaḷam* of paddy and 2 *kāśu* and two nurses who received 30 *kaḷam* of paddy and 1 *kāśu* for attending the patients and administering medicines and a barber for performing minor operations in addition to his professional duties. This lithic record also gives the information that the sick ration consisted of one *nāḷi* of rice per head per day and that a provision of 2 ¼ *kāśu* was made for a lamp to be kept burning in the hospital during nights; 15 *kaḷam* of paddy for the water-man and 40 *kāśu* for stocking medicines. A list of twenty medicines stocked in the hospital

[137] S. Sankaranarayanan, *Sanskrit Education*, p. 19.

[138] Ibid.

[139] Ibid.

is given in this inscription. K.V. Subrahmanya Ayyar, the editor of this inscription, has elaborately dealt with the preparation of various items of medicines and their multi-purpose application in curing diseases with the help of certain Ayurvedic texts like *Caraka-Saṁhitā* and *Aṣṭāṅga-Hṛdaya*.[140]

This inscription gives a very clear picture of the trouble taken during the Coḷa times to provide students with adequate facilities so that they could devote their time and energy to academic pursuits. Although only the Tirumukkūḍal inscription gives details about a hostel and hospital attached to an educational institution, it is not improbable that many other such centres were also equipped with similar facilities.

Although the Tirumukkūḍal inscription offers the best example of the functioning of a hospital, there were many other hospitals and dispensaries with well-qualified doctors in villages and towns where physicians were appointed and paid by royalty and philanthropists. The Coḷa inscriptions mention many of these dispensaries called *āturaśālai* or *vaidyaśālai* — *ātura* and *vaidya* meaning medicine and *śālai* meaning institution of charitable character.[141] For example, there is a record of the eleventh century CE of the reign of Rājendra Coḷa I from the Matsyapurīśvara temple at Koyil-Tevarāyaṇpeṭṭai, mentioning a free dispensary (*āturaśālai*) at Tañjāvūr called Sundaraśoḻa-Viṇṇagar Āturaśālai (named after King Sundara Coḷa) established by queen Āḻvār Parāntakaṉ Kundavai Piraṭṭiyār, who made grants of land to the temple.[142] The queen entrusted the charge of the whole gift to Savarṇa Arayaṉ Madhurantakan and his descendants, evidently for the proper functioning of the hospital.[143] Many of these were

140 *EI*, vol. XXI no. 38, pp. 224-25; S. Gurumurthy, op. cit., p. 53.

141 S. Gurumurthy, "Medical Science and Dispensaries in Ancient South India as Gleaned from Epigraphy", *JHS*, 1970, vol. 5 no. 1, p. 77.

142 *ARE* 248 of 1923.

143 *ARE* 1923, pt. II, para 14, p. 102.

looked after by doctors who were gifted tax-free land for their services. Such tax-free lands were called *vaidyakkāṇi, vaidyavṛtti, kāṇi* and *vṛtti,* meaning share of tax-free land.[144] These doctors were mostly educated in religious institutions like the *maṭhas* which, besides serving as educational centres, also maintained hospitals for the sick and needy. These inscriptions also go to show that there were many people learned in the ancient medicinal treatises which were in Sanskrit.

An interesting and important bilingual inscription (in Sanskrit and Tamil) of the reign of Vīra-Rājendra has been discovered in the Śiva temple (referred to as Tirukkailāyattu Parameśvara or the Supreme Lord of the holy Mount Kailāsa, in the inscriptions) in the village of Śoḷamahādevī or Coḷamahādevī in Tirucirāpaḷḷi district.[145] The first part of this inscription is engraved above the *koṣṭa* (cell) of Lord Dakṣiṇāmūrti and the rest on the eastern side of the same place, but much of this record is damaged. This epigraph records the gift of land to a scholar who was teaching a commentary (*vārttika*) titled *Prādīpaka* written by Cidānanda Bhāṭṭara on a work called *Śārīrakabhāṣya* by a person bearing the title *Bhagavatpāda*.[146] This inscription is the earliest and clearly dated epigraphical reference to Śrī Śaṅkarācārya — that too by his famous title *Bhagavatpāda* — and to his *Brahmasūtrabhāṣya* as *Śārīrakabhāṣya*.[147]

The *Śārīrakabhāṣya* (also known as *Śārīraka Mīmāṁsābhāṣya*

[144] *ARE* 1923, pt. II, para 14, p. 102.

[145] S. Sankaranarayanan, "Prādīpaka: A Forgotten Vārttika (from Tamilnadu on the Śārīrakabhāṣya of Śrī Śaṅkara)", *ALB*, vol. 57, 1993, pp. 109-23 (henceforth *Prādīpaka*).

[146] S. Sankaranarayanan, "Prādīpaka: A Forgotten Vārttika (from Tamilnadu on the Śārīrakabhāṣya of Śrī Śaṅkara)", *ALB*, vol. 57, 1993, pp. 109-23 (henceforth *Prādīpaka*).

[147] S. Sankaranarayanan, *Sanskrit Education*, p. 20.

and *Brahmasūtrabhāṣya*) of Ādi Śaṅkara has attracted, down the centuries, a long list of commentators, but an early *vārttika* on this work has not been known. Luckily, this inscription of Vīra Rājendra shows that there did exist an early *vārttika* on Śrī Śaṅkara's *Brahmasūtrabhāṣya* also.[148] This inscription opens with a verse in Sanskrit in *anuṣṭubh* metre:

rājaitam vīrarājendrassabhām rājñaśca bhāvinaḥ |
praśritaḥ prārthayati uccair dharmoyam rakṣyatām iti | |

This verse depicts the king (*rājan*), Vīra Rājendra as humbly requesting (*praśritaḥ prārtayati*), the administrative assembly of the locality (*etam sabhām*), namely Śoḷamahādevī-caturvedimaṅgalam, as well as the future kings (*rājñaś ca bhāvinaḥ*) of the country to protect and maintain the present gift that is highly meritorious (*uccair dharmo yam rakṣyatām*). This record states that the village Śrī Śoḷamahādevī-caturvedimaṅgalam (i.e. Śoḷamahādevī where this record comes from) was a *brahmadeya* (gift given to brāhmaṇas) and it was included in the territorial division Paṇḍikulāśani Vaḷanāḍu). The *peruṅgurisabhā* (the honourable administrative assembly) of this village assembled in its full strength (*kuraivarak kuḍi*) in the courtyard (*tirumuṟṟam*) in the temple of God Viṣṇu (Tirumaliruñjolai Āḻvār) and issued an order on the basis of an honourable command, obviously of the ruling monarch granting some land for the maintenance of a teacher (name not given) who was teaching (*vākkanipparkku vṛttiyāga*), the *vārttika*, a sort of commentary titled *Prādīpaka* (*prādīpakam āgira vārttikam*), written (*paṇṇina*) by a certain Cidānanda Pidārar, i.e. *bhaṭṭāra, bhaṭṭāraka*) on the work *Śārīrakabhāṣya* of a person (name not given) bearing the honorific title *Bhagavadpāda* (*Bhagavadpādīyam Śarīrakabhāṣyattukku*).[149] This is followed by a description of the land granted.

---

[148] S. Sankaranarayanan, *Prādīpaka*, p. 110.

[149] Ibid., pp. 114-15.

This record is particularly interesting as the King Vīra Rājendra had himself requested the *mahāsabhā* of the village to safeguard this grant, thus suggesting that it was this monarch who actually made the grant, while under his command, the village assembly issued the regular order confirming the grant. It also indicates the personal interest that Vīra Rājendra had taken for the propagation of philosophical knowledge in his kingdom.[150]

The date of this record falls between CE 1063-69 and therefore it is logical to assume that the *Prādīpaka-Vārttika*, for the purpose of teaching of which this grant was made, might have been composed fifty or sixty years earlier, that is, around the beginning of the eleventh century if not earlier.[151] This commentary, *Prādīpaka-Vārttika* and its author, Cidānanda Piḍārar are known for the first time from this inscription. Cidānanda's honorific epithet Piḍārar (same as Paḍārar found applied to holy persons in many other Tamil records) is an equivalent of the Sanskrit *bhaṭāra* and *bhaṭṭāraka*, often used as synonyms of *pūjya* and *pujyapāda*.[152] However, this work has not been traced and is most probably lost.

This inscription, while recording the land-grant to a scholar, for teaching the *Prādīpaka-Vārttika*, does not specifically give the exact location of where it was to be taught. The Coḷa inscriptions like the Kuṁbakoṇam Nāgeśvarasvāmi temple inscription of the reign of Parāntaka Coḷa I (tenth century CE) and the Tirukkoṣṭhiyūr Bhairava temple inscription of Rājarāja Coḷa I, the Eṇṇāyiram Narasiṁha Perumāḷ temple inscription of Rājendra Coḷa I, the Tribhuvanai Varadarāja Svāmi temple inscription of Rājādhirāja Coḷa I and the Tirumukkūḍal Veṅkaṭeśa Perumāḷ temple inscription of Vīra Rājendra Coḷa are all grants for teaching various branches of Vedas, Śāstras

[150] S. Sankaranarayanan, *Prādīpaka*, p. 115.

[151] Ibid., p. 117.

[152] Ibid., p. 118.

and Āgamas inside the premises of these temples. Therefore; it would appear that the classes in the *Prādīpaka-Vārttika* were meant to be conducted in the vicinity of the niche (*koṣṭha*) enshrining Lord Dakṣiṇāmūrti, above and by the side of which this epigraph is engraved.[153] There is an age-old custom of students of *Śāṅkarabhāṣya* classes to offer *praṇāms* to the Supreme Guru Dakṣiṇāmūrti by reciting Śrī Śaṅkara's own composition, the *Dakṣiṇāmūrti-aṣṭaka*, and therefore the Dakṣiṇāmūrti *sannidhi* itself may have been chosen as an ideal location for conducting classes in the *Śārīrakabhāṣya* with *Prādīpaka-Vārttika*.[154] It may also be very interesting to note that this location, namely the Dakṣiṇāmūrti *sannidhi*, is still in existence with the inscription in site — a rare and historical find which is of unique importance for the students of Advaita Vedānta.[155]

The gift mentioned in the inscription is a *brahmadāna* or *brahmajñānadāna*, i.e. imparting the knowledge of *Brahman*, the Supreme, through conducting classes on Advaita Vedānta treatise.[156] The inscription is the earliest and clearly dated epigraphical reference to Śrī Śaṅkarācārya — that too by his famous title *Bhagavatpāda* — and to his *Brahmasūtrabhāṣya* as *Śārīrakabhāṣya*.[157] Hence, its importance.

The Kanyākumārī inscription of Vīra Rājendra records that this emperor created many villages (*brahmadeyas*) for brāhmaṇas from the Coḷa, Tuṇḍira, Pāṇḍya, Gaṅgāvaṭī and Kuḷuta areas and gave 40,000 brāhmaṇas, who were masters in the Vedas, gifts of land and made them settle there permanently.[158] The Carāla copper-plate inscription of this

---

[153] S. Sankaranarayanan, *Prādīpaka*, op. cit., p. 118, 121.

[154] Ibid., pp. 117-18, 121.

[155] S. Sankaranarayanan, "The Bhagavatpādīyam Śarīraka Bhāṣyam in The Coḷamahādevī Epigraph: More Light", *ALB*, vol. 64, 2000, p. 106.

[156] S. Sankaranayanan, *Prādīpaka*, p. 113.

[157] S. Sankaranarayanan, *Sanskrit Education*, p. 20.

[158] Kanyākumārī inscription, op. cit., vv. 80-81, pp. 148-49.

ruler, which is identical, verse by verse, with that of the Kanyākumārī inscription as far as the *praśasti* portion is concerned, also records a donation to learned men. This epigraph records the royal gift of the village of Cheram alias Madhurāntaka-caturvedimaṅgalam to three brāhmaṇa scholars named Śrotrīya-Kramavittan, Mauṇḍaya-Kramavittan and Pallaya-Kramavittan of the Ātreya *gotra* and *Baudhāyana sūtra* and of the lineage of a certain Hṛṣikeśa Bhaṭṭa Somāyajiyār of Cheram on the occasion of the Uttarāyaṇa Saṅkrānti.[159]

Kulottuṅga I (CE 1071–1122)

Kulottuṅga I was the son of Ammaṅgādevī, the daughter of Rājendra Coḷa I and the son of Rājarāja Narendra of the dynasty of the Eastern Cāḷukyas of Veṅgi. Jayaṅkoṇḍār was the poet-laureate of his court and the Tamil work *Kaliṅgattuparaṇi* was composed by him towards the end of the reign of Kulottuṅga I. A Tamil inscription of Kulottuṅga Coḷa I inscribed in the Varadarāja Svāmi temple in Kāñcīpuram records that during his reign there was a *maṭha* in Kāñcī called Arikeśavan Maṭha situated on the north bank of the sacred tank (*tiruppoigai*).[160] It was the place where the brāhmaṇas, well-versed in the sacred lore congregated for discussion and ritual. It was presided over by one *mahāmuni* (great-sage) of *periya kovil* (big temple). The inhabitants of a nearby village called Vaidyavūr granted lands, free of taxes for feeding scholarly brāhmaṇas who studied in this *maṭha*.

A Sanskrit lexicon *Nānārthārṇava Saṁkṣepa* composed in the reign of Rājarāja Coḷa II, a descendant of Kulottuṅga Coḷa I, by a person named Keśavasvāmin records that Kulottuṅga I established a village of Śaiva brāhmaṇas who were Sanskrit scholars in the Coḷa country.[161]

---

[159] Carālā plates, op. cit., p. 263.

[160] *ARE* 635 of 1919; K.V. Raman, *The Varadarājaswāmi Temple, Kanchipuram*, New Delhi, 1975, p. 137

[161] T. Ganapati Sastri (ed.), *Nānārthārṇava Saṁkṣepa* (Ekakṣarakāṇḍa, vv. 1-200), Trivandrum, 1913.

Vikrama Coḷa (CE 1118-35)

The son and successor of Kulottuṅga Coḷa I, Vikrama Coḷa ruled jointly with his father from CE 1118 to CE 1122. The great Tamil poet Oṭṭakūttar adorned the court of Vikrama Coḷa. An inscription found on the north wall of the central shrine of the Gomuktīśvara temple in Tiruvaḍuturai (Tañjāvūr district), belonging to the reign of Vikrama Coḷa provides information about the teaching of medicinal sciences (Āyurveda) in a *maṭha* which was attached to the temple of Tiruvaḍuturaiuḍaiyar.[162] It refers to a grant of land by a Coḷa military commander (*senāpati*) to this *maṭha* for its maintenance, for feeding some brāhmaṇas, *tapasvīs*, *anādigirīśa*s (Ādiśaivas) and those studying Āyurveda works (Vaidyaśāstra) such as Bahaḍa, i.e. one or both of the *Aṣṭāṅgahṛdaya* of Vṛddha Vāgbhaṭa of *c.* sixth century CE or the *Aṣṭāṅgahṛdaya* of Bāla Vāgbhaṭa of *c.* eighth century CE and the Caraka (i.e. the *Caraka Saṁhita* of *c.* first century CE).[163] These students also studied Vyākaraṇa and the Rūpāvatāra. The *mahāsabhā* of the village exempted the gift land from taxes. The students studying in the *maṭha* were fed in the *dharma chātra* attached to the temple.[164] This *maṭha*, thus, seems to have functioned as a residential institution which trained students for the medical profession. It is also clear from epigraphical evidence that the *maṭha* played a major role in attending to the needs and welfare of the general public, with the heads of these institutions being proficient not only in religious texts, but also in other spheres of sciences.

Kulottuṅga Coḷa II (CE 1133-50)

Kulottuṅga Coḷa II was the son and successor of Vikrama Coḷa. Oṭṭakūttar who was the court-poet in his father's time continued to be so in his reign and in the reign of his son and

[162] *ARE* 159 of 1925.

[163] S. Sankaranarayanan, *Sanskrit Education*, p. 21.

[164] S. Gurumurthy, *Education in South India*, p. 21.

successor Rājarāja II as well. An interesting inscription of the thirteenth regnal year of Kulottuṅga Coḷa II, the son and successor of Vikrama Coḷa found in the Tirukkoṭīśvara temple in Peruvaḷūr (North Arcot district) records the founding of the temple of Tirukkoṭīśvaram Uḍaiyār in this village and an endowment for worship and festivals.[165] It also registers an endowment of 12 *veli*s of land for the maintenance of ten *bhaṭṭa*s well-versed in the Vedas and the Śāstras, one Śivācārya and one *vaidya,* who were all provided with house-sites on the north and west sides of the temple by Rājendraśoḷan-Sambuvarāyan. He also provided lands for the Veḷḷāla tenents of these *bhaṭṭa*s and remitted the *paḍikāval* taxes on the *devadāna* and the *agaram* lands. This donor was a subordinate of this king as well as of his predecessor, Vikrama Coḷa.[166]

Rājarāja Coḷa II (CE 1163/66–1179/82)

The son and successor of Kulottuṅga Coḷa II, Rājarāja Coḷa II was of a scholarly bent of mind as seen from his title *rāja paṇḍita.*[167] This is rather reminiscent of the title *paṇḍita coḷa* held by his illustrious ancestor Rājendra Coḷa I. Rājarāja II's contribution to the literary field and his patronage of Tamil is seen from his title *muttamiḷkkutalaivan* (the patron of the threefold Tamil) which refers to prose, poetry and drama (*iyal, iśai* and *nāṭakam,* respectively).[168] The fact that this ruler was equally favourable to Sanskrit is seen from data forthcoming from a work called *Nānārthārṇava Saṁkṣepa* which is a Sanskrit lexicon composed by a Chāndoga brāhmaṇa called Keśavasvāmin.[169] The prefactory verses of this lexicon mention

[165] *ARE* 512 of 1937-38.

[166] *ARE* 1937-38, pt. II, para 38, p. 91.

[167] T.V. Sadasiva Pandarathar, *History of the Later Coḷas*, Annamalainagar, 1949.

[168] K.A. Nilakanta Sastri, *Coḷas*, p. 351 and fn. 73.

[169] T. Ganapati Sastri, op. cit.

that Kulottuṅga I founded a village of Śaiva brāhmaṇas well-versed in Sanskrit in the Coḷa country. Keśavasvāmin, the author of this book, belonged to a family of grammarians from this village. He was in the employment of Rājarāja Coḷa II at whose instance he wrote this Sanskrit lexicon which is also called *Rājarājīya*. The *Nānārthārṇava Saṁkṣepa* is the biggest homonymous lexicon known, containing about 5,800 stanzas, divided into six *kāṇḍa*s according to the number of syllables, with the words being arranged after the initial letters of each *kāṇḍa*.[170]

Kulottuṅga Coḷa III (CE 1178-1217)

Kulottuṅga III succeeded Rājādhirāja II who was the successor of Rājarāja II, on the Coḷa throne. An important epigraph inscribed on the west wall of the first *prākāra* of the Ādipurīśvara temple in Tiruvoṟṟiyūr (near Chennai), belonging to the reign of Kulottuṅga Coḷa III gives some information about education during the later Coḷa times.[171] A person named Durgaiyāṇḍi Nāyaka, an agent of the king's subordinate, bought some cultivable lands with the permission of the king. After assigning portions of the land to a Viṣṇu temple, a Jaina *paḷḷi* and a Piḍāri (village deity) temple, he dedicated 60 *veli*s of land for maintaining a hall called *vyākaraṇadāna-vyākhyāna maṇḍapa* in the Tiruvoṟṟiyūr temple for feeding the students who studied the Vyākaraṇa-śāstra in the *maṇḍapa*, for paying renumeration to the teachers who taught the students and for the worship of Vyākaraṇadāna Perumāḷ, i.e. Śiva. This lithic inscription also states that god Vyākaraṇadāna Perumāḷ was pleased to appear before Paṇini Bhagavān for fourteen continuous days in that very place of the *maṇḍapa* and to teach him the first fourteen aphorisms

---

170 R.C. Majumdar, *The History and Culture of the Indian People* (Vol. V: The Struggle for Empire), Bombay, 1989, p. 318.

171 *ARE* 202 of 1912.

(*Pratyāhārasūtras*, i.e. those with which the Paṇinīyan grammar commences).

Another inscription in the same wall of this temple, also belonging to the reign of Kulottuṅga III, states that on the recommendation of a certain Vaṇadarāyan, the king declared that land presented for the upkeep of the *vyākaraṇadāna-vyākhyāna maṇḍapa* by Durgaiyāṇḍi Nāyaka, may be made rent-free.[172] In a later record of the time of Jaṭāvarman Sundara Pāṇḍya III, the tax *ponvāri*, which was collected in the northern and southern divisions of Tiruvoṟṟiyūr, is stated to have been assigned for maintaining the same historic *maṇḍapa* and other similar buildings in this temple.[173] The grammar hall, thus referred to as the original place where Paṇini received the first fourteen aphorisms (also known as *Māheśvara-Sūtras*), directly from Lord Śiva, is no longer pointed out at present in the Tiruvoṟṟiyūr Temple.[174]

S. Sankaranarayan points out another tradition preserved in the *Patañjalicarita* of Rāmabhadra Dīkṣita (seventeenth century CE), according to which Patañjali wrote his famous *Vyākaraṇa Mahābhāṣya* and also taught it to his pupils at Cidambaram (erstwhile South Arcot district) as ordered by Lord Naṭarāja (Śiva), the presiding deity of the temple at that place.[175] In view of all these traditions that connect the birth and development of Vyākaraṇa with god Naṭarāja Śiva, it is possible to surmise that the deity Vyākaraṇadāna Perumāḷ of the Tiruvoṟṟiyūr inscriptions is none but Naṭarāja Śiva and the *vyākaraṇadāna-vyākhyāna maṇḍapa* is the present beautiful Naṭarāja *maṇḍapa* where the deity Naṭarāja is kept and worshipped even today. This *maṇḍapa* is found spacious

[172] *ARE* 201 of 1912.

[173] *ARE* 110 of 1912; *ARE* 1912, pt. II, p. 110.

[174] Ibid.

[175] S. Sankaranarayanan, *Sanskrit Education*, p. 24.

enough to house one or two classes at a time and it is adjacent to the wall of the Ādipurīśvara shrine where the present inscriptions are found.[176] Again, if viewed from the point of architectural style also, this *maṇḍapa* could be coeval with the inscriptions under consideration.[177]

A Sanskrit inscription from the Kaṁpahareśvara temple in Tribhuvanam (near Kuṁbakoṇam) of the reign of Kulottuṅga Coḷa III, who also constructed this temple, records the name of a spiritual teacher (*guru*) of this king called Someśvara (also known as Īśvara Śiva).[178] This Sanskrit inscription in Grantha characters is a metrical composition of high order and in various metres like *śālinī*, *vasantatilakā*, *indravajrā*, *śārdūlavikrīḍitā*, *upajātī* and *āryā*.[179] It is inscribed in the temple in three places — on the south wall of the central shrine and in two places on the outer *gopuram*.[180] This inscription, in which this temple is referred to as Tribhuvanavīreśvaram, records that the consecration of Śiva and Pārvatī here was performed by Someśvara. He was the son of Śrīkaṇṭha Śambhu and this inscription praises him as one who was "well-versed in the Śaiva Darśana and the eighteen *vidyā*s and had expounded the greatness of Śaiva thought in the Upaniṣads".[181] The last stanza of this inscriptional poem which altogether comprises eleven verses states that this great scholar composed a work called *Siddhānta-ratnākara*.[182]

---

176 S. Sankaranarayanan, *Sanskrit Education*, p. 24.

177 Ibid.

178 *SII*, vol. XXIII no. 190, p.147; *ARE*, 79 and 80 of 1908.

179 H. Sarkar, *The Kampahareśvara Temple in Tribhuvanam*, Madras, 1974, p. 48.

180 Ibid., p. 16.

181 Ibid., Appendix I, pp. 66-67.

182 Ibid., v. 11, p. 67.

It is interesting to note that two Tamil inscriptions of the reign of Jaṭāvarman Sundara Pāṇḍya I (1251-68 CE) found in the Naṭarāja temple in Cidambaram register information about a library (Sarasvatī Bhaṇḍāra) in this temple.[183] These epigraphs incidentally mention only one work among the numerous manuscripts which were stored there and that too twice. This was the *Siddhāntaratnākara* which appears to have been a highly valued possession of the library and a title that was popular at that time.[184] The name of the author is not mentioned. However, it would seem identical with the work of the same name occurring in the Tribhuvanam record of Kulottuṅga III who ruled till CE 1218, i.e. just about thirty-two years before the accession of Sundara Pāṇḍya I, the king of the Cidambaram records.[185]

In support of the above identification, it is interesting to note that the inscription in the Kaṁpahareśvara temple in Tribhuvanam, in which Īśvara Śiva is said to be the author of this work contains a passage *sthāṇor yena viviktam aupaniṣadam viśvādhikatvam viboḥ* and it is significant that the land granted for the maintenance of the *bhaṇḍāra* in the Cidambaram temple was named *viśvādhikaviveka-maṅgalam* which is evidently connected with the expressions *viśvādhikatvam* and *viviktam* of the verse.[186] The *Siddhāntaratnākara* is not traceable today.

Both Śrīkaṇṭha Śambhu and Īśvara Śiva were the *rājagurus* of Coḷa kings from the time of Vikrama Coḷa to Kulottuṅga III, Śrīkaṇṭha Śambhu being called Uḍaiya Svāmidevar, epithets used in respect of Coḷa receptors in those days.[187] The name Śrīkaṇṭha Śambhu reminds us of the name Śrīkaṇṭha

---

[183] *ARE* 168 and 169 of 1961-62; *EI*, vol. XL, pp. 223-24.

[184] S. Sankaranarayanan, *Sanskrit Education*, pp. 29-30.

[185] Ibid., p. 30

[186] *EI*, vol. XL no. 47, p. 221.

[187] Ibid.

Śiva, who was the author of *Śaivabhāṣya* (*Śrīkaṇṭha-bhāṣya*) on Bādarāyaṇa's *Brahmasūtra* and who was perhaps a southerner, i.e. of the Tamil country of around CE 1122, and hence a contemporary of Kulottuṅga III.[188]

An inscription in Tamil of the reign of Kulottuṅga III dated CE 1191 found in the Varadarāja Svāmi temple in Kāñcī throws some interesting light on the tradition of imparting the works of the eminent Śrīvaiṣṇava preceptor (*ācārya*) Rāmānuja, who strove hard to propagate Viśiṣṭādvaita philosophy.[189] The impact of Rāmānuja's life and activities and his association with the Varadarāja Svāmi temple in Kāñcīpuram where he spent his formative years is profound. Many of the reforms in the temple organization and form of worship he introduced in Śrīraṅgam had their influence in this temple in Kāñcī also.[190] In recognition of his great services, Rāmānuja was deified in the Varadarāja Svāmi temple within fifty-five years after his demise.[191] This is seen from the lithic record of Kulottuṅga Coḷa III mentioned above which records that an influential Coḷa chieftain named Iḷaiāḷvān Kaliṅgarāyan of Neṭṭūr consecrated the image of Emberumanār (Rāmānuja) and donated all the taxes accruing from two villages to meet the expenses for the offerings to the deity and in addition, made special provisions for *Bhāṣyavṛtti* or exposition of *Rāmānuja-bāṣya* in this temple. Incidentally, Iḷaiāḻvān was another name of Rāmānuja and the donor was evidently a great devotee of this great preceptor whose name *Iḷaiāḷvān* he adopted as his own.[192]

A Coḷa inscription of the reign of Kulottuṅga III in the Vaṭāraṇyeśvara temple in Tiruvālaṅgāḍu registers a gift of a lamp to the temple at Tiruvālaṅgāḍu by a person named

---

188 S. Sankaranayanan, *Sanskrit Education*, p. 31.

189 *ARE* 193 of 1919; K.V. Raman, op. cit., p. 65.

190 K.V. Raman, op. cit.

191 Ibid.

192 Ibid.

Aranilaivisagan Tirailokyamallaṉ Vatsarājaṉ of Arumbākkam. This donor rendered the *Bhārata* into elegant Tamil.[193] This translation of the *Mahābhārata* does not survive to this day.[194] Three Tamil versions of this epic are known, viz. the earliest called *Bhāratavenba* by Perundevaṉār who might have lived in the ninth century CE; Villiputturāḻvār, who possibly belonged to the fifteenth century CE, translated ten *parvas* of this epic. The latest Tamil version is by Nallapiḷḷai, who is believed to have lived in the eighteenth century CE.[195] It is thus clear that none of these could be the version of the reign of Kulottuṅga III.[196]

Rājarāja Coḷa III (CE 1216-50)

Rājarāja Coḷa III succeeded Kulottuṅga III to the throne. The Coḷa empire was fast declining and it came to an end after his successor Rājendra Coḷa III. Other than the inscriptions mentioned earlier regarding medicine, an inscription of the reign of Rājarāja Coḷa III, found on the south wall of the Śiva temple in Kuṉṟattūr (Chengalpet district), gives details about a provision made for a medical practitioner.[197] This record states that a person named Kulottuṅgaśoḷa Mangaḷādhirājaṉ Śīraḷadevaṉ of Kuṉṟattūr, a *savarṇa* and a Kāśyapa was the recipient of the *vaidyakkāṇi* (i.e. land set apart for the service of a physician) of Kuṉṟattūr-nāḍu.[198] The epithets *Kaṭakameḍutta-Kūttapirāṉ*, *Śivakīrtti* and *Śaivaśikhāmaṇi* reveal that he had Śaiva leanings and he seems to have belonged to the Kāśyapa *gotra* as he had the adjunct Kāśyapaṉ attached to his name. It is noteworthy that he is called *savarṇa* since the famous

[193] *ARE* 482 of 1905.

[194] *ARE*, 1906, pt. II, para. 23, p. 52.

[195] *ARE*, 1906, pt. II, para. 23, p. 52.

[196] Ibid.

[197] *ARE* 184 of 1929-30.

[198] *ARE* 1929-30, pt. II, para. 27, p. 81.

Tirumukkūḍal inscription referred to earlier mentions the physician Kodaṇḍarāman Aśvattāma Bhaṭṭan who worked in the hospital attached to the college of the Viṣṇu temple there and is stated to be a *savarṇa*.[199] Similarly, an inscription of the seventh regnal year of Rājendra Coḷa I states that the recipient of the *vaidyabhoga* of the hospital known as Sundaraśoḷa Viṇṇagar Āturaśālai at Tañjāvūr was a *savarṇa*.[200] From these instances, it looks as if the duties of the physicians generally devolved on a *savarṇa*. The *Vaijayantī* gives the synonym of a *savarṇa* to be "the son of a brāhmaṇa by a kṣatriya woman" or a "Māhiṣya", who had various duties such as tending of cattle, and practice of astrology and medicine.[201] It is therefore clear that the institutions like the *maṭha* trained pupils in medicinal science also.

A lithic inscription from the Subrahmaṇya temple from the village of Tiruviḍaikkaḻi (Tañjāvūr district) dated CE 1229 in the reign of Rājarāja Coḷa III registers a gift of five and odd *veli*s of land by purchase by an individual named Kuṉṟattu Nārāyaṇa for maintaining a *maṭha* he had established in the village and for feeding the three brāhmaṇa students of Vedānta who had come there all the way from the Maḷayāḷam country (Kerala).[202] This gift was exempted from taxes by the *mahāsabhā* of Tiruviḍaikkaḻi. The adjective Kuṉṟattu of the donor perhaps signifies that he too hailed from the Maḷayāḷam country.[203]

Poet-Composers of the Sanskrit Inscriptions

Many of the bi-lingual inscriptions of the Coḷa emperors, at the end of the Sanskrit *praśasti,* provide the name and several details

[199] *ARE* 1929-30, pt. II, para. 27, p. 81.

[200] *ARE* 249 of 1923.

[201] *ARE* 1929-30, pt. II, para. 27, p. 81.

[202] *ARE* 276 of 1925; S. Sankaranarayanan, *Sanskrit Education,* p. 24.

[203] Ibid.

of the poets who composed the verses that constitute that section. This is in the tradition of the bilingual charters of their predecessors, the Pallavas and the Pāṇḍyas. In addition, there are a few lithic inscription of the Coḷas in Sanskrit which also provide the names of the poet-composers.

The Veḷāñjeri copper-plate inscription of Parāntaka Coḷa I (CE 932) consists of about sixteen Sanskrit verses with a Tamil portion. It records towards the end that this charter was composed by a person named Rutsa but since this epigraph is unfortunately in a damaged state, no details about this poet are available.[204] A lithic inscription of Parāntaka I, found on a boulder on the temple-town of Śoḷingūr (near Arakonam), is again bilingual in character.[205] This, too, is in a slighty damaged condition. It opens with a few Tamil words, followed by ten verses in Sanskrit and a short Sanskrit prose passage. The last verse of the ten-stanza poem states that these verses were composed by a sage (*muniḥ*) Kumāra, a Vaikhānasa of the Kāśyapa *gotra*.

The Sanskrit *praśasti* of the Anbil copper-plate grant of Parāntaka II (Sundara Coḷa) dated CE 961 contains forty-six stanzas in various metres like *anuṣṭubh, āryā, hariṇī, indravajrā, mandākrāntā, mañjubāṣinī, puṣpitāgrā, praharṣiṇī, rathoddhatā, śārdūlavikrīḍitā, śragdharā, sundarī, svāgata, upendravajrā* and *vasantatilakā*. The last verse clearly states:

vidyā nadhyambu rāśir vimalataraguṇa vrātaratnākaro yaḥ ।
pārāśaryanvayambudhi śiśirakaro bhaṭṭa-dattābhidhānaḥ ।।

tasya śrīnātha pādāmburuhayugaḷikā ṣaḍpadasya praśastim ।
putraścitrarārtha ramyām samaracayad imām mādhava bhaṭṭa yajvā ।।

---

[204] R. Nagaswamy, *TVCP*, Veḷāñjeri Plates of Parāntaka I, Plate V, p. 2.
[205] *EI*, vol. IV no. 32, v. 10, p. 224.

> Of Bhaṭṭa Datta, who was an ocean for the rivers of learning, a mine of the most spotless good qualities, a moon to the ocean which was the family of Parāśara and a bee at the lotus-like ft of the consort of Lakṣmī, i.e. Viṣṇu (or the disciple of Śrī Nātha = Nāthamunigal), the son, Mādhava Datta Yajvan composed this *praśasti* which is "bedecked with various meanings".[206]

According to T.A. Gopinatha Rao, the editor of this inscription, Parāntaka II could have been the contemporary of Āḷavandār (Yāmunācārya, the well-known Śrīvaiṣṇava preceptor and grandson of Nāthamuni, the first Śrīvaiṣṇava *ācārya*).[207] The ancestors of Aniruddha, the minister of Parāntaka II (Sundara Coḷa) who were Śrīvaiṣṇavas, must have come under the influence of the Āḻvārs and Nāthamuni (with whose time the ages of the ancestors of Aniruddha agree very well). Mādhava Bhaṭṭa, the composer of the Coḷa *praśasti* contained in the Anbil plates, calls himself the disciple of Śrīnātha.[208] In all probability, he was a student of Nāthamuni, who is reputed to have had a very long life.[209]

The Larger Leiden copper-plate inscription of the reign of Rājarāja Coḷa I, consisting of twenty-one copper sheets, is dated CE 1006.[210] This refers to the Tamil section of this bilingual inscription. The Sanskrit *praśasti* portion, consisting of 111 lines of writing in forty-eight verses, covering the obverse and reverse of five copper plates belongs to the reign of Rājaraja's son and successor, Rājendra Coḷa I. The legend on the seal of the Leiden plates reads:

---

[206] *EI*, vol. XV no. 5, v. 46, pp. 63-64.

[207] Ibid., p. 54.

[208] *Ibid.*, pp. 63-64.

[209] Ibid.

[210] *EI*, vol. XXII no. 34, pp. 213-68.

etad-rājendra coḷasya parakesarivarmaṇaḥ |
rājad rājanya makuṭa śreṇi ratneśu śāsanam | |

These verses in the *praśasti* in various metres like the Anbil plates were composed by a poet-scholar named Anantanārāyaṇa. He is described in one of the last verses of this inscription as:

grāme ramye jagatī mahite koṭṭaiyūr abhidhāne |
lakṣmī dhāmani ajani vimale yo vaṣiṣṭhanvavāye | |

sat saṁsevi vimala carito anantanārāyaṇākhyaḥ |
soyam dhīmān aracayadmimām agrajanma praśastiṁ | |

In the delightful village called Koṭṭaiyūr, famed in this world, that intelligent brāhmaṇa of stainless character named Anantanārāyaṇa, the follower of the wise, born in the spotless family of Vasiṣṭha, which was the abode of prosperity, composed this *praśasti*.[211]

According to K.V. Subrahmanya Aiyer, the editor of this inscription, poet Anantanārāyaṇa must have been the court-poet of Rājendra Coḷa I in whose reign this *praśasti* was composed.[212]

The bilingual Tiruvālaṅgāḍu copper-plate record dated CE 1018, also belongs to the reign of Rājendra Coḷa I and was issued in his seventh regnal year.[213] Consisting of thirty-one copper sheets, the Sanskrti *praśasti* portion of this grant has 137 verses in suitable metres. Verse 136 of this epigraph records:

śaṅkarasya sutenedam bhaktena muraviddviṣaḥ |
nārāyaneṇa kavinā śāsanam kṛtina kṛtam | |

---

211 *EI*, vol. XXII no. 34, v. 39, p. 242.

212 Ibid., p. 222.

213 Tiruvāḷaṅgāḍu plates, op. cit., pp. 383-439.

> The learned poet Nārayaṇa, son of Śaṅkara and a devotee of Viṣṇu, composed this grant.[214]

Yet another copper-plate inscription of the reign of Rājendra Coḷa I is the Karandai Tamiḻ Sangam epigraph which was issued in the eighth regnal year of this emperor, i.e. CE 1019.[215] The entire bilingual inscription was etched on fifty-seven plates. The Sanskrit *praśasti* section consists of seventy-six verses in seventeen metres with the last one recording that:

> *śaṅkarāryātmajena idam pārśvagrāma nivāsina* |
> *nārāyaṇena kavinā śāsanam śāśvatam kr̥tam* | |

> This everlasting grant was composed by poet Nārāyaṇa, son of Śaṅkarārya and a resident of Pārśvagrāma (the neighbouring village).[216]

K.G. Krishnan has surmised that poet Anantanārāyaṇa (Nārāyaṇa) authored the *praśasti* of the three copper-plate inscriptions of Rājendra Coḷa I mentioned above. The Sanskrit section of the Tiruvālaṅgāḍu grant, issued in the seventh regnal year of Rājendra is stated to have been composed by Nārāyaṇa, the son of Śaṅkara, evidently the same person mentioned in the Karandai plates.[217] The Larger Leiden plates state that the *praśasti* was composed by Anantanārāyaṇa belonging to the lineage of Vasiṣṭha (i.e. *gotra*). Verses 1, 3, 6, 7, 9, 13, 15, 16, 18, 23, 24 and 26 of the Karandai plates are respectively identical with verses 1, 3, 5, 6, 8, 11, 14, 15, 17, 24, 25 and 30 of the Leiden plates.[218] A comparison of the final portion of the Sanskrit section of the Larger Leiden plates and the Sanskrit verses quoted at the end of the Tiruvālaṅgāḍu

---

214 Tiruvāḷaṅgāḍu plates, op. cit., v. 136, p. 401.

215 K.G. Krishnan, *KTPR*.

216 Ibid., v. 76, p. 76.

217 Ibid., p. 53.

218 Ibid.

charter which pertain to the engravers of the respective documents brings out the hemistich — *a-kr̥ṣṇa-caritaḥ kr̥ṣṇa saṁbhāvo-pi mahāmatiḥ*, common to both these grants.[219] If these are taken into account, we can probably conclude that Nārāyaṇa of the Karandai charter and of the Tiruvālaṅgāḍu grant was the same as Anantanārāyaṇa (Nārāyaṇa for short) of the Leiden grant.[220] In that case, Pārśvagrāma (of the Karandai plates) should be identified with Koṭṭaiyūr (of the Larger Leiden plates), which would then mean the village nearby. Koṭṭaiyūr was actually on the outskirts of the new *agrahāra* which was formed in the reign of Rājendra (the details of which are in the Karandai grant), thus befitting its description as Pārśvagrāma. It would not be presumptuous to infer that the poet who had composed the Sanskrit section of all these three important Coḷa copper-plate grants was a court-poet and would have been amply rewarded for his labours, though we do not get any evidence of it.[221]

The Eśālam copper-plate grant, also of the reign of Rājendra Coḷa I, issued in his 24th regnal year (CE 1036), consists of fifteen copper-sheets engraved on both sides, of which the Sanskrit portion covers three plates and a part of the front page of the fourth plate, while the rest comprise the Tamil section.[222] This Sanskrit *praśasti* portion consists of thirty-five verses in various metres. The second last verse clearly mentions that this *śāsana* was composed by poet Nārāyaṇa, the son of Śaṅkara, belonging to Pārśvagrāma.[223]

śaṅkarasya tanujena pārśvagrāma nivāsina |
nārāyaṇena kavinā śāsanam śāsvatam kr̥tam

---

[219] K.G. Krishnan, *KTPR*, p. 53.

[220] Ibid.

[221] Ibid.

[222] R. Nagaswamy, *ECPR*, p. 10.

[223] Ibid., v. 34, p. 33.

It is clear that from the fifth year of Rājendra to his twenty-fifth year, this poet had been occupying an important position in the court of Rājendra Coḷa.[224]

A bilingual lithic inscription dated in the seventh regnal year (CE 1069) of Vīra-Rājendra is etched on six stone pillars in the *maṇimaṇḍapa* of the temple of goddess Kanyākumārī in Kanyākumārī.[225] This inscription, unfortunately damaged in several places, consists of 444 lines, the Sanskrit portion alone consisting of eighty-one verses. Unfortunately, the name of the poet who composed this poem does not find a place here. Fortunately, the Carālā copper-plate inscription of Vīra-Rājendra, dated in his seventh regnal year, discovered in Cittoor district of Andhra Pradesh and also bilingual, had eighty-one verses in the Sanskrit section and is identical verse by verse with the Kanyākumārī lithic inscription.[226] This Sanskrit section is followed by a Tamil portion after which are two Sanskrit verses, the second of which records the name of the composer of the Sanskrit section as Candrabhūṣana Bhaṭṭa.[227]

> *vīrarājendradevasya vikramasya prakāśanam* |
> *candrabhūṣaṇa bhaṭṭena racitam śuddha budhina* | |
>
> This panegyric illuminating the prowess of Vīrarājendradeva was composed by the pure-minded Candrabhūṣana Bhaṭṭa.

A few verses later, in the same inscription, this poet is referred to by the pharaphrased named Śaśibhūṣaṇa Paṇḍita.[228] He is evidently identical with Candraśekharabhūṣaṇa-Bhaṭṭa alias

[224] R. Nagaswamy, *ECPR*, p. 11.

[225] *EI*, vol. XVIII no. 4, pp. 21-55; *TAS*, vol. I no. 34, pp. 87-158.

[226] *EI*, vol. XXV no. 25, pp. 241-65.

[227] Ibid., v. 83, p. 264.

[228] Ibid., v. 87, ll. 207-08, p. 264.

Vīrarājendra Brahmādhirāja, mentioned in an inscription of this king (Vīra-Rājendra) from Gaṅgaikoṇḍacoḷapuram where a large number of the king's officers are mentioned, among whom Guṇanidhi Aruḷmoḻi alias Mīṉavaṉ Mūvendaveḷār of the Carālā record also finds mention.[229] A certain Candrabhūṣaṇa Paṇḍita figures in two records from Bellary district dated CE 1054 and 1068 and it is possible that he was identical with the composer of this copper-plate grant.[230]

Other than these copper-plate inscriptions and long lithic inscriptions, it is interesting to note that there are some short lithic records consisting of only one or two stanzas which provide the name of the poet-composers. One such example is a stone inscription of Naralokavīra (a famous army general of Kulottuṅga I) found at a Śiva temple in Siddhaliṅgamaḍam (South Arcot district) and written by Āṇḍapiḷḷai-bhaṭṭān of Tirukkovalūr.[231]

Vidyācakravartins

Other than the poets who composed the royal charters of the Coḷa emperors as mentioned above, there are many other Sanskrit inscriptions in Tamil Nadu, mostly lithic in nature, which belong to the same period, but not to the imperial house of the Coḷas. These are the Sanskrit epigraphs and the bilingual inscriptions of the vassals of the Coḷas called the Bāṇas. The poets of these inscriptions bore the title Vidyācakravartins. An analysis of the literary and epigraphical sources have revealed that there was a whole family of composers who had this title and among these, some are very well known through their literary and epigraphical works.[232] These

[229] *SII*, vol. IV no. 529, l. 27; Carālā plates, op. cit., p. 254.

[230] Carālā plates, p. 254.

[231] *SII*, vol. XXVI no. 390, p. 254.

[232] S.S. Janaki, *Gadyakarṇāmṛta*, Madras, 1981.

Vidyācakravartins were also connected with the contemporary rulers of the Hoysaḷa dynasty of the Karnataka area.

S.S. Janaki has identified the first of these Vidyācakravartins as a contemporary of the Hoysaḷa ruler Ballāla II (CE 1173–1220) and as the composer of a large number of Sanskrit and bilingual epigraphs of the Bāṇa ruler Rājarājadevan Poṉparapināṉ Magadhaipperumāḷ (*c.* CE 1181–1213) who was a contemporary of the Coḷa monarch Kulottuṅga III (CE 1178–1218).[233] This poet was also possibly the same person as Karpagavilli (Dhanvin or Dhanvimiśra) of the Coḷa records of the first quarter of the thirteenth century CE belonging to the reign of Kulottuṅga Coḷa III found in the Puṇḍarīkākṣa Perumāḷ temple in Tiruveḷḷaṟai (near Tirucirāpaḷḷi) and who also wrote a commentary *Dīpa* on the *Drahyāyana Śrauta-Sūtra* and lived at Lālgūḍi (Tirucirāpaḷḷi district).[234]

The epigraphs of Rājarājadevan Poṉparapināṉ Magadhaipperumāḷ, the Bāṇa chieftain, found in the temple of Kailāsanātha at Nāratampūṇḍi (North Arcot district)[235] and in the Oppilāmaṇīśvara temple at Aragaṇḍanallūr (South Arcot district),[236] which consists of the same set of thirteen verses mention that this poet Sakalavidyācakravartin was presented with elephants for composing these verses by this Bāṇa ruler.

Two of the verses of this poet are also found by way of an inscription in the Aruṇācaleśvara temple in Tiruvaṇṇamalai.[237] Here, in a very poetic way, the Vidyācakravartin says that this Bāṇa chief snatched the Pāṇḍyan crown on six occasions

---

[233] *SII*, vol. VIII no. 135, pp. 63-64 and *ARE* 554 of 1902; 482 of 1908; 369-71 of 1925; 117 of 1934-35 and 247 of 1941-42.

[234] S.S. Janaki, op. cit., p. 23.

[235] *ARE* 369-71 of 1934-35.

[236] *ARE* 117 of 1934-35.

[237] *ARE* 554 of 1902; *SII*, vol. VIII no. 135, pp. 63-64.

and that he handed over only one of them to the Coḷa king. He further adds that this generous Bāṇa king offered the other five crowns to Aruṇācaleśvara, the presiding deity of Tiruvaṇṇāmalai and thus had nothing to give to his supplicants! In another verse, this poet says that the Bāṇa, having won over all the kings and collected booty from them, covered the sacred hill Aruṇādri (in Tiruvaṇṇāmalai) with gold and that the sun thus mistook it for Mount Meru.

Two inscriptions from Tiruveḷḷaṟai mention that this poet was called Sakalavidyācakravartin and had the titles Kavirāja and Tribhuvanakavi Cakravartin and hailed from Madhurāntaka-caturvedimaṅgalam (Ālambākkam, near Lālguḍī).[238] He is described by the Tamil epithet Tirutter-ponmeynda-perumāḷ, evidently in deference to his patron Ponmeynda-perumāḷ Magadaipperumāḷ of Āragaḷūr.[239]

This poet was evidently extremely prosperous as seen from the two Tiruveḷḷaṟai epigraphs. One of these, which is bilingual, states that he established a *maṭha* at Svetaśaila (Sanskritized form of Tiruveḷḷaṟai) and made an endowment for feeding ninety people everyday for thirty festival days during the year in the temple at Tiruveḷḷaṟai.[240] The other inscription registers that this poet made an endowment for feeding 900 people in the Karpagavilli Maṭha, named after him during the festival in the month of Vaikāśi at Tiruveḷḷaṟai.[241]

Another Vidyācakravartin, known as Kālakalābha Vidyācakravartin or Kālakalābha Sakalavidyācakravartin, was the composer of the Sanskrit historical prose work *Gadyakarṇāmṛta*.[242] This very valuable work falls into two parts,

[238] *ARE* 207-08 of 1938-39.

[239] *ARE* 1938-39, pt. II, para 22.

[240] *ARE* 208 of 1938-39.

[241] *ARE* 207 of 1938-39.

[242] S.S. Janaki, op. cit., p. 23.

one a mythological prefatory account in which the historical events are foreshadowed symbolically, and two, the actual historical narrative.[243] The second part which is of utmost use to historians deals with the historical events associated with the Hoysaḷa and Tamil kings in the thirteenth century CE. This poet also has been identified with the composers of two lithic epigraphs of the Hoysaḷa ruler Rāmanātha (CE 1254-95) from the Raṅganātha Svāmi Temple, Śrīraṅgam.[244]

These two inscriptions mention the name of this poet as Śokkavilli Bhaṭṭar alias Mudaliyār Kaṟiyamaṟi of Pāṭakam who bore the title Sakalavidyācakravartin and also as Sakalakalāsārvabhauma.[245] The title Kaṟiyamaṟi given to this poet in this inscription is evidently the same as the word *kālakarikalabha* found in the colophon of the *Gadyakarṇāmṛta* composed by him.[246]

Incidentally, this Vidyācakravartin was also honoured by the Pāṇḍyan king who was either Māravarmaṉ Vīra Pāṇḍya II (CE 1252-67) or Jaṭāvarman Vīra Pāṇḍya II (CE 1254-75). Hence, this poet enjoyed the favour of the Hoysaḷa and the Pāṇḍya rulers. This is not surprising as it was a tradition in those days for poets and scholars to be honoured in various royal assemblies. The work *Rukmiṇīkalyāṇa* authored by another Vidyācakravartin at a slightly later date refers to his ancestors' holding positions in successive Hoysaḷa courts as well as in the assemblies of other kings and learned men.[247] It is no wonder that Śokkavilli, who bore the proud title of Sakalakala Vidyācakravartin and who was the court poet of

243 S.S. Janaki, op. cit., p. 30.

244 *SII*, vol. IV no. 498, p. 139; *SII*, vol. XXIV no. 276, p. 295; *SII*, vol. IV no. 499, p. 139; *SII*, vol. XXIV no. 295; S.S. Janaki, op. cit.

245 S.S. Janaki, op. cit., p. 10.

246 Ibid.

247 Ibid., p. 11.

Hoysaḷa Someśvara (CE 1235-54), the father of Hoysaḷa Rāmanātha (whose Śrīraṅgam inscription this poet composed), was also honoured by the Pāṇḍyan king.[248]

Another important Vidyācakravartin was the composer of the work *Rukmiṇīkalyāṇa*, commentaries on the *Kāvyaprakāśa* and the *Alaṁkārasarvasya*, the *Prayogadīpikā* and other literary works. This poet was the contemporary of the Hoysaḷa king Ballala III (CE 1291–1342) and composed Sanskrit inscriptions of this king found in the Kāmākṣi Amman Temple in Kāñcīpuram.[249] The author of this inscription is recorded as Kavicakravartin and the historical importance of this inscription is that it is an eulogy of Ballala III as a victor over the Coḷas and the Pāṇḍyas as a restorer of a Pallava king to the throne at Kāñcī.

Other Poets

S. Sankaranarayanan has drawn our attention to a very interesting link between the great Sanskrit poet Śrīharṣa, who composed the *Naiṣadīyacarita*, one of the five *pañca mahākāvya*s (five great poems of Sanskrit literature).[250] This poet lived during the period of the reigns of Vijayacandra and his son Jayacandra of the Gāhaḍavāla dynasty of Kānyakubja (i.e. Kanauj) during CE 1154-93.[251] In this poem, while describing the king of Kāñcī, the poet states that he excavated a wonderful, sacred lake in which was a Śivaliṅga and S. Sankaranarayanan has understood the words of this verse to indicate that this poet was personally in Kāñcī when he was composing that verse. S. Sankaranarayanan has concluded that the vast lake with Jaladevatā (Śivaliṅga) described by Śrīharṣa

[248] S.S. Janaki, op. cit., p. 11.

[249] *ARE* 312 of 1954-55 and S.S. Janaki, op. cit., p. 9.

[250] S. Sankaranarayanan, "Śrīharṣa and Kāñcīpuram: Their Forgotten History Traced" from *Rare Facets of Ancient History and Culture*, vol. I, New Delhi, 2009, pp. 347-56.

[251] Ibid., p. 348.

as having been excavated by the king of Kāñcī and the vast principal lake (*śiraḥsaras*) with Śaṅkara (Śivaliṅga) of the Kāñcī ruler Pallava Rājasiṁha (eighth century CE) mentioned in this ruler's own epigraphs must be one and the same, i.e. the present vast lake (Ponneri) in Kāñcīpuram.[252]

Moreover, in this poem, Śrīharṣa mentions that he was the son of a master-poet named Śrīhīra and his wife Māmallādevī. It is obvious that the name of the lady is to be derived from Māmalla, a Dravidianized version of "mahāmalla", a well-known unique title of Narasiṁhavarman I Pallava (*c.* CE 630-68), which was the title of his great-grandson Rājasiṁha also.[253] The title *mahāmalla* and its Dravidianized form *māmalla* of the most powerful and magnificent monarch might have been adopted as a popular personal name by the people of Toṇḍaimaṇḍalam and the name of Śrīharṣa's mother suggests strongly that she must have hailed from the Kāñcī region, perhaps from Kāñcīpuram (or Māmallapuram) itself.[254] Therefore, Kāñcīpuram happened to be the place of the poet's maternal grandfather (*mātamahānagara*).

Śrīharṣa flourished during the time of the Gāhaḍavāla kings Vijayacandra and Jayacandra (between CE 1154-94) and so his father Śrīhīra should have belonged to the time of Vijayacandra (CE 1154-74) and his father Govindacandra (CE 1114-54). During this period, some scholars of the Coḷa country appear to have been honoured by the Gāhaḍavāla kings — a copper-plate grant of Govindacandra dated CE 1128-29 records the king's land-grant, favouring a Buddhist scholar-monk named Vāgīśvararakṣitaka of the Coḷa country, together with his preceptor Śākyarakṣitaka, a scholar from Orissa.[255] There is

---

[252] S. Sankaranarayanan, "Śrīharṣa and Kāñcīpuram: Their Forgotten History Traced" from *Rare Facets of Ancient History and Culture*, vol. I, New Delhi, 2009, p. 353.

[253] Ibid., p. 354.

[254] Ibid.

[255] Ibid., p. 355; *EI*, vol. XI, pp. 22ff.

also an unfinished lithic epigraph of a Gāhaḍavāla princess found in the Śiva temple in Gaṅgaikoṇḍacoḷapuram (the capital of the Coḷas since the time of Rājendra Coḷa I), which belongs to the reign of Kulottuṅga Coḷa I and is dated sometime after CE 1111.[256] On the basis of this evidence, scholars have suggested that during this period, a Gāhaḍavāla princess might have been married to a prince of the Coḷa dynasty.[257] Therefore, some scholars of the Gāhaḍavāla court like Śrīhīra might have visited the Coḷa capital and also Kāñcīpuram, the secondary and northern Coḷa capital which was also an important pilgrim centre.[258] It is possible that a scholar in that city, greatly impressed by Śrīhīra on many accounts, offered his daughter Māmallādevī to this young scholar and their son was the great scholar-poet Śrīharṣa.[259] It is not improbable that the father of Māmallādevī was a scholar of some eminence in the court of the Coḷa king of the day and thus during the period under study, a Gāhaḍavāla princess married a Coḷa prince and reciprocally, a daughter of the scholar of the Coḷa court married a scholar of the Gāhaḍavāla court.[260]

S. Sathyanathaier has enumerated fourteen educational grants of the Coḷa time — eight in the Chengalpet district (from Uttaramerūr 5; Tirumukkūḍal 1; Tiruvoṟṟiyūr 1; and Kāñcīpuram 1), one at Tribhuvanai; one at Eṇṇāyiram and one at Ukkal, thus making it a total of eleven grants for Toṇḍaimaṇḍalam. There are three such educational grants from the Tañjāvūr area — Kuṁbakoṇam, Tiruvāḍuṭuṟai and Tiruviḍaikaḻi.[261] Here, the predominance of Toṇḍaimaṇḍaḷam

[256] S. Sankaranarayanan, op. cit., p. 355.

[257] *ARIE*, 1908, p. 66; R.C. Majumdar (ed.) *The History and Culture of the Indian People* (vol. V: The Struggle for Empire), Bombay, 1989, pp. 53-54.

[258] S. Sankaranarayanan, op. cit., p. 355.

[259] Ibid., p. 356.

[260] Ibid.

[261] S. Sathyanathaier, *Studies on the Ancient History of Toṇḍaimaṇḍalam*, Madras, 1987, p. 52.

is very clear and the reason for the concentration of the Brāhmanical college organization in this area could be that different streams of Indian culture blended there harmoniously, with the Buddhist example having affected the Brāhmanical educational organization here.[262] The Nalanda University, founded in the middle of the fifth century CE, where subjects like Mahāyāna, Hīnayāna, Vedas, and other Brāhmanical works, Grammar, Sāṁkhya, Yoga, Tantrism, Medicine and Astronomy were taught in the medium of Sanskrit, had become famous by the start of the seventh century CE. Toṇḍaimaṇḍalam and Nālandā were in close contact with each other and it is likely that Brāhmanical Toṇḍaimaṇḍalam must have got from the Buddhists the idea of concentration in educational effort and of the provision of all conveniences for students.[263]

There are several undated inscriptions of the Coḷa times found in temples which have a bearing on education during those times. One is from the Sundareśvara temple in Sendalai (Tañjāvūr district) which records an endowment, a portion of which was specified for exposition of the *Bhārata* (*Mahābhārata*) called *Bhāratappaṅgu* and where a stage (*aṁbalam*) was assigned for this discourse in this temple.[264] Thus, the tradition of the recitation of the *Mahābhārata* in temples seen from two Pallava records continued in the Coḷa era as well.

Another interesting Coḷa inscription of the eleventh century CE from the Udvahanātha Svāmi temple in Tirumaṇañjeri (Māyavaram district) contains verses from the *Agni Purāṇam* in praise of the God Udvahanātha enshrined in this temple.[265] The

---

262 S. Sathyanathaier, *Studies on the Ancient History of Toṇḍaimaṇḍalam*, Madras, 1987, p. 52.

263 Ibid., p. 53.

264 *ARE* 63 of 1897; ibid., pt. II, para 9, p. 3; *SII*, vol. VI no. 12, p. 4.

265 *ARE* 23 of 1919.

Kaccīśvara (Kacchapeśvara) temple in Kāñcīpuram contains a Sanskrit inscription in Grantha script of the Coḷa times datable to the tenth–eleventh centuries CE.[266] This lithic record, found on a pillar in the *maṇḍapa* in front of the Durgā shrine is very interesting as it contains six verses from the poem *Sūryaśatakam* of Mayūra in praise of the Sun God. In all probability, it was a votive pillar erected by somebody in honour of Sūryadeva, one of the *pañcasandhi* deities (Aiñjaṇḍidevar in Tamil).[267] There might have been more pillars of this type which might have contained other verses of the same *śataka*, but they are not existent now; and the presence of this pillar in the Durgā shrine has to be accounted for by its probable displacement during temple repairs in the later days — probably in the time of Kulottuṅga I when the central shrine of the Kaccīśvara temple seems to have undergone thorough overhauling.[268]

Mayūrakavi was a court-poet who flourished in the court of Harṣavardhana in the first half of the seventh century CE and is reputed to have been the father-in-law of Bāṇabhaṭṭa; while in the *Prabandhacintāmaṇi*, the relationship is mentioned as that of a brother-in-law (sister's husband).[269] His only work is the *Sūryaśatakam* popularly known as the *Mayūraśatakam*. The verses are written in the *śragdharā* metre and their literary merit coupled with the miraculous results which are alleged to attend their composition have secured for them great popularity among the orthodox.[270] The surviving pillar in the Kacchapeśvara temple stands to proclaim the popularity of this work within three centuries of its composition in so southerly a part of this vast land with the then difficulties of

---

[266] *ARE* 81 of 1921.

[267] *ARE* 1921, pt. II, para 78, pp.115-16.

[268] Ibid., p. 116.

[269] *ARE* 1921, pt. II, para 78, p. 116.

[270] Ibid.

communication, which however were no barrier against the travel of literary works and appreciation of literary beauty.[271]

Another example of a great Sanskrit work presented in inscriptions is seen in the west and east *gopura*s on the Naṭarāja temple in Cidambaram. The sculptured panels of the 108 *karaṇa*s are accompanied by the etching of the corresponding verses from the *Nāṭyaśāstram* of Bharata in the Grantha script of the Coḷa times of the twelfth century CE.[272]

The inscriptions with verses from the *Agni Purāṇam*, *Sūryaśatakam* and *Nāṭyaśāstram* go to show how literary works in Sanskrit travelled so extensively and were so popular in the Tamil country as to be etched on walls and pillars of temples where they could be read and appreciated by the common man.

The inscriptions, both lithic and the copper-plate grants of the Coḷa times provide a clear picture of the status of higher education in the Coḷa era. However, there is little evidence of a direct character on the spread of literacy or the extent to which it was generally valued, but it is possible to hazard the conjecture that the percentage of literacy in the population was of a fairly high standard.[273] There are inscriptions which reveal that the village school functioning from the shade of a tree or in the verandas of temples or *maṭha*s was a common institution and its teacher was among the staff of employees remunerated from the common land held by the village.[274] There is an inscription from the Vaidyanātha temple in Tirumālvāḍi (Tirucirāpaḷḷi district) of the period of the Coḷas which records a gift to the temple by a person named Kāman

---

[271] C. Sivaramamurti, *Indian Epigraphy and South Indian Scripts*, Chennai, 1999, p. 41.

[272] *ARE* 368 of 1913; *ARE* 343 of 1913; *ARE* 1914, pp. 74-81.

[273] K.A. Nilakanta Sastri, *Coḷas*, p. 628.

[274] Ibid.

Tāyaṉ who was a teacher (*vatti*) of Iḍaiyāṟ.[275] Another inscription from the Netroddhārakasvāmi temple in Panaiyavaram (South Arcot district), which is undated, records a provision for maintaining a teacher in a free school.[276]

Stonemasons and coppersmiths engraved the epigraphs on stone and copper, and the work was done with remarkable accuracy and art, but sometimes there are corrupt and colloquial phrases and words in many inscriptions which show that the work was generally entrusted to workmen who were just literate but no scholars.[277] The large number of educated people employed by the Coḷa monarchs in various departments of administration in their far-flung empire shows that education must have percolated down the society. In addition to all this were the expositions of the epics like the *Rāmāyaṇa* and the *Mahābhārata* in temples and also the Purāṇas and works of philosophy to educate the common man and to instill moral and ethical values in society.

[275] *ARE* 17 of 1920.

[276] *ARE* 323 of 1917.

[277] K.A. Nilakanta Sastri, op. cit.

5

Second Pāṇḍyan Empire

THE epigraphs of Tamil Nadu clearly prove that the Pāṇḍyas had been under the sway of the Coḷas, till CE 1218, i.e. until the end of the rule of Kulottuṅga Coḷa III.[1] The Coḷa empire waned in the last quarter of the thirteenth century CE and came to a close with Rājendra III in CE 1279. Subsequently, the Coḷa country became part of the Pāṇḍyan empire and the thirteenth century CE witnessed unprecedented Pāṇḍyan revival. The Pāṇḍyan power rose to the height of its glory under Jaṭāvarman Sundara Pāṇḍya I and Māravarman Kulaśekhara. The epigraphs of the monarchs of the Pāṇḍyan empire provide some information about Sanskrit education of those times.

Jaṭāvarman Kulaśekhara I

The end of Jaṭāvarman Kulaśekhara reign nearly coincides with that of Kulottuṅga Coḷa III. This Pāṇḍyan ruler, in his twenty-fifth regnal year, created the Rājagaṁbhīra-caturvedimaṅgalam consisting of 1,030 *brahmadeyas*; perhaps he held the title *Rājagaṁbhīra*. Three inscriptions in the Appan temple in the village of Śeraṇmādevī (Tirunelveli district) of the reign of Jaṭāvarman Kulaśekhara I is a typical example of a series of triple documents.[2] The gift was made by this Pāṇḍya king in the name of his brother-in-law Kodai Ravivarman. The first of these inscriptions registers that at the suggestion of his brother-

---

[1] N. Subrahmanian, *History of Tamilnad (to AD 1565)*, Madurai, 1983, p. 205.

[2] *ARE*, 664-66 of 1916; ibid., pt. II, para 8, p. 108.

in-law, Ravivarman, some land in Śeraṉmahādevī-caturvedimaṅgalam be made completely tax-free for daily offerings, the recital of the Vedas and Purāṇas and for singing and dancing.[3] The other two are also associated with the gift of land mentioned above.[4]

Māravarman Sundara Pāṇḍya I (CE 1216-38)

Māravarman Sundara Pāṇḍya I was either the son or the younger brother of his predecessor Jaṭāvarman Kulaśekhara and was a contemporary of Rājarāja Coḷa III.[5] An interesting epigraph from the Niṉṟa Nārāyaṇa temple in Rāmnāḍ district registers a gift of land as *Mahābhārata-vṛtti* by Tiruvaraṅgadevan Kunrduttan and his brother Tiruvaraṅgadevan Uyyakkolvan to provide for the reading of the *Mahābhāratam*, the *Rāmāyaṇam* and the Purāṇas in a *maṭha* built by them and in the immediate presence of the god at Tiruttangāl.[6]

There is an inscription in the Appan temple in the village of Śeraṉmādevī (Tirunelveli district) of the reign of Tribhuvanacakravartin Koṉerinmaikoṇḍāṉ in which the king promised to make a gift of tax-free land in Śeraṉmahādevī-caturvedīmaṅgalam for feeding seventeen people daily including the *tridaṇḍī sannyāsins* and for maintaining a teacher for the Śāstras in the *maṭha* of the temple.[7] Another inscription in the same place of the reign of Māravarman Sundara Pāṇḍya mentions that while he was seated on his throne at Madurai, this king promised the gift of land mentioned above.[8]

---

[3] *ARE* 664 of 1916.

[4] *ARE* 665-66 of 1916.

[5] N. Subrahmanian, op. cit., pp. 206-07.

[6] *ARE* 546 of 1922; ibid., pt. II, para 50.

[7] *ARE* 667 of 1916.

[8] *ARE* 668 of 1916.

Many inscriptions like this one relate to *maṭha*s which grew in power and popularity in the Coḷa and Pāṇḍya times. It became a common occurrence to attach *maṭha*s to temples from the tenth century CE onwards. These religious institutions were very influential and in many cases controlled the affairs of the temple. The *maṭha*s not only housed and fed pilgrims from afar, but were also educational institutions with teachers for various subjects and students residing and studying in them.

Incidentally, there is another inscription of a king (whose name is not mentioned) in the very same place which registers an order for making a tax-free gift of land for offerings in the temple of Dvārāpati Appan (Kṛṣṇa) in this village (Śeraṉmādevī) and also to grants made for the study of Ṛgveda, Yajurveda, Sāmaveda and the Atharvaveda and for the teaching of the Śāstras and the recital of the Purāṇas.[9]

Jaṭāvarman Sundara Pāṇḍya I (CE 1251-68)

The successor of Māravarman Sundara Pāṇḍya II to the throne at Madurai was Jaṭāvarman Sundara Pāṇḍya I, the greatest emperor of this dynasty. His empire extended from Nellore and Cuddapah in present-day Andhra Pradesh to Kanyākumārī in Tamil Nadu.

Two damaged Tamil inscriptions from the Naṭarāja temple in Cidambaram (South Arcot district), almost certainly belonging to the reign of Jaṭāvarman Sundara Pāṇḍya I, provide information about libraries and their organization.[10] Evidence of the existence of such libraries in the ancient Tamil country is rather rare, while in the north, many of the great educational institutions of ancient and medieval India like Nālandā, Vikramaśilā and Pāṭaliputra which strove hard for the spread of learning, are believed to have housed libraries

---

9 *ARE* 671 of 1916.

10 *ARE* 168 and 169 of 1961-62; *EI*, vol. XL, pp. 223-24.

containing hundreds of manuscripts for the benefit of students and scholars. The writings of Chinese Buddhist scholars like Hieun Tsang and Itsing who travelled to India and studied at some of these prestigious institutions provide authentic information about these libraries where many facilities such as copying manuscripts were provided to those using them. However, information about such libraries in south India is not seen from literary sources although very great educational institutions did exist here as well.

Since time immemorial, the Vedas have been taught and learnt by rote only, i.e. the teacher without looking into any book, would recite a Vedic passage, in convenient parts and the students would hear him with all attention and repeat it correctly a good number of times and memorize the same carefully.[11] Reciting the Vedas by looking into books and writing the Vedic texts have always been looked down upon in ancient times and therefore the Veda *pāṭhaśālā*s that imparted the knowledge of the Vedic text alone need not acquire or organize a library.[12] However, this was not the case with regard to the *Pāṭhaśālā*s or *ghaṭika*s which taught different Śāstras at various levels and thus the educational institutions at various temples mentioned earlier would possibly have had libraries housing manuscripts which the teachers and students had access to. Unfortunately, there is no mention of these from the important educational centres at Eṇṇāyiram, Tribhuvanai, Tirumukkūḍal and the like. Luckily, there are some lithic epigraphs of the Pāṇḍya times from Cidambaram and Tirunelveli with regard to libraries which functioned in the premises of temples in the thirteenth century CE.

The inscriptions of the reign of Jaṭāvarman Sundara Pāṇḍya I mentioned above record the orders of a body of officials

---

[11] S. Sankaranarayanan, "Sanskrit Education in Ancient Tamil Country (An Epigraphical Survey)", *ALB*, vol. 57, 1993, p. 25.

[12] Ibid.

who were collectively responsible for various affairs of the administration of the temple of Naṭarāja. These orders were to do with the details of the organization of the Sarasvatī-bhaṇḍāram or library to which lands were assigned for maintenance. The Sarasvatī-bhaṇḍāram seems to have been established by one Svāmideva and it was located in the western *maṇṭapa* (where the epigraph is etched) situated to the north of the Subrahmaṇya shrine in the *Rājādhirāja-prākāra* of the temple and its books (*granthas* and *pottagas*, i.e. *pustakas*) were stored in the adjacent stack-room known as Vikrama-śoḷan-tirukkaiyoṭṭi, i.e. a storeroom of sacred manuscripts named after Vikrama Coḷa of the twelfth century CE.[13]

This suggests that the Sarasvatī-bhaṇḍāram must have been in existence much earlier (by a century or so) than the date of the record.[14] The language of the record suggests that they were also meant to reorganize the already existing library and that they speak of the modalities of absorbing the already existing staff of the new set-up.[15] This epigraph enumerates the names of twenty scholars employed in the *bhaṇḍāram*. Of these, six were in-charge of reading and maintaining the books on Divyāgama, possibly also on Vyākaraṇa and other subjects; two persons were appointed for reading Purāṇa and Jyotiṣa works; eight persons were recruited for copying afresh the old and worn-out manuscripts; four were employed in the task of maintaining the manuscripts (like dusting, putting new planks and threads and retying them). It was stipulated that the transcript copies of the manuscripts must be compared with their originals by two scholarly staff-members of the library for the benefit of the visiting scholars. A few ascetics (*tapasvins*) were part of the staff of the library. The staff-members of the library came from different places like Guṇṭūr,

---

[13] S. Sankaranarayanan, p. 28.

[14] Ibid.

[15] Ibid.

Vaṅgipuram and Gomata in Andhra.

These employees were paid in kind (paddy) and in cash (*kāśu*) on a daily basis and provision was also made for supplying clothes to them. This interesting record also states that a portion of a village known as Vaḍanallūr was allotted for the purpose of paying the employees and that this part of the village was renamed as Viśvādhika-viveka-maṅgalam yielding an annual income of 810 *kaḷam* of paddy, out of which two-thirds were meant for the maintenance of the library and for the payment of the employees and the remaining one-third was for conducting some festivals of the deity in this temple.

The lithic epigraphs also appears to mention that there were a very large number of manuscripts stored here, although the name of only one — *Siddhāntaratnākara* — is mentioned. Incidentally, the name of this work is mentioned twice and also a reference to its being copied. The language of this inscription indicates that this particular work was a very special one and that the title was popular at that time. The author of this work is not known. However, it seems identical with the work of this same name that figures in a Sanskrit lithic record from the Kaṁpahareśvara temple at Tribhuvanam (near Kuṁbakoṇam of the time of Kulottuṅga Coḷa III, approximately thirty-two years before the accession of Jaṭāvarman Sundara Pāṇḍya I (to whom the two inscriptions of Cidambaram belong)).[16] The epigraph from Tribhuvanam states that the work was composed by a great scholar called Someśvara, also known as Īśvara Śiva, the son of Śrīkaṇṭha Śambhu and the preceptor (*guru*) of Kulottuṅga III. This inscription mentions that this work was written from the standpoint of Śaiva philosophy and that the author had established (obviously in that work), the Upaniṣadic doctrine

[16] *SII*, vol. XXII no. 90, p. 147.

that God Śiva transcends that universe (*viśvādhika*).[17] The fact that the village gifted to the library was named *viśvādhika-viveka-maṅgalam* as seen in the inscription seems to support this identification. In the Tribhuvanam temple itself is another inscription which is damaged, but appears to mention a village named *viśvādhikavive* (*kamaṅgalam*).[18]

Mention has been made on the earlier chapter on the Coḷas about inscriptions from the Tiruvoṟṟiyūr temple regarding land grants made during the reign of Kulottuṅga Coḷa III to the *vyākaraṇadāna-vyākhyāna maṇḍapa* in that temple and its connection with the great grammarian Pāṇini. A record of the time of Jaṭāvarman Sundara Pāṇḍya I found on the west wall of the central shrine of this temple records an agreement by which the tax *ponvāri*, collected both in the northern and southern divisions of Tiruvoṟṟiyūr were assigned for maintaining the same historic *maṇḍapa*.

Māravarman Kulaśekhara I (CE 1268–1308)

Jaṭāvarman Sundara Pāṇḍya I installed his son Māravarman Kulaśekhara as crown-prince and the latter later succeeded him on the throne. He was the last great Pāṇḍyan king to rule independently. It was during his reign that Marco Polo, the Venetian traveller visited the Pāṇḍyan country. An account of the social conditions of this time is also available from the writings of Wassaf, a Muslim historian.

Another Pāṇḍyan epigraph provides information about a library that existed during the twelfth–fourteenth centuries CE. This lithic record, possibly belonging to the reign of Māravarman Kulaśekhara is etched in the temple of Tuvārāpati Appan (Dvārāpati Appan) in the village of Śeraṉmādevī (Tirunelveli district).[19] It gives details of an order of the

[17] S. Sankaranarayanan, op. cit., p. 30.

[18] *SII*, vol. XXIII no. 189, p. 147.

[19] *ARE* 695 of 1916.

administrative body of the village which is called in this epigraph as Śeravaṉmahādevī-caturvedimaṅgalam, exempting from taxes, certain lands granted by an individual in favour of a Sarasvatī-bhaṇḍāram attached to the temple of Dvārāpati Appan of that village. Unfortunately, more details about this library are not given in this inscription.

An inscription dated CE 1283 of the fifteenth regnal year of Māravarman Kulaśekhara I in the Ekāmranātha temple in Kāñcīpuram registers the donation of three villages named Periya-vilattūr, Siṟṟu-vilattūr, Korapadiri and Veppañjeri, converting them into an *agrahāra* under the name Kulaśekhara-caturvedimaṅgalam to 110 brāhmaṇas for reciting the Vedas in front of the God Ekāmranātha at Kāñcīpuram during the service called Kulaśekharan-*sandhi,* instituted in the name of the king, after excluding the portion previously granted as *devadāna*.[20]

An interesting inscription of the reign of Māravarman Kulaśekhara from the Ādinātha temple in Āḻvār Tirunagari (Tirunelveli district) records a gift of special privileges in the distribution of sacred *prasāda* to a brāhmaṇa of Maṇalūr who recited the Purāṇas and the Itihāsas in the temples at Tirunagari.[21]

---

[20] *SITI*, vol. I no. 439, p. 429.

[21] *ARE* 467 of 1909.

6

Hoysaḷas

THE Hoysaḷa dynasty, which came to power after the fall of the Gaṅga dynasty in south Karnataka, ruled from *c.* CE 1006–1346 and also extended their power to parts of Tamil Nadu. The fortunes of the Hoysaḷas were closely connected to those of the contemporary powers ruling in the Tamil country. In fact, the main interest of the reign of Vīra-Someśvara (CE 1235-54) consists of his relations with the two great Tamil kingdoms, the Coḷas and the Pāṇḍyas. Around CE 1233, even during the lifetime of his father Vīra-Narasiṁha II (CE 1220-35), he erected a capital-city named Vikramapura in the midst of the Coḷa country, which is now the modern Kaṇṇanūr, a suburb of Samayapuram near Tirucirāpaḷḷi.[1] The Coḷa monarch at the time was the weak Rājarāja Coḷa III (CE 1216-50) who owed his crown to the Hoysaḷa protection and generosity.[2]

Vīra-Someśvara's sons, Narasiṁha II (CE 1254-91) and Vīra-Rāmanātha (CE 1254-95) divided their father's kingdom, probably as a matter of administrative convenience. The former ruled the home province while the latter was in-charge of the Tamil provinces including part of the east Mysore country, comprising modern Kolar district. Rāmanātha's Tamil provinces were very vast and many of his inscriptions are found in the northern part of Tamil Nadu and in the Tirucirāpaḷḷi and Tañjāvūr areas. Some of his inscriptions reveal that he was closely allied with the Coḷa ruler Rājendra III (CE 1246-79), the

[1] K.R. Venkatraman, *Hoysaḷas in the Tamil Country*, Annamalainagar, 1950, p. 16.

[2] Ibid., p. 17.

alliance being necessary in the face of a common danger, the aggression of Jaṭāvarman Sundara Pāṇḍya I.[3]

There are a number of inscriptions of the Hoysaḷas in the Śrī Raṅganātha Svāmi temple in Śrīraṅgam, many of them belonging to the reign of Vīra-Rāmanātha. One of the most important of these is a damaged epigraph in the third *prākāra* of this very vast temple-complex dated CE 1269 of the time of Vīra Rāmanātha.[4] This inscription is particularly important as it refers to the existence of a library (Sarasvatī-bhaṇḍāram) attached to the temple of Śrīraṅgam. The mention of libraries in connection with temples or religious institutions, as mentioned earlier, is somewhat rare in inscriptions. According to the Āgamas, a temple of the first magnitude should have a library attached and the Śrīraṅgam temple being of this type and being an important centre of religious activity in the medieval centuries, it is but natural that it must have been provided with such an institute for the dissemination of the Vaiṣṇava religion.[5] The Pāñcarātra Āgama work *Pauṣkara Saṁhitā* (referred to by Śrī Rāmānuja of the eleventh century CE in the *Śrībhāṣya*) prescribes that every great temple must have a shrine or temple of learning — *jñānapratiṣṭhāna* otherwise called *vidyāpīṭhapratiṣṭhāna* with a library containing collections of perfect manuscripts of the Pāñcarātra Āgama, works of the Vedas, Vedāṅgas, Smr̥tis, Itihāsas, Vyākaraṇa and Tarka; that the library must have in it an image of Sarasvatī, the Goddess of Speech seated on a lotus (*kañjastha vgīśvarī*); that different subjects must be taught near the image of the goddess; and that the library must be provided with sufficient funds, properly granted, for maintaining and preserving the manuscripts (*jñānakośānupālane*).[6]

---

[3] K.R. Venkatraman, *Hoysaḷas in the Tamil Country*, Annamalainagar, 1950,, p. 25.

[4] *ARE* 139 of 1938-39; *SII*, vol. XXIV no. 279, pp. 297-98.

[5] *ARE* 1938-39, pt. II, para 70, p. 95.

[6] S. Sankaranarayanan, "Sanskrit Education in Ancient Tamil Country (An Epigraphical Survey)", *ALB*, vol. 57, 1993, p. 26.

This record of Vīra-Rāmanātha mentions that the images of Sarasvatī Devī, Vedavyāsa Bhagavān and Hayagrīva (all the three deities presiding over learning) had been newly installed in the *maṇṭapa* constructed as an adjunct to the library (Sarasvatī-bhaṇḍāram) by Nīlakaṇṭha Nāyaka of Palapaḷḷi, a contemporary of the Hoysaḷa Vīra-Rāmanātha. He also made a gift of money for providing offerings to these deities. It is possible that this *pustaka-bhaṇḍāra* had already existed in the twelfth century CE.[7]

It would not be out of place to mention, in this connection, an inscription of the western Cāḷukyan king Tribhuvanamalla Someśvara from Nāgai (erstwhile Hyderabad state) which records the provision made for the maintenance of six *sarasvatī-bhaṇḍārika*s or curators who looked after the library attached to the college endowed by the king.[8]

[7] S. Sankaranarayanan, "Sanskrit Education in Ancient Tamil Country (An Epigraphical Survey)", *ALB*, vol. 57, 1993, p. 32.

[8] *Hyderabad Archaeological Series*, no. 8; *ARE*, 1938-39, pt. II, para 70, p. 95.

7

Vijayanagara Empire

THE Vijayanagara empire, founded in CE 1336, on the banks of the River Tuṅgabhadrā in present-day Karnataka covered, at its height, a vast portion of south India. The kings of the four dynasties — Saṅgama, Saluva, Tuluva and Aravīḍu — who ruled from Vijayanagara (present-day Hampī) over this extensive area did much for reviving the political stability, economic revival and cultural efflorescence of south India. It is therefore only to be expected that literature also flourished in their empire. The literary works in Sanskrit and the numerous lithic and copper-plate records of this era provide a clear idea of the patronage extended to Sanskrit language and literature.

Bukka I (CE 1356-77)

During the reign of Bukka I, his son Kumāra Kampaṇa, who had been governing the Tamil districts of the Vijayanagara empire as his viceroy since CE 1360-61, led an army against the Sultanate of Madurai in CE 1370, which resulted in putting an end to the latter. This great military exploit of Kumāra Kampaṇa or Vīra-Kampaṇa Uḍaiyār was the theme of a beautiful Sanskrit poem called *Madurāvijayam* (conquest of Madurā) also called *Kamparāyacaritam* (history of Kamparāya), composed by his wife, Gaṅgādevī, a talented poetess.[1] In this work, which is composed in epic style, is to be found much historical information. Composed in elegant Sanskrit, this poem

[1] S. Tiruvenkatachariar, *Madhurāvijayam of Gaṅgā Devī*, Annamalainagar, 1957.

resembles the *Raghuvaṁśa* in style. Gaṅgādevī was a student of Sanskrit classics and was well-versed in Vedic lore.[2] She mentions the names of Kālidāsa, Bāṇa Bhaṭṭa, Bhāravi, Daṇḍin, Bhavabhūti, Vyāsa and Vālmīki and in a single verse devoted to each, she brings out the special merit of the poet.[3] Gaṅgādevī's work reveals that she was a very gifted poetess among the galaxy of great poets of Sanskrit literature.

Vedānta Deśika

The illustrious Śrīvaiṣṇava scholar, philosopher and poet Veṅkaṭanātha, better known as Vedānta Deśika (*c.* CE 1268–1369), lived in the Tamil country during the turbulent times of the late thirteenth century CE and during the period of the early Vijayanagara emperors of the fourteenth century CE. Born at Tūpiḷ in Kāñcīpuram to Anantasūri Somayājī and Totarāmbā, he later moved to other Śrīvaiṣṇava centres like Tiruvahīndrapuram (Tiruvendipuram, near Cuddalore) and Śrīraṅgam (Tirucirāpaḷḷi district). His works, approximately 139 in number, are in Sanskrit, Maṇipravāḷa, Tamil and Prākṛt and cover the spheres of religion, philosophy and literature.

During his stay in Śrīraṅgam, this island was attacked by the Muslims in CE 1323 under the leadership of Ulugh Khan. Vedānta Deśika fled to Satyamaṅgaḷam on the Kāverī (sometimes identified with a place called Satyagalam, near Kollegal).[4] The Śrīvaiṣṇava work, *Guruparamparaprabhavam,* as well as the *Koil Olugu* (a chronicle of the Raṅganātha Svāmi temple, Śrīraṅgam) mention that on the eve of the Muslim invasion, the authorities of the Śrīraṅgam shrine removed the image of Aḻagiyamanavāḷa Perumāḷ (the processional image of

---

[2] S. TiruvenkatacharIar, *Madhurāvijayam of Gaṅgā Devī,* Annamalainagar, 1957, Canto I.

[3] Ibid.

[4] V.N. Hari Rao, *History of the Śrīraṅgam Temple,* Tirupati, 1976, p. 119.

the Raṅganātha Svāmi temple) to Tirunārāyaṇapuram (Melkoṭe, near Mysore in Karnataka) and to many other places and finally to Tirumala (Tirupati in Andhra Pradesh).[5] An official of the Vijayanagara empire, named Gopaṇa Uḍaiyār, who resided at Senji (Ginji in Viḻḻupuram district) took this image from Tirupati to Śiṅgapuram (near Senji) where it was safeguarded and worshipped. Finally, Gopaṇa defeated the Muslim troops and brought the processional images of Raṅganātha Svāmi and His consorts to Śrīraṅgam and reconsecrated them there. Gopaṇa, also known as Gopaṇārya and Gopaṇangal was a brāhmaṇa officer of Kumāra Kampaṇa belonging to the *Āpastamba sūtra* and Bhāradvāja *gotra*.[6] He was initially a general supervisor-in-charge of temples in the Tamil country and was later appointed as the governor of Senji by Kumāra Kampaṇa.[7]

According to the hagiological work, the *Prapannāmṛtam*, Vedānta Deśika, who had to leave Śrīraṅgam on account of the disturbed state there, returned to this island and witnessed with great happiness the re-consecration of the images and composed verses commemorating this memorable event.[8] These verses are found in a fourteenth-century inscription etched in Grantha alphabet on the wall of the Śrīraṅgam temple. The first verse is as follows:

āniya ānīla śṛṅga dyutiracita jagadrañjanād añjanādreḥ |
ceñjyamārādhya kañcitsamayamatha nihatyoddhanuṣakān turuṣkān | |
lakṣmī kṣmābhyāmubhābhyām saha nijanagare sthāpayan raṅganātham |
saṁyagvaryām saparyam punarakṛta yaśodarpaṇo gopaṇāryaḥ | |

[5] *EI*, vol. VI no. 33, pp. 322ff.

[6] A. Krishnaswami, *The Tamil Country Under Vijayanagara* (hereafter *TCUV*), Annamalai University, 1964, p. 55.

[7] Ibid., pp. 55-60.

[8] V.N. Hari Rao, op. cit.

> Having brought (the god) from the Añjanādri (mountain), the splendour of whose darkish peaks gives delight to the whole world; having worshipped Him at Senji for some time, then having slain the Tuluṣkas, whose bows were raised, Gopaṇārya, the mirror of fame, placing Lord Raṅgānātha together with both Lakṣmī and the Goddess Earth in his own town, again duly performed excellent worship.[9]

The second verse inscribed beneath this one is as follows:

> *viśveṣam raṅgarājam vr̥ṣabhagiritatād gopaṇaḥ kṣoṇīdevaḥ* |
> *nītva svām rājadhānim nijabalanihatotsikta tauluṣkasainyaḥ* | |
>
> *kr̥tva śrīraṅgabhūmim kr̥tayugasahitam tam tu lakṣmī mahībhyām* |
> *saṁsthāpyāsyām sarojodbhava iva kurute sādhucaryām saparyām* | |

> Having carried Raṅgarāja, the Lord of the World, from the slope of the Vr̥sabhagiri (mountain) to his capital; having slain by his army the proud Tauluṣka soldiers, having made the site of Śrīraṅgam united with the golden age (Kr̥ta Yuga) and having placed there this (God) together with Lakṣmī and the Earth, the brāhmaṇa Gopaṇa duly performs like the lotus-born one (Brahmā), the worship which has to be practised.[10]

In the Vijayanagara epoch too, like in previous times, the temple continued to play a major role in disseminating learning and education. In the premises of the temples were located the *maṭhas* (monasteries) which rendered yeoman service in teaching certain schools of religion and philosophy. An interesting and informative Tamil inscription dated CE 1359 is found engraved on the north wall of the second *prākāra* of the Varadarāja Svāmi temple in Kāñcīpuram.[11] This inscription

[9] *EI*, vol. VI no. 33, p. 322.

[10] Ibid.

[11] *EI*, vol. XXV no. 34, pp. 318-26.

states that by a Divine Order, the title Brahmatantra Svatantra Jīyar was conferred on a certain Vaiṣṇavadāsa who was placed in-charge of a *maṭha* and its properties so that he could propagate the tenets of the *Rāmānuja Darśanam* to the Vaiṣṇava laity and to maintain the library he had collected, probably on the *maṭha* premises.[12] The *Rāmānuja Darśanam* referred to here, refers to the *Viśiṣṭādvaita-siddhānta* as codified and expounded in his *Śrībhāṣya* by the well-known Śrīvaiṣṇava preceptor (*ācārya*) Rāmānuja, who raised this system to an unassailable eminence and had arranged for its propagation by training a number of able exponents and seventy-four *siṁhāsanādhipatis*.[13] Regarding the person mentioned in this record from Kāñcīpuram, Brahmatantra Svatantra Jīyar, some information is available from the Śrīvaiṣṇava work *Guruparampara-prabhavam*. Brahmatantra Svatantra Jīyar, whose original name was Vīravaḷḷi Peraruḷāḷayyaṉ, was well-versed in the Śāstras and was an ardent disciple of Śrī Vedānta Deśika. He once defeated a scholar from north India in a polemical contest at Śrīraṅgam and was honoured by Vedānta Deśika with the title Brahmatantra Svatantra Jīyar (he who is a master in Brahmatantra). He had a number of disciples and authored two works *Divyasūri Stuti* and the *Ācāryāvatāra-ghattārtha*.[14] The *maṭha* which was thus started in Kāñcīpuram under the pontificate of this Brahmatantra Svatantra Jīyar in CE 1360 grew in importance and appears to have moved its headquarters later to Melkoṭe in Karnataka where it became popular under the name of Parakāla Maṭha.[15]

An important point of interest in this inscription is the reference to a collection of manuscripts (or library) which was kept in this *maṭha* and a stipulation made for its proper upkeep

[12] *EI*, p. 319.

[13] Ibid.

[14] Ibid., p. 322.

[15] Ibid.

as envisaged in the expression *ivan tedina postakaṅgaḷum iduku vendum upakaraṇaṅgaḷum*. It would not be out of place to mention here, a slightly later inscription dated CE 1406 from Vyntyāla in South Kanara district which registers a gift of one village and income from other villages to Paurāṇika Kavi Kr̥ṣṇa Bhaṭṭa of Śr̥ṅgerī for the renovation and maintenance of a library (*pustaka-bhaṇḍāra*) belonging to the Śr̥ṅgerī Maṭha when Narasiṁha Bhāratī who probably succeeded Vidyāraṇya Tīrtha as its pontiff.[16]

At about the same time (CE 1377), there was a *maṭha* named the Veda Maṭha in the Śrī Varadarāja Svāmi temple which was presided over by a certain Vedasāgara Śrīpāda and which most likely specialized in teaching the Vedas.[17] This *maṭha* was probably patronized by the Mādhvas, who are the followers of the Dvaita philosophy propounded by Śrī Madhvācārya.

Harihara II (CE 1377–1404)

Harihara II who succeeded his father Bukka I on the throne of Vijayanagara assumed the enviable titles *rāja-vyāsa, rāja vālmīki* and *karnaṭaka vidyā vilāsa* which reveal in unmistakable terms that he was himself an author of great works of literature, besides being a patron of literary men.[18] The Nallūr copper-plate inscription of this ruler dated CE 1399 states that he gave Aubala Yajvan and his younger brother Nr̥siṁha Yajvan, the village known as Śrīnallūr.[19] The donees of the inscription, Aubala and Nr̥siṁha belonged to the Bhāradvāja *gotra*. Aubala is referred to as *adhvarin* and *yajvan* in this inscription[20] which

[16] *ARE*, 1936-37, pt. II, para 55, p. 81.

[17] K.V. Raman, *Śrī Varadarājaswāmi Temple, Kāñcīpuram*, New Delhi, 1975, p. 137.

[18] *E.C.*, VI, Kp. 34; *ARE*, 11 of 1915; Rep., 1915, para 41; T.V. Mahalingam, *Administration and Social Life Under Vijayanagara* (hereafter *ASLV*), Madras, 1940, p. 354.

[19] *EI*, vol. III no. 19, vv. 29-31, p. 126 (Nallūr plates).

[20] Ibid., vv. 29-30, p. 123.

appear to be synonymous with *adhvaryu* "a student of the Yajurveda".[21] Nṛsiṁha is described as one "who had crossed the ocean of the Vedas" (*śruti-sāgara-pāragaḥ*). Harihara gave them the village of Śrīnallūr when he was "surrounded by several pious and amiable scholars who walked the path prescribed by the Vedas, who were full of eloquence and who were headed by the family priest" (*paritaḥ priyataiḥ snigdhaiḥ purohita purogamaiḥ, vividhaiḥ vibudhaiḥ śrautapatikairadhikairgira*).

The village of Śrīnallūr, also called Nallūri and Sāvaṇarājiyapuram in the inscription, was situated in the ancient territorial subdivision of Toṇḍaimaṇḍalam (erstwhile North Arcot, South Arcot and Chengalpet districts of Tamil Nadu) and has been identified with Vaḍakku-Nallūr which is to the south-west of River Āraṇi.[22] Incidentally, the inscription describes Toṇḍaimaṇḍalam as "adorned by learned men" (*vidvadbhiḥ upaśobhite*).

This inscription mentions many titles of Harihara II, one of them being *vedabhāṣya-prakāśakaḥ* (the publisher of the commentaries of the Vedas).[23] This *biruda* clearly refers to the commentaries on the Vedas which were published under the king's authority by Sāyaṇācārya, the celebrated Vedic scholar.[24] An inscription from Śrīsailam (Andhra Pradesh) records that this king caused the *Veda-Bhāṣya*, i.e. the commentary on the Vedas to be written and the institutions of the Vaidikas (brāhmaṇas) to be established on a firm basis.[25] Sāyaṇa was the younger brother of Mādhavācārya, the illustrious literary celebrity who has generally been considered to have assumed the yellow robes and is identified with Vidyāraṇya of the Śṛṅgerī Maṭha.[26]

---

[21] *EI*, vol. III no. 19, fn. 3, p. 126.

[22] Ibid., p. 119.

[23] Ibid., p. 122.

[24] Ibid., p. 118.

[25] *ARE*, 11 of 1915; *ARE* 1915, pt. II, para 41, p. 105.

[26] T.V. Mahalingam, *ASLV*, p. 354.

Many details regarding the relations and contemporaries found in Mādhava's and Śāyaṇa's works are corroborated by a mutilated inscription etched in the Śrī Varadarāja Svāmi temple (Aruḷāla Perumāḷ temple) in Kāñcīpuram.[27] This lithic epigraph, found embedded on the right side of the *gopura* leading to the *abhiṣeka-maṇḍapa* (place of sacred bath of the deities) in this temple, is in Sanskrit and etched in the Grantha script. This undated inscription is addressed to Sāyaṇa, the younger brother of Mādhava and gives details such as the parentage and other details of the brothers. The three brothers mentioned in this inscription are Mādhava, the eldest (who was to be known as Vidyāraṇya after he became an ascetic), Sāyaṇa, his younger brother (who was to be known as Bhāgīrathī-Tīrtha after he became an ascetic) and Bhoganātha, the youngest brother.[28] All three brothers were at one time or another to be councillors of emperors or kings; Mādhava and Sāyaṇa to the Vijayanagara emperors and Bhoganātha to King Saṅgama II. The reference to the family being of the Bhāradvāja *gotra* is especially important as it makes a distinction from Mādhava-to-be-Vidyāraṇya (who is sometimes called Mādhavamantrī) from another Mādhava belonging to the Āṅgīrasa *gotra* who was also an erudite scholar and who served the early Vijayanagara emperors as *mantrī* in the capacity of provincial governor in the areas of modern Goa.[29] Sāyaṇa's mother is called Śrīmāyī and his father as Māyaṇa in this epigraph. His preceptor (*guru*) was Śrīkaṇṭhanātha, the great poet (*kavivaraḥ*). According to the Biṭraguṇṭa grant, Śrīkaṇṭhanātha was the preceptor of Saṅgama II.[30] This king issued the Biṭraguṇṭa grant in his capacity as the viceroy of the

[27] Nallur plates of Harihara II, op. cit., pp. 118-19; *Uttankita Sanskrit Vidya-Aranya Epigraphs*, vol. I (*Vidyaranya*) (hereafter *USVAE*), Bombay, 1985, pp. 33-34.

[28] *USVAE*, p. 34.

[29] *USVAE*, p. 34.

[30] Nallur plates, op. cit., p. 119.

Udayagiri province to which post he succeeded on the death of his brother Kaṁpaṇa I, the brother of Harihara I.[31]

The eminent scholar-statesman Sāyaṇācārya mentions in his *Alaṁkāra-Sudhānidhi* that he was the minister of Kaṁpa I, his son, Saṅgama II and later served in the court of Bukka I and saw the enthronement of Harihara II.[32] Sāyaṇa was a great scholar and writer. He compiled the *Subhāṣita-Sudhānidhi*, a literary anthology during the time of Kaṁpa I; *Dhātuvṛtti*, a work on Sanskrit verbs; *Prāyaścitta-Sudhānidhi*, also known as *Karmavipāka*, a work describing penances; *Yajñatantra-Sudhānidhi*, a treatise on ritual and *Alaṁkāra-Sudhānidhi*, explaining the figures of speech — all during the time of Saṅgama II.[33] During the time of Bukka I and Harihara II, he wrote his commentaries on the Vedas which were *Taittirīyāraṇyaka Bhāṣya*, *Śukla Yajurveda-Saṁhitā Bhāṣya*, *Vaṁśabrāhmaṇa Bhāṣya*, *Taittirīya Saṁhitā Bhāṣya*, *Sāmaveda-Saṁhitā Bhāṣya*, *Atharvaveda-Saṁhitā Bhāṣya* and *Ṛgveda Bhāṣya*.[34] The composition of the Vedic commentaries is often attributed to Mādhavācārya, as the term *Mādhavīyam* occurs in the colophons of many of them; or at least they were considered as joint productions of Mādhava and Sāyaṇa.[35] However, the colophons of all of them state that they were the productions of Sāyaṇa and were called *Mādhavīyam*. In the introductory verses of *Puruṣārtha-Sudhānidhi* and *Yajurveda Bhāṣya*, it is said that King Bukka I asked Mādhavācārya to compose the treatises, but he told the king that his brother Sāyaṇa was proficient in these subjects and consequently Bukka asked Sāyaṇa to compose these works.

---

[31] T.V. Mahalingam, *ASLP*, pp. 359-60.

[32] Ibid., p. 359.

[33] Ibid.

[34] Ibid., pp. 359-60.

[35] Ibid.

Virūpākṣa I

Virūpākṣa I, who crowned himself ruler immediately after the death of his father Harihara II, ruled only for one year. He was succeeded by his brother Bukka II, who proclaimed himself king and who, in turn, was succeeded by his brother Devarāya I. Virūpākṣa was a scholar and composed two Sanskrit dramas, namely the *Nārāyaṇīvilāsam* in five acts and the *Unmattarāghava* in one act describing Rāma's lamentations in the loss of Sītā.[36]

An inscription found at the Śrī Raṅganātha Svāmi temple, Śrīraṅgam, consisting of two Sanskrit verses, etched on the capital of two pillars in the *maṇḍapa* of the Cakrattāḷvār shrine in this temple, belongs to the reign of this king.[37] One verse states that the king was the son of Harihara and the grandson of Bukka and the daughter's son of Rāmabhūpati, while the other records the construction by the king of the *vimāna*, *gopura* and *maṇḍapa* and his gift of the village of Paccil to the temple. The first of these verses is identical with the one occurring in the drama *Nārāyaṇīvilāsam*, the authorship of which is claimed by the king.[38] This verse is the opening stanza of the *Nārāyaṇīvilāsam* in which the *sūtradhāra* introduces King Virūpākṣa as the author of that play. As this verse is apparently copied from that drama, it may be surmised that the king took keen interest in popularizing this composition.[39] Another inscription in Sanskrit verse inscribed on the south wall of the *candana maṇḍapa* in the same temple states that only he who imparts knowledge is a father, that all those who do good are

---

36 R.C. Majumdar (ed.), *The History and Culture of the Indian People* (vol. 6: The Delhi Sultanate), Bombay, 1990, p. 469.

37 *ARE*, 153 of 1938-39; *SII*, vol. XXIV no. 292, p. 306.

38 *ARE*, 1938-39, pt. II, para 42, p. 85.

39 B.Bh. Chhabra, N. Lakshminarayana Rao and M. Ashraf Hussain, "Ten Years of Indian Epigraphy (1937-46)", from *Ancient India (Bullettin of the Archaeological Survey of India)*, no. 5, January 1949, p. 57.

(real) relations and only she who is faithful (to her husband) is a wife.[40] The authorship of this verse can perhaps be assigned to the king himself.[41]

A lithic inscription of Virūpākṣa found on the east wall of the fourth *prākāra* of the Śrī Raṅganātha Svāmi temple, Śrīraṅgam mentions this king's disenchantment with worldly life and his visit to Svāmi Vidyāraṇya.[42] The composer of this epigraph presents the turmoil in the mind of this noble king and his reverence of his preceptor as follows:

> At one time, seeing the grave troubles and torments undergone by beings passing everlastingly through the cycle of birth, death and rebirth, and moved by the deepest compassion for them, approached and prostrated himself before his own preceptor and the refuge of the whole world, namely Paramahaṁsa Parivrājakācārya Vidyāraṇya Śrīpāda, who was the most distinguished of all ascetics, vision of whom was easy to the virtuous, whose mind was always engaged in meditation involving the self and the soul and who was like Śaṅkarācārya incarnate. He then realized that without serving at the holy of this enlightened Soul, he could not hope to get rid of hauteur born of shortcomings attributable to the body, the mind and speech, that he could not hope to see the dispelling of darkness (spiritual ignorance) and the dawning of light (spiritual knowledge) and that he could not hope to achieve that spiritual height that would yield him the fruit of the four requisites of human existence (righteousness, wealth, fulfilment of desire and salvation).[43]

It is known that Virūpākṣa crowned himself immediately after the death of Harihara II, but was displaced after a short period

[40] *ARE*, 86 of 1938-39; *SII*, vol. XXIV no. 291, p. 306.

[41] *ARE* 1938-39, pt. II, para 42, p. 85.

[42] *ARE* 54 of 1936-37; *SII*, vol . XXIV no. 244, p. 304.

[43] *USVAE*, vol. I, p. 124.

by Bukka II. The spirit of disenchantment and his realization that salvation lay only in the service of Sage Vidyāraṇya, as revealed by this inscription, may have made Virūpākṣa's exit from the throne not wholly involuntary.[44]

Some of the copper-plate inscriptions of Virūpākṣa register his gifts of villages to scholarly brāhmaṇas well-versed in the Vedas. One of these, the Ālaṁpūṇḍi plates is dated CE 1383 and therefore Virūpākṣa must have been a prince in the reign of his father Harihara II when he gave this grant of land to the donees. This inscription, one of the earliest of the Vijayanagara copper-plates inscriptions of Tamil Nadu, mentions that Virūpākṣa granted to certain unnamed learned brāhmaṇas the village of Ālaṁpūṇḍi.[45] The village had been the object of a previous grant by Harihara II and had then received the surname Jannāmbikābdhi.[46] The pronouns *mama* and *mayā* in lines 17 and 21 show that both Harihara's previous grant and the present donation of Virūpākṣa were made at the instance of a princess who was the sister of Harihara II and consequently the paternal aunt of Virūpākṣa and whose name must have been Jannāmbikā, because the village of Ālaṁpūṇḍi received the surname Jannāmbikābdhi (i.e. Jannāmbikā-samudram) after her own name.[47] Interestingly, the village of Ālaṁpūṇḍi mentioned in this inscription still bears the same name and was found in this village which is near the town of Senji (Ginji).[48]

Another copper-plate inscription of Virūpākṣa dated CE 1386 also falls in the reign of his father Harihara II.[49] It appears

---

44 *USVAE*, vol. I, p. 121.

45 *EI*, vol. III no. 32, vv. 9-12, pp. 227-28 (Ālaṁpūṇḍi plates).

46 Ibid., v. 10.

47 Ibid., p. 225.

48 Ibid., p. 224

49 *EI*, vol. VIII no. 31, pp. 298-306 (Śoṟaikkāvūr plates).

that Virūpākṣa made the grant as a provincial governor.[50] The inscription records that Virūpākṣa or Vīra-Virūpaṇṇa Uḍaiyār granted the village of Śiṟaikkāvūr together with some land adjoining it as an *agrahāra* under the name Vijayasudarśanapuram to fourteen brāhmaṇas of various *gotras*. From the names of the donees (*bhaṭṭas*) given in this inscription namely Nārāyaṇa Bhaṭṭa, Govinda Bhaṭṭa, Śrī Narasiṁha Bhaṭṭa, Śrī Vāsudeva Bhaṭṭa, Devarāja Bhaṭṭa Yakṣyamāna, Śrīraṅgarāja Bhaṭṭa, Yajñamūrti Bhaṭṭa, Dāmodara Bhaṭṭa, Śrīraṅganātha Bhaṭṭa, Yajñātma Bhaṭṭa, Śrī Narasiṁha Bhaṭṭa, Śrīraṅganātha Bhaṭṭa, Maṇḍaḷapuruṣa Somayājin and Śrīparvatanātha Bhaṭṭa, it is seen that most of them bear Śrīvaiṣṇava names.[51] Interestingly, some of the donees have family names which are distinctly those of a few well-known Śrīvaiṣṇava *ācārya-puruṣas* like Vedagomapurattār, Gomatattār, Vaṅgīpurattār, Uṟupputturār, Śoṭṭaiyār and Kārambicchettu.[52] The Śrīvaiṣṇava work of the Vaḍagalai sect, the *Vaḍagalai-Gurupramparāprabhavam* records that the work *Śrutaprakāśikā* consists of notes taken by Sudarśana Bhaṭṭa, the grandson of the famous Śrīvaiṣṇava Ācārya Parāśara Bhaṭṭa from the discourses of the Śrīvaiṣṇava teachers Ambalācārya on the *Śrībhāṣya*.[53] According to the Vaḍagalai tradition, Sudarśana Bhaṭṭa was an elder contemporary of the great Vedānta Deśika. It thus appears that in case the author of the *Śrutaprakāśikā* was not living at that time of the Śoṟaikkāvūr grant, his memory must have been quite fresh in the minds of the Vaiṣṇavas.[54] As most of the donees of the grant are Vaiṣṇavas, it is not unlikely that the granted village was called Vijayasudarśanapuram after the *ācārya*, provided

[50] *EI*, vol. VIII no. 31, p. 299.

[51] Ibid., pp. 298-306 (Śoṟaikkāvūr plates). p. 300.

[52] Ibid., fn. 8.

[53] Ibid., p. 305, fn. 1.

[54] Ibid.

Vijayasudarśana was not a surname either of Virūpākṣa or of his father Harihara II.[55] Incidentally, the village of Śiṟaikkāvūr which is mentioned in this inscription is the same as the modern Śoṟaikkāvūr where these copper plates were discovered, very near Kuttāḷam in Tañjāvūr district.[56]

Devarāya I (CE 1406-22)

Devarāya I was fond of learning and extended his patronage to men of letters, philosophy and artists whom he invited to his court and discoursed with them on the arts and sciences in which they were proficient.[57] He honoured poets, philosophers and artists in the Pearl Hall of his palace by bathing them in showers of gold coins and gems.[58] An inscription of this monarch, dated CE 1410-11 records that he made Bhūpati, son of Bukka as governor of the Tamil country. The village of Nelvayi, situated in Tuṇḍiramaṇḍala, was given by Bhūpati as an *agrahāra* to Vāmana, son of Govinda Yajvan of the Bhāradvāja *gotra* and who had studied the three Vedas.[59]

An inscription, found at Attipākkam in erstwhile South Arcot district in characters of the fifteenth century CE belonging to either the reign of Devarāya I or Devarāya II, mentions a donation to a brāhmaṇa, who was well-versed in the Vedas and Śāśtras and who belonged to the Bhāradvāja *gotra* and the *Āpastamba Sūtra*.[60]

Devarāya II (CE 1422-46)

Devarāya II also called Prauḍha Devarāya was also a scholar and a patron of poets and scholars. He appears to have been

---

[55] *EI*, vol. VIII no. 31, pp. 298-306 (Śoṟaikkāvūr plates).

[56] Ibid., p. 300.

[57] R.C. Majumdar (ed.), op. cit., p. 288.

[58] Ibid.

[59] *ARE*, 1972-73, no. A11.

[60] *ARE*, 263 of 1968-69.

the author of the *Ratiratna-dīpikā* and the *Brahmasūtravṛtti*, a gloss on the *Brahmasūtras* of Bādarāyaṇa, following the Advaita tradition of Śaṅkara.[61] His court was the meeting place of Jaina, Vaiṣṇava, Śrīvaiṣṇava and Vīraśaiva scholars.[62] Sarvajña Siṅgama who wrote the *Nāṭakaparibhāṣā*, *Saṅgīta-Sudhākara*, *Saṅgīta-Cintāmaṇi* and *Rasārṇava-Sudhākara* was the greatest Sanskrit scholar of his reign. Some of the other Sanskrit scholars were Vāmanabhaṭṭa who composed *Bhāva-sṛṅgāra-bhūṣaṇa*, Komaṭi Vema, the composer of *Śṛṅgāra-dīpika*, Sāḷuva Gopa Tippa, the grandson of Harima, a sister of Devarāya II and his viceroy at Mulubāgal who wrote *Kāmadhenu*, a commentary on Vāmana's *Kāvyālaṁkāra Tāḷadīpikā*; Maggeya Mayideva's compositions were *Anubhava-sūtra* and *Viśeṣārtha-Prakāśikā*; *Vaiśya-Vaṁśa-Sudhārṇava* was written by Kalacala Mallinātha; a commentary on *Amara* was composed by Bommalakaṇṭī Appalācārya under the patronage of Sarvajña Siṅgama and Irugappa Daṇḍanātha, the army general of Devarāya who was also a scholar wrote *Nānārtha-Ratnamālā*.[63] Other poets at Devarāya's court were Candrakavi who has described himself as an *aṣṭabhāṣā kavi* (a poet in eight languages) and thus he must have composed in Sanskrit also, and Rājaśekhara who composed the Śrīraṅgam copper-plate grant of this king.[64] There are many other copper-plate grants of this ruler like the Satyamaṅgalam copper-plate inscription which were also composed by talented poets but unfortunately their names have not been etched on these plates. Thus, Devarāya, other than being a patron of well-known Sanskrit scholars and poets,

---

[61] *Vijayanagara Sexcentenary Commemoration Volume*, Dharwar, 1936, p. 397.

[62] S. Srikanta Sastri, "Development of Sanskrit Literature Under Vijayanagar," from *Sexcentenary Commemoration Volume*, Dharwar, 1936, p. 309.

[63] H.M. Nagaraju, *Devaraya II and His Times*, Mysore, 1991, p. 184.

[64] Ibid.

also encouraged other poets of his empire to compose the verses of his inscriptions etched on copper plates.

Devarāya extended patronage to scholars by granting them villages for their upkeep and the details are found in his inscriptions. The Satyamaṅgalam copper-plate inscription of Devarāya II dated CE 1424 records that he bestowed the village of Ciṭeyāṭyūru, which was surnamed Devarāyapura after this king, as an *agrahāra*, along with presents (*dakṣiṇā*) to eight excellent brāhmaṇas (*dvijottama*) of the Bhāradvāja *gotra*.[65] The eight donees who received the shares (*vṛtti*) of this village were Śiṅgapārya, Narahari, Nāgapa, Viṭṭhapa, Śaṅkaṇārya, Narapati and Vallabha, each of whom had "thoroughly studied the *Ṛgveda*" (*ṛg-śākhā pāradrśaṇaḥ*).

A copper-plate grant dated CE 1424 (of the reign of Devarāya II), issued by prince Śrīgiribhūpāla, the younger brother of Devarāya II who ruled over Maratakapuri (Maragatapuri, which has been identified with Viriñcipuram in erstwhile North Arcot district), records that he gifted the village (*agrahāra*) named Nīpataṭāka (identified with the village of Kaḍapperi in North Arcot district) to a learned brāhmaṇa physician named Sampatkumāra Paṇḍita.[66] The donee, belonging to Kāśyapa *gotra* is eulogized here as "the foremost of physicians" (*bhiṣajam-agrayāyin*), whose father Govinda Paṇḍita was one "who had seen the further shore of the ocean of the whole of Āyurveda and the Vedāṅgas" (*sarvāyurveda vedāṅga sārasvat pāradṛṣvanaḥ*). The village of Nīpaṭaṭaka, the gift of which is recorded in this inscription, had been given to the same donee by this donor's father Vijayabhubhuj (King Vijaya I or Vijayabhūpāla).[67] Due to some reason, the grant

---

[65] *EI*, vol. III no. 5, vv. 25-32, pp. 38-39 (Satyamaṅgalam plates).

[66] *EI*, vol. VIII no. 32, vv. 13-20, pp. 310-11 (Madras Museum plates of Śrīgiribhūpāla).

[67] *EI*, v. 16, pp. 310-11.

had lapsed in the interval and at the time of Śrīgiribhūpāla's grant, it was renamed as Vijayapura or Vijayarātpura, evidently in honour of its original donor, Vijayarāya.[68]

Subsequently, Sampatkumāra divided the village of Vijayarātpura into fifty-six shares, gave two shares to the temples of Śiva and Viṣṇu, set apart one share for the yearly feeding of brāhmaṇas, reserved twenty-two shares for himself and gave the remaining to his brothers, relatives and learned men.[69] The editor of this inscription has suggested that since Sampatkumāra is a Sanskrit rendering of the Tamil Selvapiḷḷai, the name of the deity at Melkoṭe near Mysore, it seems possible that the chief donee belonged originally to the Karnataka country and his father's native place, mentioned in the inscription as Rambhāmayūranagarī, may be in that area.[70] One of the minor donees, Hampaṇa Bhaṭṭa mentioned in this inscription was evidently called after the Pampāpati temple in Hampī.[71]

The famous Diṇḍima family of Sanskrit poets of the Vijayanagara court are very well-known. Two interesting Tamil inscriptions from the Svayaṁbhūnātheśvara temple at Mullaṇḍrum in erstwhile North Arcot district[72] of the sixteenth century CE refer to a poet called Diṇḍimakavi and the other to Kumārar-Diṇḍimar-Aṇṇamalaināthar, perhaps a son of the former.[73] One of these inscriptions[74] records that the *agrahāram*, Agaram-Mullaṇḍrum was otherwise called Prauḍhadevarāyapuram perhaps on account of being originally

[68] *EI*, v. 16, p. 308.

[69] *EI*, vv. 21-23, pp. 311-12.

[70] Ibid., p. 308, fn. 1.

[71] Ibid.

[72] *ARE*, 396 and 397 of 1911.

[73] *ARE*, 1912, pt. II, para 72, pp. 83-84.

[74] *ARE*, 396 of 1911.

ganted to brāhmaṇas by the Vijayanagara king Prauḍhadevarāya and that Diṇḍimakavi was one of the *mahājana* residents of this *agrahāra*. A work called *Viveka Vibhāgapatrikā* states that Mullaṇḍrum was granted to eight brāhmaṇa families during the reign of Prauḍhadevarāya of Vijayanagara and therefore called Prauḍhadevarāyapuram.[75]

Vīra-Nṛsiṁha (CE 1503-09)

Vīra-Nṛsiṁha, the son of Narasa Nāyaka, ruled only for a brief period of six years. Very few inscriptions of his time with regard to education are found in the Tamil country. One of these is a copper-plate grant of the village of Śadarimaṅgalam to Hastigiri Dīkṣita, a scholar of the Saṁkṛti *gotra*, Baudhāyana *sūtra* and Yajus *śākhā*. This village was renamed Vīra-Śrī-Narasiṁhendrapuram after this king, Vīra-Nṛsiṁha, at the time of the grant. The donee, Hastigiri Dīkṣita, in turn, distributed the land in the gift village to several brāhmaṇas of various *gotras* and *sūtras*.[76]

Vīra-Nṛsiṁha gave generously to the famous Kāmakoṭi Maṭha at Kāñcīpuram, a famous centre of Advaita philosophy. A copper-plate grant of his reign dated CE 1506 records that this ruler gave two villages to the pontiff of this *maṭha* named Mahādeva Sarasvatī, disciple of Sadāśiva Sarasvatī, who is described in this record in glowing terms as Paramahaṁsa Parivrājakācārya, seeking liberation (*mumukṣave*), whose body is smeared with ashes (*bhasmadhūlita-gātrāya*), and adorned with *rudrākṣa* garlands (*rudrākṣāvalī dhārṇe*), who was a great person (*mahātmane*), who has thoroughly studied all the Śāstras (*samasta-śāstra-pāṭhodhi pāragāya*), a *tapasvī*, who has attained the eight *yoga sādhanas*, namely *yama*, *niyama*, etc. (*aṣṭāṅga-yoga-yuktāya*), who is full of grace (*dayāśīlāya*), who is of bright

---

[75] *ARE*, 1912, Pt. II, p. 84.

[76] *ARE*, 1954-55, no. A 9.

intellect (*dhīmate*) and resembles Lord Śiva Himself (*svarūpiṇe*).[77] Another record of Vīra-Nṛsiṁha mentions that he gave a village named Kuḍiyantaṇḍal to this teacher who is described in exactly the same glowing terms as in the previous record.[78]

Kṛṣṇadeva Rāya (CE 1509-29)

The most illustrious and powerful of the emperors of the Vijayanagara empire, Kṛṣṇadeva Rāya was also the most scholarly. The *Mādalasacaritra*, *Satyavadhūpreṇanam*, *Sakalakathāsāra-Saṁgraham*, *Sūktinaipuṇi Jñānacintāmaṇi* and *Rasamañjarī* were authored by him.[79] The well-known Sanskrit drama called *Jāmbavatīkalyāṇam* was also written by him.

In the prologue, the drama is said to have been enacted before the people assembled to witness the Caitra (spring) festival of Śrī Virūpākṣa, the tutelary deity of the Vijayanagara empire.[80] This drama in five acts describes the marriage of Jāmbavatī, daughter of Jāmbavān and one of the eight *paṭṭamahiṣī*s of Śrī Kṛṣṇa.[81] He also wrote the *Āmuktamālyada* or *Viṣṇucittīya*, one of the five great *kāvya*s of Telugu literature. It describes the story of Periāḻvār or Viṣṇucitta, his foster-daughter Āṇḍāl and the marriage of Āṇḍāl with Śrī Raṅganātha of Śrīraṅgam.[82] This work is dedicated to Lord Veṅkaṭeśvara of Tirumala. Among all the works of this voluminous writer

---

[77] T.A. Gopinatha Rao (ed.), *Copper-plate Inscriptions Belonging to the Śrī Śaṅkarācārya of the Kāmakoṭi-Pīṭham*, Madras, 1916, pp. 24-26.

[78] *EI*, vol. XIV no. 17, pp. 231-40 (Kuḍiyantaṇḍal plates).

[79] T.V. Mahalingam, *ASLV*, p. 365.

[80] S. Krishnaswami Ayyangar, op. cit., p. 142.

[81] Nidhathavolu Venkat Rao, *Kṛṣṇadeva Rāya and His Literary Circle, in Vijayanagara: History and Legacy*, ed. S. Krishnaswami Ayyangar et al., New Delhi, 2000, p. 232.

[82] Ibid., pp. 132-33.

and great patron of letters, only the Telugu *Āmuktamālyada* and the Sanskrit drama *Jāmbavatīkalyāṇam* have come down to us.[83] In his court were eight great literary luminaries called the *aṣṭadiggajas*, namely Allasani Peddaṇa, Nandi Timmaṇṇa, Dhūrjaṭi, Piṅgaḷi Sūraṇṇa, Tenāli Rāmakṛṣṇa, Ramabhadraih, Rāmarāja Bhūṣaṇa and Madagari Mallaṇa.

Many villages were gifted as *agrahāras* by Kṛṣṇadeva Rāya as gleaned from the copper-plate inscriptions of his times. One such epigraph from the Śrī Raṅganātha Svāmi temple, Śrīraṅgam dated CE 1514[84] registers that this king granted the village of Eṇṇākuḍi under the name Kṛṣṇarāyapuram to a brāhmaṇa named Allāla Bhaṭṭa of the Ātreya *gotra* and Āpastamba *sūtra* and of the Yajus *śākhā* "who was a master of the six systems of philosophy" (*ṣaḍ-darśanyāmbudeḥ*) and the Vedas (*śruta śobhine*), "who officiated as priest during the *go-sahasra mahādāna*" (*go-sahasra-mahādāne*) and "who was like Sarasvatī in male form" (*puruṣāyai sārasvatyai*).[85] The inscription states that Kṛṣṇadeva Rāya made this donation in the presence of God Virūpākṣa in the temple at Vijayanagara (Hampī) on the bank of River Tuṅgabhadrā near the Hemakūṭa hill and surrounded by his *purohitas* and a number of brāhmaṇas well-versed in the Śrauta.[86]

Another similar copper-plate grant from Śrīraṅgam dated CE 1528 mentions that Kṛṣṇadeva Rāya granted as an *agrahāra*, the village of Vaḍambūr-Ekāmbarapuram to a number of brāhmaṇas of various *gotras*, *sūtras*, *śākhās* and of different names "who were well-versed in the Vedas" (*veda-vedāṅga*

---

[83] Nidhathavolu Venkat Rao, *Kṛṣṇadeva Rāya and His Literary Circle, in Vijayanagara: History and Legacy*, ed. S. Krishnaswami Ayyangar et al., New Delhi, 2000, p. 11.

[84] *EI*, vol. XVIII no. 21A, pp. 160-65 (Śrīraṅgam I plates of Kṛṣṇadeva Rāya).

[85] Ibid., vv. 29-35.

[86] Ibid., v. 45.

pāragaḥ). This fertile village was located on the south bank of River Kāverī and its name was changed to Kṛṣṇarāyapuram at the time of the donation.[87]

The Kāñcīpuram copper-plate grant of Kṛṣṇadeva Rāya dated CE 1521 registers a gift of villages called Poḍavūr, renamed Kṛṣṇarāyapuram at the time of the grant, and Kāṭappaṭṭu to Candracūḍa Sarasvatī, the disciple of Mahādeva Sarasvatī, who was a resident of Kāñcīpuram.[88] This epigraph eulogizes this learned pontiff as a "well-known and high-souled saint" (*vikhyātaya mahātmane*), "who was a disciple of Mahādeva Sarasvatī" (*mahādeva sarasvatyāḥ śiṣyaḥ*), "a devotee of Śiva" (*śiva cetase*), "the famous commentator on all the Śāstras" (*vyākhyātākhila śāstraya*), "an expert on Māyāvāda" (*māyāvādāmbudīndave*) and "who was a resident of Kāñcīpuram" (*kāñcīpuranivāsinaḥ*).[89]

This is supported by the terms of the grant *śiṣyapraśiṣyair bhogyam*, i.e. the land was to be enjoyed by the donee and his descendants in the apostolic line.[90] The above-mentioned villages, with clear-cut boundaries was given in perpetuity as *sarvamānya* by the king who reserved no right for himself, on the advice of the learned men of his court.[91] Incidentally, Kṛṣṇarāyapuram has been identified with the village of the same name about 45 km to the south of Kāñcīpuram and Kalapatu has been identified with Kātpāḍi, now a well-known railway junction.[92]

---

[87] *EI*, vol. XVIII no. 21B, vv. 26-40, pp. 167-68 (Śrīraṅgam II plates of Kṛṣṇadeva Rāya).

[88] *EI*, vol. XIII no. 8, pp. 122-32 (Kāñcīpuram plates of Kṛṣṇadeva Rāya).

[89] Ibid., vv. 30-31, p. 129.

[90] Ibid., p. 123.

[91] Ibid., vv. 36-40, p. 130.

[92] Ibid., p. 124.

Another copper-plate grant of Kr̥ṣṇadeva Rāya dated CE 1527, records the gift of a village called Udayambākkam by this emperor to Sadāśiva Sarasvatī, the disciple of Candraśekhara Sarasvatī (Candracūḍa Sarasvatī) of the Śaṅkarācārya Maṭha at Kāñcīpuram.[93] The village of Udayambākkam was renamed Kr̥ṣṇarāyapuram at the time of the grant. It has been identified as a village near Tirukkaḻukuṉṟam near Chengalpet.[94] The verses of this epigraph extol this learned saint thus, "whose body is besmeared with holy ashes" (*bhasma dhūḷita ghātrāya*), who wears a necklance of *rudrākṣa* beads (*rudrākṣāvaḷī dhāriṇe*), who is high-souled (*mahātmane*), who has practised the eight-fold path of yoga (*aṣṭāṅga-yoga yuktāya*), who is compassionate to all beings (*dayāśīlāya*), who is above the pairs of opposite like heat and cold (*śītoṣṇādi dvandva dukhātitaya*), who is possessed of knowledge and freedom from attachment (*jñāna vairāgya śāline*) and who is master of himself (*sarvatantra svatantrāya*).[95]

The donee, in this inscription is mentioned as Sadāśiva Sarasvatī, a disciple of Candraśekhara Sarasvatī. According to the editors of this copper-plate grant, Candraśekhara and Candracūḍa are variant forms of the same name. Moreover, Candraśekhara here is an engraver's error for Candracūḍa.[96] The metre of the verse *candraśekhara sarasvatyas śiṣyāy-amita tejase* has one syllable more than that allowed by the rules of metre in the *pada* of the *anuṣṭubh* verse.[97] If it is Candracūḍa instead of Candraśekhara, there is no such metrical difficulty. If this is so, the donee, Sadāśiva of this grant was a disciple of Candracūḍa, the donee of the earlier grant of this king.

[93] *EI*, vol. XIV no. 12, pp. 168-75 (Udayambākkam plates).

[94] Ibid., p. 169.

[95] Ibid., vv. 32-33, p. 173.

[96] Ibid., p. 169.

[97] Ibid.

Sometime between the intervals of the two grants (CE 1521 and 1527) Candracūḍa must have died and his pupil Sadāśiva must have succeeded him.[98]

The four grants mentioned above give the names of four successive pontiffs of the Kāmakoṭi Maṭha at Kāñcīpuram, namely Sadāśiva, Mahādeva, Candracūḍa and Sadāśiva, who were contemporaneous with the Vijayanagara kings Vīra-Nṛsiṁha and Kṛṣṇadeva Rāya (from CE 1506-29).[99] One of the pontiffs of this *maṭha*, the third in apostolic descent from Sadāśiva (CE 1527) composed a work *Guru-Rāja-Ratna-Mālā-Stava* in which the names of the above-mentioned teachers are given in the same order.[100] The copper-plate inscription of Vīra-Nṛsiṁha and Kṛṣṇadeva Rāya recording the donations they made to this *maṭha* at Kāñcīpuram reveal the reverence that these monarchs had towards the learned and holy pontiffs of this *maṭha*. The benefactions of these Vijayanagara monarchs would have helped to a great extent in the maintenance of this sacred centre of learning including the boarding and lodging of the students who came there to study the sacred texts.[101] Besides the inscriptions mentioned here, there are many other copper-plate inscriptions of the reign of Kṛṣṇadeva Rāya which record his gifts of villages as *agrahāra*s to scholars in the Vedas and other sacred texts.

Acyuta Rāya (CE 1530-42)

Acyuta Rāya, the half-brother and successor of Kṛṣṇadeva Rāya, was also a scholar. He has been credited with the authorship of the work *Tāḷamahodadhi*, which was commented on by Somanātha, his contemporary.[102] Rājanātha Kavi of the

[98] *EI*, vol. XIV no. 12, p. 169 (Udayambākkam plates).

[99] Ibid.

[100] Kuḍiyantaṇḍal plates, op. cit., pp. 233-34.

[101] *ARE*, 1953-54, A no. 18; *ARE*, 1954-55, A no. 10; *ARE*, 1936-37, A. no. 10.

[102] T.V. Mahalingam, *ASLV*, p. 366.

Diṇḍima family, the son of Sonagirinātha, the illustrious author of many literary works like *Bhāgavata Campū*, was the court-poet of Acyuta Rāya and wrote the historical poem in Sanskrit called *Acyutarāyābhyudaya* during the lifetime of this monarch. The *Bhāgavata Campū* was dedicated to his patron.[103] In the long tradition of the emperors of Vijayanagara, he too was very supportive of scholars and poets as seen from the details recorded in his inscriptions. In the Kṛṣṇāpuram copper-plate inscription of Sadāśiva Rāya, he is described as one "who made gifts satisfying the desires of the learned" (*vidvadsta pradāta*).[104]

An interesting bilingual inscription in Sanskrit and Tamil of the period of Acyuta Rāya is engraved on the east wall of the old Sabhānāyaka shrine in the Ekāmranātha temple in Kāñcī. The Sanskrit portion of this lithic epigraph is in verse-form in the *anuṣṭubh* metre, intercepted by a prose passage.[105] This record is interesting from the point of view of literary history as it throws light on the authorship and date of four literary compositions in Sanskrit. This inscription mentions that during the reign of Acyuta Rāya, a certain Bhogarāja was the governor of Kāñcī and that an important event happened during his governorship. Bhogarāja, who was a devotee of Lord Ekāmranātha, summoned an assembly of learned Śiva brāhmaṇas, Māheśvaras and temple-officials before God Ekāmranātha. On this occasion, this assembly of scholars listened to four literary works composed by a person named Śrīnivāsa namely the *Śivabhaktivilāsa*, *Caraṇādīstava*, *Bhogāvaḷī* and *Nāmāvaḷī*. The *Śivabhaktivilāsa*, a poem (*kāvya*) had, as its theme, the lives of the sixty-three devotees of Lord Śiva and is the same as that of the Tamil poetical work called

---

103 S. Krishnaswami Ayyangar, *Sources of Vijayanagara History* (hereafter *Sources*), Madras, 1919, op. cit., p. 176.

104 *EI*, vol. IX no. 52, v. 24, p. 334 (Kṛṣṇāpuram plates).

105 *ARE*, 274 of 1955-56; *EI*, vol. XXXIII no. 39, pp. 200-04 (Kāñcīpuram inscription of Acyuta Rāya).

Periyapurāṇam also known as *Tiruttoṇḍarpurāṇam* composed by Śekkiḷar in the first half of the twelfth century CE during the reign of Kulottuṅga II. *Caraṇādīstava* and *Pādādikeśastava* in the Tamil portion of this bilingual record is probably the same as the *Ekāmranāthastava*.[106] These works are assigned by Aufrecht to Śrīnivāsa Dīkṣita who is no doubt identical with Śrīnivāsa Yajvan of this record as the title *yajvan* is synonymous.[107] *Caraṇādīstava*, was no doubt, a description of Śrī Ekāmranātha commencing from His sacred ft to the top of His crown or head. The *Bhogāvaḷī* and *Nāmāvaḷī* were evidently the names of two types of compositions, both on Śrī Ekāmranātha.

Śrīnivāsa Dīkṣita is mentioned in this epigraph as the son of Sītārāma of the Bhāradvāja *gotra* and as a resident of Ceyārūr. He was a great scholar in the *Sāmaveda* and is said to have performed the Vājapeya sacrifice and thereby acquired the singular privilege of carrying the white umbrella (*śveta cchatra maṇḍala maṇḍitaḥ*). He was also well-versed in grammar and the fine-arts like Bharatanāṭyam (*pada vākya pramāṇeṣu bharatādi kalāsu ca prathitaḥ*). As a reward for composing these four Sanskrit works, the *sabhā* gave to Śrīnivāsa Yajvan presents of ornaments and clothes, and also arranged for the poet's permanent residence in Kāñcī by buying a house for him, which was situated to the south of the outer *prākāra* of the Ekāmranātha temple. This poet also received a *śivamana* of rice daily and five *bhāra*s of grains and five *paṇa*s per month to be enjoyed hereditarily. The members of the *sabhā* were to see that this gift was to be continued uninterruptedly. The munificence of the gifts made to the poet is sufficient indication of the patronage that men of letters enjoyed during this period.[108]

---

[106] *ARE*, p. 201.

[107] Kāñcīpuram inscription of Acyuta Rāya, op. cit., p. 201.

[108] Ibid.

The Kaḍalāḍi copper plate of Acyuta Rāya dated CE 1529, fully composed in Sanskrit verse mentions a donation to a Vedic scholar.[109] It records in detail the grant of the village of Kaḍalāḍi alias Patendal by this monarch to a brāhmaṇa named Rāmacandra Dīkṣita, described as a great person and "the best of brāhmaṇas" (*bhūmidevāgrayāyine*), the son of Nāga Bhaṭṭa of the Yajus *śākha* who "well deserved this gift of land".

The donee, Rāmacandra Dīkṣita, in turn, split up the village into 110 *vṛttis* and distributed them among forty-six brāhmaṇas, the division ranging from half a *vṛtti* to eight *vṛttis*. He also gave one *vṛtti* to Viṣṇu and one for Śiva and kept twenty-seven shares for himself. The inscription mentions that the village was granted as *ekabhogya* which implies exclusive ownership of the property and the rights over it by a single individual. However in effect, this grant was not an *ekabhogya* as part of it was divided among others and a portion reserved for deities. Land which is thus enjoyed by two or more parties goes by the name *gaṇa-bhogya* and *tri-bhogya*. In this particular context, the word *eka-bhogya* can be explained only by the fact that the grant in the first instance was made only to a single individual, Rāmacandra Dīkṣita who divided the land among the brāhmaṇas of the sect to which he belonged.[110]

It is also interesting to note from the data supplied by the Kaḍalāḍi copper plates that the donees belonged to an important sect of brāhmaṇas — the Poysala Kannaḍa sect — judging from the names and from the fact that there are two of the *Sāma śākhās*. The Poysala brāhmaṇas appear to be the only sub-sect of the Kannaḍa brāhmaṇas where there are Sāmavedins.[111]

---

109 *EI*, vol. XIV no. 22, pp. 310-23 (Kaḍalāḍi plates).

110 *EI*, p. 313.

111 Ibid.

Another important copper-plate grant of the time of Acyuta Rāya, the Uṇāmāñjeri inscription (CE 1540), also provides important information regarding the benefactions given to the scholars of the Vijayanagara epoch.[112] This epigraph, which is also entirely in Sanskrit verses, states that Acyuta Rāya, having been requested by his trusted minister Virūpākṣa, granted the village of Uhinai (Uṇamāñjeri), also known as Acyutendramahārāyapura, to a number of brāhmaṇas, learned in the Vedas and famous for their knowledge of the Śāstras. This inscription states in detail that this village was divided into sixty *vṛtti*s or shares. While one *vṛtti* and a quarter were set aside for Lord Raghunātha and an equal amont for Lord Caṇḍīśvara, the rest was distributed, in amounts ranging from a quarter of 1 *vṛtti* to 5 *vṛtti*s among forty-eight brāhmaṇas who are named in the verses. Each of these verses states the exact amount allotted to each person and other details such as the name of the father of the recipient, the *gotra* of the latter and the Vedic texts studied by him. Twenty-one of the donees were students of the Ṛgveda (Bahvṛca), eighteen were students of Yajurveda (Yājuṣa), and one was a student of Sāmaveda (Sāmaga). Six followed the *sūtra* of Drahyāyana and one that of Āpastamba. The brāhmaṇas to whom the 60 *vṛtti*s had been assigned made up an additional 30 *vṛtti*s and gave these preferential shares to the minister and the secretary (*rāyasa*) Veṅkatādri who was a distinguished student of the Yajurveda.

Like the illustrious poet Gaṅgā Devī, the consort of Kumāra Kampaṇa, a queen of Acyuta Rāya named Tirumalāmba or Tirumalā Devī was a talented poet. She composed *Varadāmbikāpariṇayam*, a Sanskrit *campū-kāvya* (work composed partially in prose and partly in poetry), the theme of which is

---

[112] *EI*, vol. III no. 24, pp. 147-57 (Uṇamāñjeri plates).

the marriage of Acyuta Rāya with Varadāmbikā.[113] The lady, who was greatly admired in the court of Acyuta Rāya for her literary achievements, records all her accomplishments in the long colophon at the end of this literary work. This quasi-historical work seems to have been written during the time of Acyuta's predecessor Kṛṣṇadeva Rāya because it comes to a close soon after the description of the youth of Cinna Veṅkatādri, son of Acyuta. It is known that when Acyuta ascended the Vijayanagara throne in CE 1530, his son Cinna Veṅkatādri was already old enough to be installed as the heir-apparent, according to the *Acyutarāyahṛdayam* of Rājanātha Diṇḍima.[114] This book, *Varadāmbikāpariṇayam* ends with the installation of Cinna Veṅkatādri as *yuvarāja* (crown prince). Though not of great literary merit, it is interesting and important because of the information it contains about the contemporary political and social life. While most of this work could have been written during the time of Kṛṣṇadeva Rāya, the portion relating to the anointment of the prince as heir-apparent could have been supplemented after CE 1530, when Acyuta was coronated and Veṅkatādri was also anointed.[115]

In addition to all this, there are a lot of epigraphical sources to prove the literary prowess of Tirumalāmbā. A bilingual epigraph engraved on the east wall of the second *prākāra* of the Śrī Raṅganātha Svāmi temple in Śrīraṅgam, dated CE 1461, of the reign of Acyuta Rāya is a very interesting record from the viewpoint of literature.[116] This inscription contains an introductory portion in Tamil which states that on the occasion of this king performing the *tulābhāra* ceremony, his *rājamahiṣī*, Oduva Tirumalaidevī Ammāṇavargaḷ, composed two Sanskrit

---

[113] S. Krishnaswami Ayyangar, op. cit., pp. 170-76.

[114] Ibid., p. 70.

[115] *EI*, vol. XXIV no. 41, p. 286 (Śrīraṅgam inscription of Acyuta Rāya).

[116] *ARE*, 15 of 1938-39; Śrīraṅgam inscription of Acyuta Rāya, op. cit., pp. 285-90.

*śloka*s and had them engraved in several holy places, Śrīraṅgam being one of them so that the descendants of prince Cikka Veṅkatādri may rule as emperors (*sārvabhauma*). This Tamil portion is followed by the two Sanskrit verses which are in the *śārdulavikrīḍita* metre. While the Sanskrit verses, etched in the Grantha script, mention the gift of *ānandanidhi* made by the king in Śaka 1461 (CE 1559), the Tamil portion refers to the performance of a *tulābhāra* on the same day which was also probably celebrated in the Viṭṭhaleśvara temple on the bank of the River Tuṅgabhadrā at Bhāskara-kṣetra (Hampī), the venue of the *ānandanidhi-dāna* which is mentioned in the Kannaḍa preamble of the Gadag version of this inscription.[117] Regarding these two verses, mention must be made that more than a dozen copies exist in different scripts in various places in the Vijayanagara empire. They are found in Tamil, Telugu, Kannada, Grantha and Nāgarī scripts, and in places as far apart as Annigere in the north to Śrīraṅgam in the south and in other places like Hampī, Anantaśayanāguḍi, Kamalāpur, Harihar, Nirgunda and Gadag.

However, in none of them is there the additional information furnished by the Śrīraṅgam inscription about the *tulābhāra* ceremony being performed on the same day as given in the Tamil portion.

The verse in the Śrīraṅgam inscription is as follow:

śake candra rasa amarendra gaṇite varṣe vikāryāhvaye
pakṣe bhādrapadasya poṣita vidhau dvāśabdike tithau |

vāre bhūmisutasya viṣṇavādhipatau tāre ācyuta
kṣmāpatir datvā ānandanidhim dvijān dhanadayan āmodayan | |

In the Śaka (year), counted by *candra* (1), *rasa* (6) and *amarendra* (14), in the (cyclic) year Vikarin, on the day of the *tithi* called

[117] *ARE*, 15 of 1938-39; Śrīraṅgam inscription of Acyuta Rāya, op. cit., p. 288.

> *dvādaśīm* in the increasing fortnight of Bhādrapada, which was a Tuesday, with the *nakṣatra* presided over by Viṣṇu (Śravaṇa), King Acyuta, by bestowing (gifts of) *ānandanidhi*, made brāhmaṇas like Dhanada (Kubera) and pleased Lord Mahādeva.

The second verse with a pun on the word *nava* (meaning nine and now) is very poetic:

> *puṇyaoghaiḥ paripālitasya purato bhūtāḷisamveṣita*
> *ṣaḍvargaiḥ śabhaḷīkṛtyasya satatākarnatā bhujaṅga vrajaiḥ* ǀ
>
> *prāptasya āti nava praśastim adhika prakyāta śaurya acyuta*
> *kṣmāpānanta nidheḥ navāpi nidhayaḥ kiṁ te labhante tulām* ǀ ǀ

> Though (themselves) *nava* (nine), how can the *nidhis* (of Kubera) attain equality with the *ānandanidhi* of King Acyuta of renowned valour, which has earned *nava* (new) celebrity (or eulogy) — for, while the former are surrounded by hosts of demons and are seized by crowds of serpents, the latter is protected by meritorious deeds and is coveted (only) by the assemblage of the good?

The idea in the first verse is that the brāhmaṇa recipients of the rich gifts of *ānandanidhi* were made to resemble Dhanada (Kubera), the possessor of the nine *nidhis*, while the second verse says that king Acyuta's gifts, however, outrivalled Kubera's *nidhis* for specified reasons.[118]

The gift of *ānandanidhi* is described in detail in the *Caturvarga-cintāmaṇi* of Hemādri in the Dānakhaṇḍa.[119] This *dāna* consists of presenting to learned brāhmaṇas, after some ceremonial preliminaries, pots made of *uḍumbara* wood and filled with precious stones and coins of gold, silver, etc. The days prescribed for the performance of this *dāna* are days in the months of Kārttika, Māgha and Mādhava (Vaikaśa), days

---

[118] *ARE*, 15 of 1938-39, p. 290, fn. 5.

[119] Ibid., p. 288.

of Ayana, Viśu, Manvādi and Yugādi, and the days of the lunar and solar eclipses. The merit accruing from this ceremony is said to be longevity, perfect health and imperial sovereignty.

It is stated in the Tamil portion that is found at the end of the inscription after the Sanskrit verses that these two stanzas which were "graciously sent by the *svāmi* (king) were engraved on stone during the regime of Śrīraṅgappā Nāyaka, an officer under Acyuta Rāya. Voḍuva Tirumalāmmā composed a Sanskrit verse (CE 1533) to commemorate the gift of *suvarṇameru* by Acyuta Rāya and the verse is inscribed in the Viṭṭhala temple in Hampī.[120]

There is also a Sanskrit inscription in Grantha script, consisiting of three verses inscribed on the north veranda near the hillock atop which is enshrined Lord Varadarāja in the Śrī Varadarāja Svāmi temple in Kāñcīpuram.[121] This epigraph, dated CE 1533 records that Acyuta Rāya, son of Narasa Nāyaka performed the ceremony of the *tulābhāra* of pearls (*mukta-tulābhāra*) of himself and his queen, Varadāmbikā at Kāñcīpuram and that his son Cinna Veṅkatādri gave munificent gifts to brāhmaṇas. Incidentally, the same verses are re-engraved above this inscription in Kanarese, Nāgarī and Telugu alphabet, respectively. It is possible that these three versions were also the compositions of Tirumalāmbā.[122]

It may be inferred that poetess Tirumalāmbā (composer of *Varadāmbikāpariṇayam*) was identified with Oḍuva Tirumalaidevī-Ammaṇavargaḷ (Voḍuva Tirumalāmmā) who was originally a "reader" (*oḍuva*) at the royal court and subsequently rose to the position of co-queen (*rājamahiṣī*) herself.[123] She was one of the galaxy of poets, royal and

---

[120] *ARE*, 709 of 1922; see also T.V. Mahalingam, *ASLV*, p. 367.

[121] *ARE*, 511 of 1919.

[122] Śrīraṅgam inscription of Acyuta Rāya, op. cit., p. 286.

[123] Ibid.

otherwise, who attained to literary fame under the patronage of the Vijayanagara kings.[124]

Sadāśiva Rāya (CE 1542-76) and Rāma Rāya

Sadāśiva Rāya, who became the monarch after Acyuta Rāya's son and immediate successor Veṅkaṭa was murdered in CE 1541, ruled from CE 1542-76. He was a weak monarch and his reign was dominated by his minister Rāma Rāya who wielded all power and was the *de facto* ruler of the empire. The British Museum copper-plate grant of Sadāśiva Rāya, dated CE 1556, described Rāma Rāya as "a king Bhoja in exercising imperial sway over the sentiments of poetry" (*sāhitya rasa sāmrājya bhoga bhojamahībujaḥ*).[125] This makes it clear that Rāma Rāya was a poet, or at least a patron of poets.[126] This inscription also gives details of a donation made by Sadāśiva Rāya at the request of Rāma Rāya. This grant was of thirty-one villages to "the great Sage Rāmānuja" for the proper worship of Lord Viṣṇu and for the support of his devotees.[127] As the great reformer Rāmānuja lived about 500 years before Sadāśiva Rāya, the meaning of this can only be that the donation was made in favour of the sect founded by Rāmānuja, or more particularly, of those of its members who were settled at the sage's birthplace Śrīperumbudūr.[128] This inscription registers that the donation was made

> to him who has become the best of instructors in inaugurating the path of the Veda; who knows the *Dramiḍa* doctrine which is the essence of the rays of light of such Veda; who is the foremost instructor in establishing the tenets of the six *darśanas*; who breaks the pride of mind of those who maintain

124 Śrīraṅgam inscription of Acyuta Rāya, op. cit., p. 286.

125 *EI*, vol. IV no. 1, v. 142, p. 21 (British Museum plates of Sadāśiva Rāya).

126 Ibid., p. 4.

127 Ibid., vv. 142-46.

128 *EI*, vol. IV no. 1, v. 142, p. 5.

> (the doctrine of) illusion; who has conquered disputants; who takes away the conceit of crowds of those most learned in magical formulas; who is termed a Garuḍa of the dissolute; while he protects those who come for refuge; who repeatedly has sanctified the earth by his circumambulations and whose mind is quite spotless from his bathing at various holy places; whose mind's eye is busy in discerning the course of the past, present and future; whose fame deserves to be proclaimed before that of Prahlāda, Nārada, Vyāsa, Parāśara, Śuka and other great devotees of the Holy One; who is always full of bliss; whose mind is always given to truth; who gladdens the circle of the good and who is thus another form of Lakṣmī's husband and who was always approached by His foster father Nanda; whose heart is devoted to His wife Satyabhāmā and who possesses a discus and his sword *nandaka;* whose soul is ever engaged in meditation on the footsteps of Nārāyaṇa; who, in order that he may worship Ādikesava (Viṣṇu), has assumed the form of an image in the sacred place, the excellent town named Pirumpūndūru, to him who also is called the holy Emperumāḷ, to the great sage Rāmānuja, ever-mindful to propitiate Rāma.

The real object of the grant was to enable the devotees to carry on the worship of Lord Viṣṇu with "incense, lights, oblations of food, flowers, dancing, singing, music, umbrellas, *cāmaras*, etc., and to celebrate in proper style, the yearly festival of Viṣṇu on the holy *nakṣatra,* the yearly car-festival and to provide food of all kinds for the Vaiṣṇava brāhmaṇas and their families and aged people in the extensive hall of the holy Rāmānuja". The editor of this inscription has opined that this hall should be the Rāmānuja *maṇḍapa* in Śrīperumbudūr.[129]

Āliya Rāma Rāya's spiritual teacher (*guru*) was Tātārya of Kāñcīpuram who wrote a Sanskrit work, *Pañca-Mata-Bhañjanam,* and is therefore called Pañca-Mata-Bhañjanam

---

[129] *EI*, vol. IV no. 1, v. 142, p. 6, fn. 2.

Tātācārya and who lived with this monarch for some time in Candragiri before settling down in Kāñcī.[130] His son was the famous Śrīnivāsārya, better known by the name Lakṣmīkumāra Tātācārya and Koṭikanyādānam Tātācārya who was the *guru* of Veṅkaṭa II and who performed the *abhiṣeka* ceremony during the coronation of this king.[131] The family of Tātācārya's took a leading role in popularizing Śrīvaiṣṇavism in south India, particularly in the post-Rāmānuja period.[132]

The *Prapannāmṛta* is a Sanskrit work on the hagiology of the Śrīvaiṣṇavas, written by a disciple of Raṅganātham a grandson of Lakṣmīkumāra Tātācārya and who belonged to the family of Āndhrapūrṇa (Vaḍagunṇambi), one of the favourite disciples of Rāmānuja. The literary work mentions that the Tātācāryas were descendants of Śrī Śailanātha or Tirumalai-Nambi, the uncle and teacher of Rāmānuja.[133] Two members of this family, Siṅgarācārya, i.e. Narasiṁhācārya and his younger brother Śrīraṅgācārya, were specialists in the exposition of the *Rāmāyaṇa* and are said to have migrated from Tirupati to Eṭṭūr and from there to Hampi, the capital of Vijayanagara empire where they were highly respected by the Vijayanagara monarchs.[134] One of the descendants of this family was the well-known Pañcamatabhañjanam Tātācārya, who lived in the court of Rāma Rāya, mentioned earlier in this chapter.

The *Prapannāmṛta* clearly mentions that this scholar was the son of Śrīnivāsa Guru and was learned in all the Śāstras.

---

130 *EI*, vol. XII no. 38, p. 347 (Arivilimaṅgalam plates).

131 Ibid.

132 G. Harihara Sastri and V. Raghavan, "The Hanumad Viṁśati of Lakshmikumara Tatacharya," *JOR*, XVIII, p. 32.

133 Ibid., pp. 32-33; K.V. Raman, op. cit., pp. 82-83.

134 K.V. Raman, op. cit., p. 82.

He was the *ācārya* (preceptor) of Rāma Rāya. A great Śrīvaiṣṇava Sanskrit scholar Vādhūla Doḍḍācārya also known as Mahācārya who lived at Ghaṭikācala (Śoḷingūr) at this time had defeated many Śaiva scholars in Citracūṭa (Cidambaram). He was able to accomplish his desire of establishing the worship of Śrī Govindarāja Perumāḷ in that temple, from where the images had been earlier removed, with the help of emperor Rāma Rāya and his *guru* Tātācārya.[135]

Diṇḍima Poets

Rājanātha Diṇḍima, as mentioned earlier, flourished in the court of Acyuta Rāya. Two interesting Tamil inscriptions of the sixteenth century CE found on the walls of the Svayambhūnātheśvara temple in Nullandram in erstwhile North Arcot district, refer to a poet called Diṇḍimakavi and Kumāra-Diṇḍimar Aṇṇāmalaināthar.[136] The first of these is found on the south wall of the Svayambhunātheśvara temple and records that the *mahājanas* of Prauḍhadevarayāpuram alias Agaram-Mullāndram, including the poet Diṇḍimakavi, assigned house-sites to certain stone-masons.[137] The second lithic record is inscribed on the south wall of the Aruṇācaleśvara shrine in the same temple and refers to a gift of land by a brāhmaṇa lady to the shrine of Aṇṇāmalainātha constructed by her in the temple of Svayambhūnātha for the merit of herself and her husband Kumāra-Diṇḍimar-Aṇṇamalaināthar.[138] The second record is dated Śāka 1472 (CE 1550), which is of the reign of Sadāśiva Rāya. As mentioned earlier in this chapter, it is clear that Agaram Mullāndrum was otherwise called Prauḍhadevarāyapuram (perhaps on account of its originally having been granted to brāhmaṇas

---

135 S. Krishnaswami Ayyangar, *Sources*, p. 202.

136 *ARE*, 396-97 of 1911.

137 *ARE*, 396 of 1911.

138 *ARE*, 396 of 1911.

by Prauḍhadevarāya and that Diṇḍimakavi was one of the *mahājana*s of that village.[139] As mentioned earlier in this chapter, a work called *Viveka Vibhāgapatrikā* records that the village named Mullāndrum was originally granted to eight brāhmaṇa families during the reign of Prauḍhadevarāya of Vijayanagara and was therefore called Prauḍhadevarāyapura. Most of the original donees were poets, Rājanātha being one of them. It is not unlikely that Diṇḍimakavi also called Kumāra Diṇḍimar, as hinted in the Mullāndrum record was a descendant of them, who had established his reputation as a poet.[140]

Śrīraṅga Rāya I (CE 1572-85)

Śrīraṅga Rāya I, a patron of scholars, as seen from his inscriptions, appears to have been a student of Koṭikanyādānam Lakṣmīkumāra Tātācārya, the famous scholar of Kāñcīpuram who wielded much power during the time of his successor Veṅkaṭa II. A Tamil record in Grantha letters on the west wall of the Vāmana shrine in Śrīraṅgam states that Śrīraṅgadeva Rāya, the disciple (*śiṣya*) of Tātācārya, caused the construction of the *garbhagṛha, ardhamaṇḍapa, mahāmaṇḍapa* and *gopura* of this shrine and also endowed a village to it.[141] The date of the record is wrongly quoted, but if the inscription belongs to Śrīraṅga I, then Tātācārya figuring in the inscription and bearing the epithet Śrīraṅgadeva-Śikhāmaṇi may be identical with the famous Vaiṣṇava teacher Koṭikanyādānam Tātācārya, who is known to have been the *guru* of Veṅkaṭa II, successor of Śrīraṅga I.[142]

The Arivilimaṅgalam copper-plate inscription dated CE 1577 of the reign of Śrīraṅga Rāya (CE 1572-85) sates that at the request of Sevappa Nāyaka of Tañjāvūr, Śrīraṅga Rāya

[139] *ARE*, 1912, pt. II, para 72, p. 83.

[140] Ibid., p. 84.

[141] *ARE*, 320 of 1952-53.

[142] *ARE* 1952-53, pt. II, p. 16.

granted the village of Aruḷmoḻimaṅgalam alias Acyutappasamudra situated on the south side of the River Kāverī to the Mādhava guru Vijayīndra Tīrtha.[143] This grant had already been made by Acyuta, son of Sevappa Nāyaka, but now the formal sanction from the Vijayanagara overlord was obtained and the village was given to the donee.[144] Vijayīndra Tīrtha, after receiving the village, divided it among a number of brāhmaṇas of various *gotra*s and *sūtra*s for his own merit and for that of Sevappa and his son Acyuta. This inscription, composed entirely in Sanskrit, extols the donee, Vijayīndra Tīrtha as being well-read in *pada* (Vyākaraṇa), *vākya* (Pūrva-Mīmāṁsā) and *pramāṇa* (Tarka); one who had defeated his enemies because of his knowledge; who was a scholar in the Śāstras; who "had sharp words which cut down the opinion of Māyāvādins" and who had been ordained by Surendra Tīrtha.[145]

The donee of this grant was known by the name Viṭṭhalācārya in his Pūrvāśrama. Surendra Tīrtha of the Pūrvādhi or Sumatindra Maṭha, who was the twelfth in descent fom Madhavācārya, the founder of the Dvaita school of philosophy, was the spiritual *guru* of Vijayīndra.[146] It was from him that he received the robes of *saṁnyāsa* and eventually also succeeded him on the pontifical seat as the thirteenth preceptor. Vijayīndra, like Vādhirāja Tīrtha of the Saude Maṭha, received all his education in philosophy from the great Vyāsarāya Tīrtha of the Vyāsarāya Maṭha. The latter was a contemporary of Kṛṣṇadeva Rāya by whom he seems to have been held in high esteem. Vijayīndra is said to have held the pontificate for a period of fifty years, five months and sixteen days. He seems to have spent the last part of his life at

[143] Ariviḷimaṅgalam plates, op. cit., pp. 340-58.

[144] *ARE,* 396 of 1911 p. 342.

[145] Ariviḷimaṅgalam plates, op. cit., vv. 27-44.

[146] Ibid., p. 344.

Kuṁbakoṇam where he passed away. Incidentally, he was the contemporary of Appaya Dīkṣita, the great Advaita philosopher. At the same time also lived the Śrīvaiṣṇava scholars and preceptors, Doḍḍācārya of Coḷasiṅgapuram and Tātācārya of Kāñcīpuram.[147] When Appaya Dīkṣita wrote condemning the Mādhava philosophy, Vijayīndra Tīrtha wrote many refutation of his works, most of which are said to have been written in the temple of Maṅgalāmbikā at Kuṁbakoṇam.[148] He also wrote many commentaries on important Mādhva works. Some of the important works of Vijayīndra Tīrtha, who was one of the most famous Mādhava *āchāryas* were *Cakra Mīmāṁsā, Candrikodahṛta, Nyāya Vivaraṇa, Nyāyamṛta-Vyākhyā, Appayya-Kapola-Capetka*, etc.[149]

Veṅkaṭa II (CE 1586–1614)

The reign of Veṅkaṭa II, lasting for almost three decades, was marked by a revival of strength and prosperity for the empire.[150] His capital was Candragiri. The numerous copper-plate inscriptions of his reign show him to be a patron of scholars and poets.

The Daḷavāy-agrahāram plates dated CE 1586 mention that Veṅkaṭapatideva Mahārāya granted to a number of brāhmaṇas the village of Gaṅgāvarapaṭṭi, together with a few other villages at the request of the Madurai Nāyaka prince, Vīra-Bhūpa (Vīrappa Nāyaka), the son of Kṛṣṇappa Nāyaka I and that these lands were clubbed under the name Vīrabhūpasamudram.[151] These brāhmaṇa donees are described as well-versed in the Śāstras and the Veda.[152] Another copper-

147 Ariviḷimaṅgalam plates, op. cit., p. 346.

148 Ariviḷimaṅgalam plates, fn. 3.

149 Ibid.

150 K.V. Raman, op. cit., p. 33.

151 *EI*, vol. XII no. 21, pp. 159-87 (Daḷavāy-agrahāram plates).

152 Ibid., v. 32, p. 174.

plate inscription, dated CE 1586, mentions that he gifted two villages named Yāṁpeḍu alias Veṅkaṭamahārāya Samudram to a brāhmaṇa named Kaimili Kṛṣṇam Bhaṭṭa.

One more copper-plate inscription, the Padmaneri epigraph dated CE 1598 of the reign of Veṅkaṭa II, mentions that his king gave the village of Padmaneri to numerous brāhmaṇas of various *śākhās*, *gotras* and *sūtras*, most of whom were very well-versed in the Vedas.[153] This village, given at the request of Kṛṣṇappa Nāyaka II, was surnamed Tirumalāmbāpuram, presumably after Kṛṣṇappa Nāyaka's mother, Tirumalāmbikā. This village was divided by this king (Kṛṣṇappa Nāyaka) into eighty-three shares and bestowed on these brāhmaṇas. This inscription also praises Kṛṣṇappa Nāyaka as having founded numerous *agrahāras* for the exclusive use of brāhmaṇas proficient in the Śāstras and bestowed villages on them in perpetuity. The village of Padmaneri, which is described as getting a regular supply of water from the Śyāma-nadī *anicut* and which had ownership of two dams across the mountain streams between Coḷagiri and Vaḷḷigiri as also numerous canals, has been identified with its namesake near Nāṅguneri in Tirunelveli district.[154] It is interesting to note that some of the donees of the Padmaneri grant seem to have come from distant provinces. Akkala Bhaṭṭa is stated to be the son of Peru Bhaṭṭa of Vodya or Orissa; Tirumala Nambikoṇḍa, the son of Pīna Mādhava of Maḍavāḍa or Mārwāṛ; Bhūma Bhaṭṭa, the son of Nāga Bhaṭṭa of Mahaṁkāḷi or Mahākāḷī which is perhaps Ujjain and Nārāyaṇa son of Yallaṁ Bhaṭṭa of Huggi or Hoṭgi.[155] It is also worthy of note that the donees belong to various Brāhmanical sects and to different *śākhās*, *gotras* and *sūtras*, from which it is apparent that the king was very tolerant and

---

[153] *EI*, vol. XVI no. 22, pp. 287-97 (Padmaneri plates of Veṅkaṭa II).

[154] Ibid., p. 288.

[155] Ibid., p. 291.

confined his munificence to no particular sect or class.[156]

Yet another copper-plate inscription of Veṅkaṭa II, the Vellaṅguḍi plates, dated CE 1598, records that at the request of Kr̥ṣṇa Bhūpati (Kr̥ṣṇappa Nāyaka II), son of Vīra Bhūpati and Tirumalāmbikā, king Veṅkaṭa II gifted an *agrahāra* to a number of scholarly brāhmaṇas, the village of Veḷḷaṅguḍi, together with three villages, all clubbed together under the name Vīrabhūpa Samudram.[157] It is interesting to know that this village was granted to some brāhmaṇa ladies also; it is a very rare thing to meet with allotment of shares to women in the *agrahāra*s which are conferred on the brāhmaṇas.[158] It is stated that the *agrahāra* was divided into 261 *vr̥tti*s and that each *vr̥tti* was further divided into five *aṁśa*s, thus making a total of 1,305 *aṁśa*s and the gift to each donee is made in terms of the *aṁśa*s. It is stated that each *vr̥tti* was sufficient to meet the needs of five people; it appears that the shares were granted perhaps proportionate to the number of members in the family of the donee.[159]

The Vilāpāka copper-plate inscription of this ruler, dated CE 1601 registers the gift of the village of Vilāpāka, surnamed Jvaraharaliṅgasamudra to Tiruveṅgaḷanāthārya, son of Ananta Bhaṭṭa, who was well-versed in the eighteen Purāṇas and belonged to the Śrīvatsa *gotra, Āpastamba Sūtra* and Yajus *śākhā*.[160] The copper-plate grant also states that the donee Veṅgaḷabhaṭṭa (Tiruveṅgaḷanāthārya), assigned one share of the village to the writer Rāmaya and to the engraver (*śilpin*) Kāmaya to meet the cost of writing materials.[161] This grant

---

[156] *EI*, vol. XVI no. 22, p. 291.

[157] *EI*, vol. XVI no. 23, pp. 298-329 (Veḷḷaṅguḍi plates).

[158] Ibid., p. 302.

[159] Ibid.

[160] *EI*, vol. IV no. 39, pp. 269-78 (Viḷāpāka plates).

[161] Ibid., vv. 62-63.

was made by Veṅkaṭa II at the request of a subordinate prince Liṅga, son of Bomma of Veḷūrū.[162] Liṅga's father, Veḷūrū-Bomma, i.e. Bomma of Veḷūrū, is identical with Sinna Bomma Nāyaka of Veḷūrū and with Cinna Bomma, son of Cinna Vīra, father of Liṅgamma Nāyaka and patron of Appaya Dīkṣita.[163] While the Advaita scholar Appaya Dīkṣita is known through his literary works it is only through invaluable copper-plate grants that we come to know that there lived other great scholars who were also honoured by the kings and chieftains of the same time, but whose names have unfortunately not come down to us through any other source.

A copper-plate inscription, dated CE 1602, mentions the grant of four villages named Citturu, Māmbāka, Agaram and Puruvalupāka, situated in Aṭṣarvaka (Accharapākka) in Paḍaivīḍu-mahārājya by King Veṅkaṭa II to a scholar named Vāsudeva Bhaṭṭa, who belonged to the Ātreya *gotra, Āśvalāyana Sūtra* and Ṛk *śākhā*. The four villages were constituted into one unit and renamed Dattātreyapuram.[164] This king granted the *sarvamānya* gift of the village of Kṛṣṇāpura in Paḍaivīḍu-rājya to Tūpil Nārāyaṇācārya, son of Appayācārya of the Kauśika *gotra, Āpastamba sūtra* and Yajuṣ *śākhā*, who was a great devotee of Raghuvīra (Rāma) and a scholar in the *Śrīmad Rāmāyaṇa*.[165] According to an inscription dated CE 1611, this ruler gifted the village of Cittūrū renamed Raghupatisamudram with its hamlet situated in Paḍaivīḍu-mahārājya to a brāhmaṇa named Ammalācārya of the Bhāradvāja *gotra, Āpastamba Sūtra* and Yajus *śākha* who was a scholar in Ubhaya-Vedānta, Tarka, Mahābhāṣya and the eighteen Purāṇas.[166] A gift of a village named Katrapāḍi Cinatimmapuram, also known as

---

[162] *EI*, vol. IV no. 39, vv. 57-61.

[163] Ibid., p. 271.

[164] *ARE*, 1957-58, no. A32.

[165] *ARE*, 1931-32, no. A2.

[166] *ARE*, 1935-36, no. A13.

Kṛṣṇañjamasamudram by Veṅkaṭa II to a very large number of brāhmaṇas of various *gotras* and *śākās*, is registered in a copper-plate epigraph dated CE 1613.[167]

Eṭṭūr Lakṣmīkumāra Tātācārya

Śrīnivāsārya, better known as Eṭṭur Lakṣmīkumāra Tātācārya and Koṭikanyādānam Tātācārya, is known from many of the copper-plate grants of Veṅkaṭa I as the *guru* of this king and who officiated at his coronation ceremony. The Daḷavāy Agrahāram plates,[168] the Padmaneri plates,[169] the Veḷḷāṅguḍi plates[170] and other inscriptions clearly mention this fact. Koṭikanyādānam Tātācārya made many benefactions to the Śrī Varadarāja Svāmi temple in Kāñcī as attested to by the numerous Sanskrit and Tamil inscriptions discovered there. These epigraphs, dated between CE 1587 and 1614 in the reign of Veṅkaṭa II, mention the benefactions and other acts of this spiritual preceptor.[171] He is said to have weighed himself against gold and silver and to have utilized that wealth in the service of Śrī Varadarāja Svāmi in erecting the Kalyāṇa-koṭi *vimānam* for Goddess Lakṣmī in this temple.[172] This shrine for Goddess Lakṣmī was already there, but the *vimāna* was rebuilt and covered with gold-coated plates in his time and in emulation of the Puṇyakoṭi *vimāna* (above the sanctum of Śrī Varadarāja Svāmi) set up by Kṛṣṇadeva Rāya. The *vimāna* was named *kalyāṇakoṭi*, probably as a rememberence of Tātācārya's title Koṭikanyādānam (as he gave liberally to the poor, especially for celebrating the marriages of their daughters).[173]

---

167 *EI*, vol. XIII no. 22B, pp. 233-35.

168 Daḷavāy Agrahāram plates, op. cit., v. 28, p. 174.

169 Padmaneri plates, op. cit., v. 29, p. 292.

170 Veḷḷaṅguḍi plates, op. cit., v. 29, p. 313.

171 K.V. Raman, op. cit., p. 83.

172 *ARE*, 363 of 1919; *SITI*, vol. III, pt. II, p. 1358; K.V. Raman, op. cit., p. 83.

173 *SITI*, vol. III, pt. II, p. 1353.

According to the *Hanumad Viṁśati* of Lakṣmīkumāra Tātạcārya, this *vimāna* got the name *kalyāṇakoṭi* because of the numberless marriages celebrated there.[174] His benefactions also include many *vāhanas* or processional vehicles and some jewels to this temple.[175] He was the manager (*śrīkārya durandhara*) of the Śrī Varadarāja Svāmi temple in Kāñcīpuram. A temple for Hanumān was constructed by him and a tank named *Tātasamudram* was dug next to it in the village of Ayyankuḷam (now called Ayyangārkuḷam), near Kāñcīpuram.

Tātācārya was an eminent scholar. An inscription praises him as an "emperor among muses", who was "worshipped by the kings of the Karnāṭa country whose crowns were worn as a garland at the ft of this scholar" and that his fame had spread far and wide.[176] This statement was not an empty boast as it is learnt from the literary work *Prappanāmṛtam* that Lakṣmīkumāra Tātācārya performed the coronation of Veṅkaṭa II and that the king "entrusted the whole kingdom to his preceptor and himself led a life of retirement."[177] Eṭṭur Lakṣmīkumāra Tātācārya had many titles like *vedamārga-pratiṣṭhāpanācārya* and *ubhayavedānta-sthāpanācārya*. He was the author of a work of philosophy known as *Sāttvika Brahma Vidyā Vilāsa*.[178] He also wrote the *Pāṇḍuraṅga-māhātmya* about the Viṣṇu temple at Panḍharpur in Maharashtra.[179] This literary celebrity also composed a Sanskrit poem consisting of twenty verses on Hanumān called *Hanumad Viṁśati*. This poem has been inscribed in the Grantha script on the walls of the Hanumān temple which he constructed at Ayyankuḷam

---

[174] G. Harihara Sastri and V. Raghavan, "The Hanumad Viṁśati", p. 34, fn. 1.

[175] *ARE*, 475 of 1919; K.V. Raman, op. cit., p. 83.

[176] *SITI*, vol. III, pt. II, pp. 1354-55.

[177] Ibid., p. 1354.

[178] T.V. Mahalingam, *ASLV*, p. 368.

[179] Ibid.

(Ayyangārkuḷam). The inscription at this temple (mentioned in this epigraph as the temple for Sañjīvirāyār) states that the consecration ceremony was celebrated in a grand manner and Veṇkaṭa II was present to witness the same.[180] This poem was re-engraved on the north, west and south walls of the shrine for Thāyār (Goddess Lakṣmī) in the Śrī Varadarāja Svāmi temple, Kāñcīpuram as also on the east and north walls of the "rock" and the outermost *gopura*, right at the entrance.[181] The repeated engraving of this inscription at Kāñcīpuram provides an idea of the importance enjoyed at that place by the great *ācārya*.[182]

There is an interesting legend connected with the composition of the *Hanumad Viṁśati*. Lakṣmīkumāra Tātācārya, while travelling, was accousted by robbers at the place where the temple stands today at Ayyangārkuḷam. Being a devotee of Hanuman and also a Sanskrit scholar, he at once composed the twenty verses on this deity. The robbers immediately left the place. In gratitude, Tātācārya constructed this temple consecrated the image and had the verses inscribed on the walls of this shrine. It should be remembered that Hanumān was a favourite deity of the Vijayanagara kings.[183] Lakṣmīkumāra Tātācārya also founded an *agrahāra* for scholarly brāhmaṇas.[184]

Appayya Dīkṣita

It was during the reign of Veṅkaṭa II that the great Advaita scholar Appayya Dīkṣita lived. He was a contemporary of Pañcamatabhañjanam Tātācārya and Vādhula Doḍḍācārya or

---

180 *ARE*, 92 and 95 of 1923.

181 *ARE*, 651 of 1919.

182 G. Harihara Sastri and V. Raghavan, *The Hanumad Viṁśati*, p. 34.

183 K.V. Raman, op. cit., pp. 83-84.

184 G. Harihara Sastri and V. Raghavan, "The Hanumad Viṁśati", pp. 33-34.

Mahācārya, author of the famous *Caṇḍamārutam*. Both Doḍḍācārya and Tātācārya defended the tenets of Viśiṣṭādvaita philosophy and refuted the criticisms of Appayya Dīkṣita.[185] The *Prapannāmṛtam* states that Appayya Dīkṣita wrote the *Advaita Dīpikā* and in refutation of this work, Mahācārya wrote the *Caṇḍamārutam* and Tātācārya the *Pañcamata Bhañjanam*.[186]

Appayya Dīkṣita was the son of Rangārya Dīkṣita (Raṅgarāja Makhin) of Aḍayapālam, a village in erstwhile North Arcot district.[187] By the age of twelve, he had a complete knowledge of the Vedas and other Śāstras. He was a protégé of Cinna Bomma Nāyaka of Velūr who was a subordinate of the Vijayanagara kings. In the colophon of the *Kuvalayānanda* which he wrote, he mentions that Veṅkaṭapati (Veṅkaṭa II) was his patron. This philosopher was a follower of Śrīkaṇṭha and was known as *Śrīkaṇṭhamaṭha Pratiṣṭhāpanācārya* (the establisher of Śrīkaṇṭha's school of philosophy).[188] He is credited with the authorship of 104 works, one being the *Śivārkamaṇidīpikā*, a commentary of Śrīkaṇṭha's Śaiva *Bhāṣya* from which work is very evident. Appayya Dīkṣita had a thorough knowledge of Mīmāṁsā, Vyākaraṇa, Nyāya, Alaṁkāra and practically the whole field of Sanskrit literature.[189] The *Śivārkamaṇidīpikā* is also known as *Śivādityamaṇidīpikā*.[190] The fact that he was a staunch follower of Śrīkaṇṭha's philosophy is seen from an epigraph dated CE 1582-83 found in the Kālakaṇtheśvara temple at Aḍayāpālam.[191] This epigraph is dated in the reign of Cinna Bomma Nāyaka, the ruler of Velūr,

[185] K.V. Raman, op. cit., p. 82.

[186] S. Krishnaswami Ayyangar, sources, op. cit., p. 202.

[187] T.V. Mahalingam, *ASLV*, p. 368.

[188] *ARE*, 1912, pt. II, para 71, p. 82.

[189] Ibid.

[190] Ibid., p. 369.

[191] Ibid., p. 82.

and a subordinate of Veṅkaṭa II.[192] Running around the central shrine of the Śiva temple in Aḍayāpālam, this inscription confirms the great literary activities of the polyhistor and the great influence that he wielded over his patrons.[193] This record registers that Appaya Dīkṣita constructed the Kālakaṇṭha temple and that by his association, King Cinna Bomma Nāyaka's fame spread far and wide and that the *Śrīkaṇṭha Bhāṣya* was raised (from its obscurity) to establish the superiority of Śiva in the Godhead.[194] It was in the Kālakaṇṭha temple that Appaya Dīkṣita wrote his commentary *Śivārkamaṇidīpikā* with the particular object of teaching the *Śrīkaṇṭha Bhāṣya* to 500 learned men. It was perhaps on this account that he was bathed in gold (*kanakābhiṣeka*) by Cinna Bomma Nāyaka.[195]

In addition to the information given in the inscription, there is, incidentally a verse, the authorship of which is unknown, which describes the ceremony of *kanakābhiṣekam* or bathing in gold that Cinna Bomma Nāyaka performed in order to honour the scholarship of Appaya Dīkṣita. He is said to have poured the gold coins by is own hands from a vessel.[196] Appaya Dīkṣita then went to Velūr and there induced him to make grants of gold and *agrahāra* villages to those 500 learned men who were to be taught the *Śivārkamaṇidīpikā*, raised Cinna Bomma Nāyaka (from his petty position) to the status of a famous ruler and composed 100 standard works (*prabandha*) such as *Nyāyarakṣāmaṇi*, *Kalpataru* and *Parimaḷa*.[197] This interesting document bears at the end, besides the name of Appaya Dīkṣita, those of Nīlakaṇṭha Dīkṣita, Aruṇagiri Dīkṣita, Viśvajid-Appai Dīkṣita, Umāmaheśvara Dīkṣita and Yajñeśvara Dīkṣita.[198]

---

192 *ARE*, 1912, pt. II, para 71, p. 82.

193 *ARE*, 395 of 1911.

194 *ARE*, 1912, pt. II, para 71.

195 Ibid.

196 S. Krishnaswami Ayyangar, *Sources*, pp. 250-52.

197 Ibid.

198 Ibid.

From the way in which Appaya Dīkṣita earnestly set himself to revive the school of Vedānta philosophy as expounded by Śrīkaṇṭha Śivācārya, it appears as if that philosophy had become almost obsolete and that many scholars of the time were opposed to it, if they had not condemned it altogether.[199] Being a staunch supporter of the Śaiva (Pāśupata) school of Advaita philosophy as expounded by Śrīkaṇṭha Śivācārya, he must have infused the same spirit in the Nāyakas of Velūr who patronized him — one of their family titles being "the foremost of those who assert the priority of Śiva".[200] Of the works mentioned here, *Nyāyarakṣāmaṇi* is, according to its colophon, a work on Vedānta, being a compendium of *Caturmatasāra*, which was apparently a voluminous one and was also a work of Appaya Dīkṣita and was also known as *Nayāmayukhamālika*. The *Caturmatasāra* contains four sections, each devoted to a system of philosophy, namely Advaita, Viśiṣṭādvaita, Śivādvaita and Dvaita. *Kalpataru* (i.e. *Vedāntakalpataru*) is noted by Aufrecht to be a commentary on *Bhāmatī* and is attributed to Amalānanda.[201] A commentary on this, the *Vedāntakalpataruparimaḷa* (or *Parimaḷa*) is stated to have been written by Appaya Dīkṣita. Perhaps, the latter was himself the author of a *Kalpataru*, different from the book of the same name written by Amalānanda; and *Parimaḷa* attributed to Appaya Dīkṣita in the Aḍayapālam record may here have been a work different from his commentary on Amalānanda's *Kalpataru*.[202] Appaya Dīkṣita also frequented the court of the Nāyaka of Tañjāvūr and was greatly honoured by him.[203]

He also wrote many works on Viṣṇu. Although in his *Śīvārkamaṇidīpikā*, Appaya Dīkṣita tries to maintain the

[199] S. Krishnaswami Ayyangar, *Sources*, pp. 250-52.

[200] Ibid., p. 82.

[201] Ibid., p. 83.

[202] Ibid., pp. 250-52.

[203] *MAR*, 1917, paras, 135-36; Y. Mahalinga Sastri, *JOR*, 1929-30.

supremacy of Śiva, his equal reverence for Viṣṇu is seen from his work *Varadarājastavam* in praise of Śrī Varadarāja Svāmi of Kāñcīpuram and *Kṛṣṇa Dhyāna Paddhati* in praise of Kṛṣṇa.[204] He also wrote a commentary called *Yādavābhyudaya Vyākhyā* on the great Sanskrit poem *Yādavābhyudaya* by Śrī Vedānta Deśika, the well-known Śrīvaiṣṇava preceptor (*ācārya*), philosopher and scholar-poet.[205] As a great scholar in rhetoric (*alaṁkāra*), he wrote three works on the subject — the *Kuvalayānanda, Chitra-Mīmāṁsā* and *Vṛttivārtikam*.[206] A verse mentions that Appaya Dīkṣita wrote the *Kuvalayānanda* at the instance of King Veṅkaṭapati Rāya (Veṅkaṭa II).[207]

Veṅkaṭa III (CE 1630-42)

Veṅkaṭa III was also a patron of scholars as seen from some inscriptions. Two copper-plate records of his reign, the Kūniyūr[208] and the Nīlmaṅgaḷa[209] plates register that when he was crowned as an emperor, the learned (of his kingdom) were presented with plenty of gold (*tadā abhiṣiktaḥ sudhīyaḥ api hemnā*). The Kūniyūr[210] and the Nīlmaṅgaḷa[211] plates also mention that "he was like the tree of India (*kalpataru*) to wise men" (*sūtramasakhī sudhi sārthanam*), thereby meaning that he gave to the learned all that they desired. The Kūniyūr record, in the concluding portion states that this king was "a moon to the lilies (which are) learned men" (*sudhijana kuvalaya candraḥ*).[212] The main purpose of the Kūniyūr inscription dated CE 1634 is to

[204] T.V. Mahalingam, *ASLV*, p. 369.

[205] S. Krishnaswami Ayyngar, *Sources*, pp. 209-10.

[206] T.V. Mahalingam, *ASLV*, p. 369.

[207] S. Krishnaswami Ayyangar, *Sources*, p. 250.

[208] *EI*, vol. II no. 34, v. 32, p. 244 (Kūniyūr plates).

[209] *EI*, vol. XXXVIII no. 39, v. 32, p. 218 (Nīlmaṅgaḷa plates).

[210] Kūniyūr plates, op. cit., v. 37, p. 344.

[211] Nīlmaṅgaḷa plates, op. cit., v. 37, p. 219.

[212] Kūniyūr plates, op. cit., v. 124, p. 250.

register the gift of the village of Kūniyūr (situated in the Tirunelveli area, south of the River Tāmraparaṇī which was surnamed Muddukṛṣṇapuram) at the request of Tirumala Nāyaka of Madurai to a number of learned brāhmaṇas deeply versed in the Vedānta (*viprah vedāntapāragāḥ*).[213] In the names of the donees given in this epigraph, there are very many of Tamil origin.[214] Interestingly, the names of most of these scholars are derived from the designations of certain temples of Viṣṇu and Śiva in south India. Aḷagādri is called after the sacred hill of Aḷagar near Madurai; Veṅkaṭādri, Veṅkaṭapati, Veṅgaḍattappa, Timmarāsu, Tirumala, Tiruveṅgaḍa, Vaḍamala and Śeśādri are derived from different names of the temple in the hill at Tirupati; Varadabhaṭṭa owes his name to the Varadarāja (Aruḷāla Perumāḷ) temple in Cinna Kāñcī; Raṅga and Raṅgarāja refer to the temple in Śrīraṅgam and Ahobala is the name of the village in Kurnool district which contains the famous shrines of Narasiṁha. Among the names connected with Śiva temples, Ārura is derived from Tiruvārur; Kanakasabhāpati and Cidambaravadhanin after the god at Cidambaram; Cokkanāthamakhin and Cokkanāthāvadhanin are derived from Cokkanāthasvāmin, one of the names of the god at Madurai; Kāḷahasti is the name of the famous Śaiva place of pilgrimage; and Aruṇagiri and Aruṇādri are Sanskrit names of Tiruvaṇṇāmalai.[215]

The Nīlmaṅgaḷa copper plate of this king, dated CE 1632, records the gift of the village of Nīlmaṅgaḷa, also called Rāghavaśrīpura and its hamlet Kūttanūr Manambākkam, to a learned brāhmaṇa named Nāgambhaṭṭa who belonged to the Bhāradvāja *gotra*, *Āpastamba Sūtra* and Yajus *śākhā*. Nīlmaṅgaḷa was situated in the well-known ancient territorial subdivision called Jayaṅgoṇḍa-Coḷamaṇḍalam (roughly identical with

[213] Kūniyūr plates, op. cit., vv. 55-59.

[214] Ibid., vv. 60-118, pp. 246-50.

[215] Ibid., p. 240.

erstwhile Chengalpet and South Arcot districts) and Nīlmaṅgaḷa may be identified with Nīlamaṅgaḷa, situated to the north-east of Oraṭṭūr.[216]

Another copper-plate inscription dated CE 1634 records the grant of the village of Cittūru, purchased from Ambalācārya (same as Ammalācārya who received this village from Veṅkaṭa II) together with the hamlet Karanai surnamed Prasanna Veṅkaṭapuram as an *agrahāra* to a number of Vaiṣṇavas by the king at the request of a brāhmaṇa officer named Bhaṇḍāram Veṅkaṭapati by Veṅkaṭa III.[217]

Poet-composers of the Sanskrit Inscriptions

Just like the poems of the copper-plate grants of the Pallavas, Pāṇḍyas, Coḷas and their feudatory chieftains, the verses of the copper-plate grants of the Vijayanagara monarchs were also composed by poets of calibre chosen by the rulers for this specific task. Many of these epigraphs bear the name of the poets at the end of the inscriptions with some of the epigraphs also supply additional information by way of educational qualifications, family, etc.

A verse in the Nallūr copper-plate record of Harihara II, which is fully in Sanskrit, mostly in verse and a partly in prose, mentions that the composer of the verses (*śloka*) of this edict (*śāsana*) was Mallanārādhyavr̥ttika (*śāsana-śloka-kartta*), who was the son of Koṭiśārādhya, who was wise and who had frequently performed sacrifices (*yajakodhmān*).[218] Composed in as many as thirty-five verses, interspersed with a prose-passage, this poet has used numerous metres in this composition which like all royal charters is eulogistic in nature, but still bears the mark of a poet of good calibre.

---

216 Nīlmaṅgaḷa plates, op. cit., p. 213.

217 *ARE*, 1935-36, no. A14.

218 Nallūr plates, op. cit., v. 34, p. 123.

The Śrīraṅgam plates of Deva Rāya II, which is almost completely in Sanskrit except for a short section inbetween in the *deśabhāṣā* Tamil, mentions that the forty-eight verses in this poem were composed by poet Rājaśekhara.[219] However, no other details about him are given in this grant. Moreover, the name of Rājaśekhara is also not known in any of the other grants of the first Vijayanagara dynasty.[220]

Two Sanskrit inscriptions of Deva Rāya II, one from Śrīraṅgam dated CE 1429[221] and the other from Tiruveḷḷaṟai dated CE 1430,[222] record the donation of two villages named Hasticoḷendra-maṅgalam and Pannanguḍi to the Śrīraṅgam and Tiruveḷḷaṟai temples, respectively. The donor was Vyāsa Bhāratī, a disciple of Rāmacandra Sarasvatī and the son of Dakṣiṇamūrti and Maragatavalli of Cillamantāgrahāram. The two records consist of several Sanskrit verses which are stated to have been composed by the donor himself.[223] This Vyāsa Bhāratī is also mentioned in another inscription from Lālguḍī of the time of the same king.[224] This inscription from the Saptaṛṣīśvara temple at Lāḷgudī is in Tamil and dated CE 1430. In this epigraph, he is mentioned as the chief disciple of Rāmacandra Sarasvatī, who bore the epithets *paramahaṁsa-parivrājakācārya, padavākyapramāṇa-pratiṣṭhāpaka* and *bhogavardhana-pariṣad-dhurandhara*. The poet, who composed the Sanskrit verses of the royal charters on the copper-plate inscriptions found in Tamil Nadu of the reign of Kṛṣṇadeva Rāya, was Sabhāpati. One copper-plate grant of this king from the Raṅganātha Svāmi temple in Śrīraṅgam dated CE 1514 in

219 *EI*, vol. XVIII no. 17, v. 41, p. 143 (Śrīraṅgam copper plates II of Devarāya II).

220 Ibid., p. 140.

221 *ARE*, 55 of 1938-39.

222 *ARE*, 199 of 1938-39.

223 *ARE*, 1938-39, pt. II, para 45, p. 86.

224 *ARE*, 131 of 1929.

fifty-one stanzas records in one of the last verses that this copper-plate inscription was composed by Sabhāpati at the command of Kṛṣṇadeva Mahārāya:

kṛṣṇadeva mahārāya śāsanena sabhāpatiḥ uktavān |
mudasandattam tadidam tāmraśāsanam | |[225]

Another similar copper-plate inscription in forty-five verses of this king from the same temple, dated CE 1528, also mentions the same details.[226] The Kāñcīpuram copper-plate inscription of this ruler, which consists of fifty-one stanzas in Sanskrit, records that it was composed by Ūrukavi.[227] The name of the poet is not specified in this inscription; perhaps his name was Ūrukavi, which may, however, simply mean "great poet".[228] According to the editors of this epigraph, a blank in the next line may well be filled with the word Sabhāpati as the metre requires it. Sabhāpati was the famous rhymester of the Rāya's court. If so, Ūrukavi was another name for Sabhāpati or a title assumed by him.[229] The Udayaṁbākkam copper-plate record of Kṛṣṇadeva Rāya which runs into fifty Sanskrit verses was also composed by Sabhāpati.[230] Incidentally, many verses in these inscriptions of Kṛṣṇadeva Rāya composed by Sabhāpati, especially the portions which contain the genealogy of this monarch, are identical. For example, verses 1 to 28 of the Śrīraṅgam copper-plate charter dated CE 1514 are identical with the Kāñcīpuram inscription of this emperor.[231] Similarly, many of the stanzas in both the Śrīraṅgam records of this ruler are identical.

225 *EI*, vol. XVIII no. 21A, v. 47, p. 164 (Śrīraṅgam I plates).

226 *EI*, vol. XVIII no. 21B, v. 44, p. 169 (Śrīraṅgam II plates).

227 Kanchipuram inscription of Kṛṣṇadeva Rāya, op. cit., vv. 44-45, p. 130.

228 Ibid., p. 126.

229 Ibid.

230 Udayambākkam plates, op. cit., v. 44, p. 174.

231 Śrīraṅgam inscription (21A) of Kṛṣṇadeva Rāya, op. cit., p. 162.

The same poet Sabhāpati composed some of the inscriptions of Acyuta Rāya also. The Kaḍalāḍi plates[232] which consist of 111 verses in Sanskrit record at the end of the document that it was composed by this poet by the order of this king.

acyutendra mahārāya śāsanena sabhāpatiḥ |
abhanimṛtpada saṁdarbham taditam tāmraśāsanam | |

The same verse is repeated in the Uṇamāñjeri copper-plate inscription of this monarch.[233] Many of the verses in these inscriptions are the same as the earlier Vijayanagara epigraphs.

The copper-plate inscriptions of Sadāśiva Rāya, namely the British Museum plates[234] and the Kṛṣṇāpuram plates[235] mention that these epigraphs were composed by Sabhāpati Svayambhū.

mṛdupatamiti tāmraśāsanārthammahita sadāśivarāya śāsanena |
abhanat anuguṇam vacomahimnā sarasatareṇa sabhāpati svayaṁbhuḥ | |

> By the order of Sadāśivarāya, Sabhāpati Svayambhū due to his capacity in speech, composed with eloquence and respect, the copper-plates.

The poet was obviously the son of Sabhāpati. The British Museum plates consist of 157 verses of which the first thirty-eight are the same as the Uṇamāñjeri inscription of Acyuta Rāya. There are 112 stanzas in the Kṛṣṇāpuram inscription. The Arivilimaṅgalam plates of Śrīraṅga Rāya, consisting of seventy-one verses state at the end that this deed was drafted by Svayambhū, son of Sabhāpati (*sabhāpatisūnuḥ*).[236]

[232] Kaḍalāḍi plates, op. cit., v. 105, p. 222.

[233] Uṇamāñjeri plates, op. cit., v. 110, p. 158.

[234] British Museum plates of Sadāśiva Rāya, op. cit., v. 151, p. 22.

[235] *EI*, vol. IX no. 52, vv. 105-06, p. 339 (Kṛṣṇāpuram plates of Sadāśiva Rāya).

[236] Ariviḷimaṅgalam plates, op. cit., v. 65, p. 355.

At the end of the long Daḷavāy-agrahāram plates of Veṅkaṭa II, which consists of 206 verses, is a verse that states the name of the poet of this inscription as Kṛṣṇakavi, the son of Kāmakoṭi and grandson of Sabhāpati.[237]

> *veṅkaṭapatirāya kṣmāpatya ādeśena śāsana ślokan* |
> *kṛṣṇakavi kāmakoṭiḥ sarasam abhanit sabhāpateḥ pautraḥ* | |
>
> Kṛṣṇakavi, son of Kāmakoṭi, the grandson of Sabhāpati, on the orders of Veṅkaṭapati Rāya, composed with eloquence, these copper plates.

The Veḷḷaṅguḍi inscription of this king, a portion of which is lost, also mentions the very same details about the composer Kṛṣṇakavi.[238] The Padmaneri grant, also of Veṅkaṭa II consisting of 159 verses, was also the poem of Kṛṣṇakavi.[239] The first of the two British Museum plates of Veṅkaṭa II (dated CE 1586), which has sixty-four verses was also the composition of this poet,[240] while the second (dated CE 1613), which has eighty-three verses was composed by Cidambara Kavi, the nephew of Śivasūrya Kavi.[241] The Vilāpāka grant of Veṅkaṭa II, which has seventy-one verses, was composed by Rāmakavi, the son of Kāmakoṭi.[242] Another copper-plate record, dated CE 1602, mentions that this poem was composed by Cidambara Kavi, the nephew of Śivasūrya.[243]

Incidentally, lines 5-94 and verses 3-42 of the Padmaneri plates are the same as those in the Daḷavāy agrahāram and in the two inscriptions from the British Museum.[244] Lines 5-110

[237] Daḷavāy-agrahāram plates, op. cit., v. 200, p. 185.

[238] Veḷḷaṅguḍi plates, op. cit., ll. 555-59, p. 318.

[239] Padmaneri plates, op. cit., vv. 152-53.

[240] *EI*, vol. XIII no. 22/A, v. 64, p. 231.

[241] Ibid., no. 22/B, v. 82, p. 235.

[242] Viḷāpāka plates, op. cit., v. 65, p. 277.

[243] *ARE*, 1957-58, A-32.

[244] Padmaneri plates, op. cit., p. 292.

containing verses of the Veḷḷaṅguḍi and Padmaneri grants are also similar.[245]

The Nīlmaṅgaḷa inscription of Veṅkaṭa III, consisting of fifty-three verses was composed by Rāmakavi, son of Kāmakoṭi and grandson of Sabhāpati.[246]

> *śrī veṅkaṭapatirāyagirā śāsasam abhanit sabhāpateḥ pautraḥ* I
> *kāmakoṭisutaḥ rāmakaviḥ śāsanam vāṅgmayam* I I
>
> Sabhāpati's grandson and Kāmakoṭi's son, Rāmakavi, on the orders of Veṅkaṭapatirāya, eloquently composed the words of this record.

Similarly, the Kūniyūr plate of the same ruler, which has 126 verses, mentions in a slightly different way that it was also the composition of the same poet.[247]

> *vīraveṅkaṭarāya ukta prāha pautraḥ sabhāpateḥ* I
> *kāmakoṭisutaḥ rāmakaviḥ śāsanavāṅgmayam* I I
>
> At the command of Veṅkaṭapatirāya, Rāmakavi, grandson of Sabhāpati and son of Kāmakoṭi, composed this grant.

The actual authorship of some of the verses which are repeated in several inscriptions leads to a certain degree of confusion. The person who composed the Daḷavāy-agrahāram plates was Kṛṣṇakavi Kāmakoṭi, the grandson of Sabhāpati. A considerable number of the verses in this document are found in the Maṅgalampad grant of Veṅkaṭa I where it is stated that the composer of the verses was one Cidambara Kavi, sister's son of Śivasūrya, king of poets.[248] But, the Kūniyūr, Vilāpāka, Koṇḍyatā and Kallakurśi grants, which contain many of the same verses of the Daḷavāy-agrahāram inscriptions are said

[245] Vellaṅguḍi plates, op. cit., p. 313.

[246] Nīlmaṅgaḷa plates, op. cit., v. 50, p. 220.

[247] Kūniyūr plates, v. 125, p. 250.

[248] Daḷavāy-agrahāram plates, p. 163.

to be the composition of Rāma, the son of Kāmakoṭi and the grandson of Sabhāpati. A similar grant belongs to the Kuḍli Śṛṅgerī Svāmi's *maṭha* and the writing is claimed there by Kṛṣṇakavi Kāmakoṭi, the grandson of Sabhāpati.[249] Thus, there is a great deal of divergence in the statement as to the actual authorship of the composition. It appears that some of the earlier members of the family, Sabhāpati or someone else was the actual author and everytime his verses were repeated and added to in drawing up fresh documents by various later members of the family, the composition was claimed to be his by the copyist.[250]

The names of the composers of a large number of Vijayanagara inscriptions are thus known: Sabhāpati, Svyambhū, Kāmakoṭi, Rāma-kavi, etc. From various sources it is possible to know something about the relationship between these persons.[251] From the Viḷāpāka and the Kūniyūr plates, it is known that Rāmakavi, their author, was the son and grandson, respectively, of Kāmakoṭi and Sabhāpati. The Arivilimaṅgalam plates and the British Museum plates of Sadāśiva Rāya state Svayambhū was the son of Sabhāpati. A later inscription of the time of the Pāṇḍyas reveals that Rājanātha, the son of Svayambhū was the composer of that document.[252] The enterprising son of the *śāsana*-composer of the court of the Vijayanagara emperors seems to have sought and obtained a place similar to that of his father at the court of the Pāṇḍyas who had already become the vassals of the Vijayanagara monarchs.[253] Thus, it is clear that Sabhāpati had two sons, namely Svayambhū and Kāmakoṭi. Rājanātha was the son of Svayambhū and Rāmakavi was the son of Kāmakoṭi.

249 Daḷavāy-agrahāram plates, p. 163.

250 Ibid.

251 Ariviḷimaṅgalam plates, op. cit., p. 347.

252 *TAS*, vol. I, p. 142.

253 Ariviḷimaṅgalam plates, op. cit., p. 348.

In the comedy named *Somavallī-Yogānanda Prahasana*, the following account of the author, Aruṇagirinātha is given: Nāgaṇṇa Kavi, who bore the *birudas* *Kavi-prabhu, Aṣṭabhāṣā-kavi, Kavi-nāga-kesarin*, etc., who was of the *Sāmaveda* and who was a follower of the *Śrīkaṇṭhāgama*, had a son named Rājanātha Deśika.[254] He was married to Abhiramā Nāyikā, the daughter of Diṇḍima-prabhu and sister of Sabhāpati of the Kāśyapa *gotra* and the *Sāmaveda*, whose ancestors bore the title *Aghoraśivācāryas*. To these was born Aruṇagirinātha, who held several distinguishing titles like *Diṇḍimakavi-sārvabhauma, Cera-Coḷa-Pāṇḍya-Prathamārādhya-Diṇḍima Kavi*, etc. According to the *Saḷuvābhyudayam*, the father of its author (i.e. of Rājanātha Kavi), was Sonādrinātha.[255] The author of the *Bhāgavata-campū, Acyutarāyābhyudayam*, etc. was also a Rājanātha Kavi whose father was also Sonādrinātha. It is therefore possible to conclude that the Rājanātha Kavi of *Sāḷuvarāyābhyudayam, Acyutarāyābhyudayam* and *Bhāgavata-campū* was one and the same person. It is difficult to explain why he wrote the *Sāḷuvarāyābhyudayam* (about Sāḷuva Narasiṁha) who ruled in the fifteenth century CE, long after the hero of that work was dead.[256] It is possible that Sāḷuva Narasiṁha first entertained the maternal ancestor of Rājanātha Kavi as his court *śāsana* writer, in gratitude for which he might have written this poem in praise of Sāḷuva Narasiṁha. A verse in the *Sāḷuvābhyudaya-Kāvya* makes it clear that the author did not write it in the reign of the hero.[257] Nor can it be asserted that the author of the *Saḷuvarāyābhyudayam* was different from the author of the *Acyutarāyābhyudayam*.

A detailed study of the Sanskrit copper-plate inscriptions or the Sanskrit portions of the copper-plate grants as also the

[254] Ariviḷimaṅgalam plates, op. cit., p. 348.

[255] Ibid.

[256] Ibid.

[257] Ibid., fn. 10.

lithic epigraphs of the Vijayanagara time reveals that the poets of these verses were talented and also had a sound knowledge of the epics, Purāṇas and other ancient lore. The numerous verses are composed in a number of metres, the most commonly used being *anuṣṭubh, āryā, dodhakā, gītī, hariṇī, indravajrā, mālinī, mandākrāntā, pr̥thvī, puṣpitāgrā, rathodhatā, śālinī, śikhariṇī, śailaśikhā, śārdulavikrīḍitā, śragdharā, vasantatilakā* and *upajatī*. Many of the invocatory verses in praise of Gaṇeśa, Viṣṇu, Śambhu, etc. are couched in beautiful language and brim with devotion.

Maṇipravāla Inscriptions

Among the innumerable inscriptions found in Tamil Nadu, the majority are written in Tamil and a small number in Sanskrit. There are also some epigraphs especially the copper-plate grants which are bilingual, the first or *praśasti* portion composed in Sanskrit and the second or operative portion of the record written in Tamil.

However, in addition to these, there are a few lithic and copper-plate epigraphs in Tamil Nadu which are composed in the quaint *maṇipravāla* style. In the ancient period in the Tamil country there was a unique development of composing inscriptions in this style which involves the use of clusters of Sanskrit expressions along with fine Tamil expressions sometimes set in the form of versified prose.[258] The word *maṇi* meaning pearl and *pravāḷa* meaning coral are indicative of the beautiful combination of Tamil and Sanskrit words used together in the composition of literary works of this genre. The *maṇipravāla* style is characteristic of Vaiṣṇava literature and was used extensively by the Vaiṣṇava commentators of the *Nālāyira Divya Prabandham* or the 4,000 hymns of the Āḻvārs or Tamil Vaiṣṇava saints of the ancient Tamil country who

258 K.G. Krishnan, *Sanskrit in the Inscriptions of Tamilnāḍu from Svasti-Śrī (B.Ch. Chhabra Felicitation Volume)*, New Delhi, 1984, p. 23.

flourished between the sixth and eighth centuries CE. This style of writing attained a very extensive usage in the thirteenth and fourteenth centuries CE as can be seen from the works of eminent scholars like Vedānta Deśika, Periyavāchan Piḷḷai and Pillai Lokācārya.

The Madurai (Vaigai Bed) inscription of the Pāṇḍyan king Cendan belonging to the second half of the seventh century CE is the first inscription in the *maṇipravāla* style.[259] This epigraph is engraved in the Vaṭṭeḷutu and Grantha characters in Tamil with Sanskrit expressions used in between to describe the king.[260] In many of the bilingual Pāṇḍyan epigraphs such as the Veḷvikuḍi,[261] Śrīvaramaṅgalam[262] and Daḷavāypuram[263] copper plates and also in many Coḷa copper-plate grants the Tamil portion is interspersed with numerous Sanskrit expressions and phrases.

Many *maṇipravāla* inscriptions were issued during the Vijayanagara period in Tamil Nadu. One such example is a lithic epigraph of Sadāśiva Rāya dated CE 1545 engraved in the third *prākarā* of the Raṅganāthasvāmi temple at Śrīraṅgam (Tiruchirāpaḷḷi district) which contains some information about a Vaiṣṇava preceptor named Nantigal Nārāyaṇa Jīyar who was associated with the administration of the Śrīraṅgam temple and who did yeoman service with regard to flood control in this temple town.[264] The scripts used in this record are Grantha and Tamil and the language provides a good example of the

---

259 K.G. Krishnan, *Sanskrit in the Inscriptions of Tamilnāḍu from Svasti-Śrī (B.Ch. Chhabra Felicitation Volume)*, New Delhi, 1984, p. 23.

260 *EI*, vol. XXXVIII no. 4, p. 27.

261 *EI*, vol. XVII no. 16, pp. 298-304.

262 K.G. Krishnan, *Inscriptions of the Early Pāṇḍyas* (*c.* 300 BC – 984 AD), New Delhi, 2002, pp. 17-21.

263 T.N. Subrahmanian, "The Daḷavāypuram Copper-plate Grant of Parāntaka Vīra Nārāyaṇa," *TASSI* (1962-63), pp. 1-31.

264 *EI*, vol. XXIX no. 9, pp. 76-78.

typical Vaiṣṇava *maṇipravāla* style with a fair admixture of Sanskrit and Tamil words as employed by the great Tamil commentators.[265]

Another such *maṇipravāla* record is found on a slab near the outermost eastern *gopura* of the Jambukeśvaram temple at Tiruvānnaikā (Tirucirāpaḷḷi district).[266] It is dated CE 1584 and thus belongs to the period of Veṅkaṭa I of the Vijayanagara dynasty. This inscription records the appointment of Candraśekharaguru-Uḍaiyār to the headship of the Pāśupata Maṭha with the right of worship and management of the temple of Tiruvānnaika-Uḍaiyār. This epigraph is composed in a high-flown *maṇipravāla* style and appears to be an apologia for the selection of a married person (*gr̥hastha*) to the pontificate of the Pāśupata Maṭha at Tiruvānnaika which had till then only been headed by a celibate.[267] This record contains numerous quotations from several works in support of this change in tradition and ends with several benedictory and imprecatory verses.[268]

Yet another similar inscription[269] is seen in the east and north walls of the second *prākāra* of the Śrīraṅgam temple dated CE 1612 and is also a good specimen of the *maṇipravāla* style. This record registers an endowment of a certain amount of money, out of the interest on which certain offerings were to be made to Lord Raṅganātha during the recitation (*tiruvadhyāyana*) of *Tiruvāymoḻī* (of Nammālvar) along with other sacred verses on the day of the asterism Tiruvādirai of Emberumanār (Rāmānuja), the famous Śrīvaiṣṇava preceptor in the month of Chittirai (April–May). The offerings were to

---

265 *EI*, vol. XXIX no. 9, p. 71.

266 *ARE*, no. 135 of 1936-37.

267 Ibid., 1936-37, pt. II, p. 91.

268 Ibid.

269 *SII*, vol. XXIV no. 523, pp. 505-06.

be distributed among the Śrīvaiṣṇavas, pilgrims and Ekāṅkīs. Interestingly, this epigraph quotes the *Divya-Śrīsūkti* (*Nālāyira Divya Prabandham*) of the Vaiṣṇava saint Periāḻvār in giving the ingredients of the preparation called Akkāravaḍisil which is referred to in the work as Tiruvoṇam. Extracts from the *Rāmānuja Nuṟṟandādi*[270] are quoted freely while describing the famous Śrīvaiṣṇava preceptor (*ācārya*) Rāmānuja. This inscription ends with a Sanskrit *śloka* invoking prosperity to Rāmānuja's teachings. This record too is written in the Tamil script with the Sanskrit expressions in Grantha characters.

These *maṇipravāla* inscriptions reveal the skill of the composers of these records who were well-versed in both Sanskrit and Tamil, and who had attained mastery in this quaint style of composition.

---

[270] *SII*, vol. XXIV no. 523, pp. 505-06.

8

Nāyakas

Nāyakas of Madurai

THE history of the Nāyakas of Tamil Nadu, who were the feudatories of the Vijayanagara emperors marks a very interesting epoch in the history of Tamil Nadu. The Nāyaka kings of Madurai ruled for approximately 200 years from the second quarter of the sixteenth century CE to nearly the second half of the eighteenth century CE, while the Nāyakas of Tañjāvūr ruled from about the mid-sixteenth century CE to the last quarter of the seventeenth century CE. The foundation of the Madurai Nāyakship started with the appointment of Viśvanātha Nāyaka (*c.* CE 1529-64) as the viceroy of the south with the titles "Chief of the Pāṇḍya Country" and "Lord of the Southern Throne" by Kr̥ṣṇadeva Rāya.[1] Viśvanātha Nāyaka was succeeded by his son Kr̥ṣṇappa Nāyaka I (CE 1564-72) and subsequently by many able princes who all contributed in great measure in following the footsteps of their overlords, the monarchs of the Vijayanagara empire. In the field of education too, they contributed much to the dissemination and enrichment of Sanskrit learning and literature. However, the information available from inscriptions is not as copious as that of the other epochs prior to the time of the Nāyakas. The data available from some of their epigraphs and pieces of literature are presented here.

---

[1] R. Sathyanatha Aiyar, *Nāyaks of Madura*, Madras, 1991, p. 51.

VĪRAPPA NĀYAKA (CE 1572-95)

Vīrappa Nāyaka succeeded his father Kṛṣṇappa Nāyaka I to the throne in CE 1572. The Kūniyūr plates dated CE 1634 of the reign of Veṅkaṭa III describe Vīrappa Nāyaka as "the support of scholars" (*bhūdānāṁ ālaṁbanam*).[2] The Daḷavāy-agrahāram copper-plate grant of the same Vijayanagara ruler dated CE 1586 records that at the request of Vīra Bhūpa (Vīrappa Nāyaka), the son of Kṛṣṇappa Nāyaka I, King Veṅkaṭapati (Veṅkaṭa II) granted to a number of brāhmaṇas well-versed in the Vedas and Śāstras the village of Gaṅgāvarapaṭṭi, together with a few other villages, clubbed under the name Vīrabhūpa-samudram.[3] This inscription provides a detailed list of the donees numbering 120 and also their *gotra*s, *sūtra*s and place of origin.[4] The names of these places correspond to modern place names like Coimbatore, North Arcot, Madurai, Tañjāvūr, Chengalpet, Kurnool, Tuṁkūr, Kolār, Guntūr, Godāvarī, Gulbargā, Bellāry and Sholapur.[5]

KṚṢṆAPPA NĀYAKA II (CE 1595–1601)

Vīrappa Nāyaka had three sons — Kumāra Kṛṣṇappa, Viśvappa and Kastūri Raṅgappa and was succeeded by the eldest who ruled for approximately five years. The Padmaneri copper-plate grant, also of the reign of Veṅkaṭa II, dated CE 1598, praise Kṛṣṇappa Nāyaka II, eulogizing his many benefactions to the temple of Śrī Raṅganātha Svāmi in Śrīraṅgam. This inscription also adds that he founded *agrahāra*s for the use of brāhmaṇas well-versed in the Śāstras and bestowed villages on them in perpetuity.[6] The focus of this inscription is the gift

---

[2] *EI*, vol. III no. 34, v. 51, p. 245.

[3] *EI*, vol. XII no. 21, vv. 41-79, pp. 175-78 (Daḷavāy-agrahāram plates).

[4] Ibid., pp. 163-67.

[5] Ibid., pp. 167-70.

[6] *EI*, vol. XVI no. 22, p. 288 and vv. 78-151, pp. 295ff.

of the village Padmaneri to a number of scholars of various *gotras* and *sūtras*, who were well-versed in the Vedas.[7] This village was surnamed Tirumalāmbāpuram, presumably after Kṛṣṇappa Nāyaka's mother.[8]

The Veḷḷāṅguḍi copper-plate grant, also dated CE 1598 of the reign of Veṅkaṭa II, mentions that at the request of Kṛṣṇa Bhūpati (Kṛṣṇappa Nāyaka II), the son of Vīra Bhūpati and Tirumalāmbikā, King Veṅkaṭa II granted as an *agrahāra* to a large number of learned brāhmaṇas the village of Veḷḷangoḷḷi, together with other villages, all clubbed together under the name Vīrabhūpa-samudram.[9] The names of the donees, their *śākhās* and *gotras* are listed in this epigraph as well as their place of origin. From this list, it would seem that most of the donees were residents of the Telugu country and had already migrated into the Tamil country or had come down south at the invitation of the donor.[10] The record is of great importance in that it accounts for a large number of Telugu brāhmaṇa families in the Tirunelveli district.[11] Themselves Telugus by birth and possessing a strong liking for the men of their own country, speaking their own language, the Nāyakas of Madurā would have imported large colonies of Telugu brāhmaṇas from the north and settled them down in Madurai and Tirunelveli districts.

The Veḷḷaṅguḍi plates, which praise Kṛṣṇamahīpati (Kṛṣṇappa Nāyaka II) as being "very well-read in all the Nītiśāstras" (*vijñāta amita nītiśāstra vitati*),[12] also mention that he granted enough money to the brāhmaṇas of other kingdoms

---

[7] *EI*, vol. XVI no. 22, vv. 46-48, p. 293.

[8] Ibid., p. 288.

[9] *EI*, vol. XVI no. 23, vv. 53-98, pp. 313-17.

[10] Ibid., p. 302.

[11] Ibid.

[12] Ibid., v. 80, pp. 315-16.

to redeem their lands which they lost to their kings owing to their inablility to pay the taxes thereon.[13] It can be understood from this that the government of other kings was so oppressive even in the case of brāhmaṇas and consequently much more so in the case of other castes, that the former had, on account of their inability to make good the heavy taxes imposed upon their lands, to abandon them; whereas the government of Kr̥ṣṇa Mahīpati was so good as to attract brāhmaṇas even from other countries to the benefit of his munificence.[14] That this statement was not a mere boast can be seen from the list of villages from which came the brāhmaṇa donees of this grant.[15]

TIRUMALA NĀYAKA (*c.* CE 1623-59)

Tirumala Nāyaka, the son of Muttu Kr̥ṣṇappa Nāyaka (CE 1601-09) and younger brother of Muttu Vīrappa Nāyaka (CE 1609-23), succeeded the latter on the throne. He was the greatest of the Nāyaka kings of Madurai. The palace, the *Pudu-maṇḍapa*, the renovation of numerous temples and numberless public works he undertook — these justify his title to greatness as a sympathetic administrator and magnificent builder.[16]

The Kūniyūr copper-plate grant of Veṅkaṭa III dated CE 1634 records that the village of Kūniyūr was gifted by this king at the request of Tirumala Nāyaka to a number of brāhmaṇas "who were celebrated for their learning in the Śāstras and deeply versed in the Vedas" (*nānā śākhābhid gotrasūtrebhyaḥ śāstravittāya, vikyātebyo dvijendrebyo vedavidbhyo viśeṣataḥ*).[17] The village was surnamed Muddukr̥ṣṇapuram

[13] *EI*, v. 80, p. 301.

[14] Ibid.

[15] Ibid.

[16] N. Subrahmanian, *History of Tamilnad* (AD *1565-1984*), Madurai, 1977, p. 17.

[17] *EI*, vol. III no. 34, vv. 40-48, p. 245.

evidently after Muddukṛṣṇa (Muttu Kṛṣṇappa Nāyaka), the father of Tirumala Nāyaka.

The famous scholar Nīlakaṇṭa Dīkṣita was patronized by Tirumala Nāyaka.[18] He was the minister of this king.[19] Nīlakaṇṭa Dīkṣita was a versatile writer, the son of Śrīnivāsa Dīkṣita and grand-nephew of Appayya Dīkṣita.[20] Among his numerous poetical works, *Śivalīlārṇava* and *Gaṅgāvataraṇa* rank very high — the former is a *mahākāvya* in twenty-two cantos detailing the sixty-four *līlā*s of God Śiva Hālasyanātha by which name He is worshipped in Madurai and his *Gaṅgāvataraṇa* deals in eight cantos with the story of the penance of Bhagīratha and the descent of the celestial Gaṅgā on earth.[21] He also wrote, in 1637, his *Nīlakaṇṭa-Vijaya-Campū*, dealing with the legend of Samudramanthana.[22] This great scholar contributed to various branches of Sanskrit literature during the seventeenth century.

Nāyakas of Tañjāvūr

According to tradition, the Tañjāvūr Nāyakas were first appointed to the regular charge of the Coḷa country by the Vijayanagara emperor, Acyuta Rāya.[23] This is confirmed by the evidence of Telugu literature like the Tañjāvūri *Āndhra Rājulu Caritamu* which says that Sevappa Nāyaka who married Mūrtimāmbā, the sister of Tirumalāmbā, a consort of Acyuta Rāya, was appointed to the governorship of the Coḷa country which was given away as dowry to Mūrtimāmbā.[24]

---

[18] C.S. Sundaram, *Contribution of Tamil Nadu to Sanskrit*, Chennai, 1999, p. 7.

[19] R.C. Majumdar, *History and Culture of the Indian People*, vol. VII (*The Mughal Empire*), Bombay, 1994, p. 607.

[20] Ibid.

[21] Ibid.

[22] Ibid., p. 610.

[23] V. Vriddhagirisan, *The Nāyaks of Tañjore, Madras*, 1985, p. 9.

[24] Ibid.

SEVAPPA NĀYAKA (*c.* CE 1532-80)

Sevappa Nāyaka, also known as Cinna Seva, Sevanṛpati and Sevabhūpa in Sanskrit and Siru Seva in Tamil was the real founder of the Nāyaka dynasty in Tañjāvūr. His reign is noted for his contributions to works of charity and religious tolerance. Some epigraphical material is available to find out the level of Sanskrit learning and literature in his land.

RATNAKHEṬA ŚRĪNIVĀSA DĪKṢITA

The lithic inscriptions of the Nāyaka times also record the names of some of the poets who composed the Sanskrit epigraphs. A bilingual record of Sevappa Nāyaka found on the eastern *gopura* of the Aruṇācaleśvara temple in Tiruvaṇṇamalai contains verses of Śrīnivāsa Dīkṣitar of Śaktimaṅgalam, Ellappa Nāyinar, Kaliṅgarayar Unnamalai Nāyinar, Ellappar and Kalmaḍattu Mudāliyar in praise of the *gopura* of eleven storeys built at Soṇācala (Tiruvaṇṇamalai) by Timmayya Cinna Cevva at the request of the brothers Śivaneśa and Lokanātha.[25] Four of the Sanskrit verses in this bilingual record were composed by Śrīnivāsa Dīkṣita. The first of these verses mentions that in the month of Siṁha in the year Aṅgīras, corresponding to Śaka 1494 or CE 1572 (expressed by the chronogram *vedhobhāgya*), Śrīmat Timmayya Cinna Cevva Nṛpati constructed, or rather, completed this tall *gopura*. In the *Sāhityaratnākara* of Yajñanārāyaṇa Dīkṣita, the *Raghunāthābhyudaya* of Ramabhadrāmbā, reference is made to the building of this *gopura* by Sevappa Nāyaka.[26] It is therefore evident that Cinna Cevva was the Tañjāvūr Nāyaka ruler, Cevappa, the second son of Timmayya.[27] The second verse of Śrīnivāsa Dīkṣita states that the *gopura* was constructed at the request of two ascetics (*tapasvins*), Śivaneśa and Lokanātha.

---

[25] *ARE*, 419 of 1928/29.

[26] *ARE*, 1928-29, pt. II, para 69, p. 86.

[27] Ibid.

These two persons were evidently devout ascetics in-charge of the general administration of the temple since another record, found on the same *gopura*, refers to Śivaneśa and another person named Āṇaiyappa Piḷḷai in this capacity.[28]

Yet another lithic record in the same place registers the name of Lokanātha as being "renowned among ascetics" (*sarvatapasvīloka mahita*).[29] In the third verse, Śrīnīvāsa Dīkṣita gives some information about himself. The names of his parents were Āṇḍampiḷḷai and Lakṣmī, he had a son named Keśava Dīkṣita and he had the title *divapradīpa*. From these facts, it is possible to identify him with Śrīnīvāsa Dīkṣita of Satyamaṅgalam, a village in the Vellore taluk of erstwhile North Arcot district who was much honoured in the court of the Tañjāvūr Nāyaka rulers, especially in that of Raghunātha from whom he is said to have received the surname *Ratnakheṭadhvari* in commemoration of a particularly fine Sanskrit verse he had composed describing the beauty of the evening twilight.[30]

Śrīnivāsa Dīkṣita also had two more sons named Ardhanārīśvara Dīkṣita and Rājacūḍāmaṇi Dīkṣita, the latter of whom attained much literary celebrity as an author.

The fourth verse of this inscription, probably composed on a different occasion, but etched in continuation of the above three stanzas, is purely an eulogistic one in praise of the *gopura*.[31] While the above are the details about Śrīnivāsa Dīkṣitar sourced from epigraphical data, more information about this great scholar in the field of Sanskrit, who wrote eighteen plays and sixty poems, can be seen from other sources. Bālayajña Vedīśvara, in his introductory verse of the

[28] *ARE*, 423 of 1928-29.

[29] *ARE*, 425 of 1928-29.

[30] *ARE* 1928-29, pt. II, para 69, p. 87; C.S. Sundaram, op. cit., p. 222.

[31] Ibid.

commentary on *Rukmiṇīpariṇaya*, gives a list of his works. Śrīnivāsa Dīkṣita, whose patron was also Sūrappa Nāyaka of Senji, who hailed from Satyamaṅgalam had several titles like *Advaitavidyācārya*, *Sadbhāsacatura*, *Abhinava bhavabhūti* and *Daṇḍidyoti divāpradīpa*.[32] Ratnakheṭa Śrīnivāsa Dīkṣita lived in the court of Sūrappa Nāyaka and dedicated to him the drama *Bhāvanāpuruṣottama*.[33] Sūrappa Nāyaka was an agent (*kāryakarta*) of Sadāśiva Rāya (CE 1542-76) and exercised authority over Tiruvaḍi-rājya or erstwhile South Arcot region, where he gave numerous benefactions to temples.[34] Ramacandra Dīkṣita, the fifth in descent from Ratnakheṭa Śrīnivāsa Dīkṣita (Ratnakheṭa → Keśava → Patañjali → Keśava → Rāmacandra), lived during the latter part of the seventeenth century CE and wrote the *Keraḷābharaṇacampū*.[35]

ACYUTAPPA NĀYAKA (*c*. CE 1560–1614)

Acyutappa Nāyaka, the son and successor of Sevappa Nāyaka, ascended the throne in c. CE 1580. However, his early connection with the administration of the kingdom and his joint rule as co-regent with his father which must have started at least from CE 1560 are best seen from his epigraphs and the literary evidence records that he was appointed *yuvarāja* by his father in the latter part of his rule.[36]

Another Sanskrit poet and scholar whose name appears in the lithic records of the Nāyaka times is Soṇādrinātha. A Sanskrit epigraph in the Grantha script of this poet is found on the eastern *gopura* of the Aruṇācaleśvara temple at

---

[32] C.S. Sundaram, op. cit., p. 176.

[33] S. Krishnaswami Ayyangar, *Sources of Vijayanagar History*, Madras, 1919, p. 272, fn.

[34] K.V. Raman, *Śrī Varadarājaswāmi Temple, Kāñchī*, New Delhi, 1975, p. 31.

[35] C.S. Sundaram, op. cit., p. 178.

[36] Ibid., p. 35.

Tiruvaṇṇamalai.[37] The verses in this inscription record the setting up of the gold pinnacles on the *gopura* of Soṇādri by King Sevappa Acyuta. The details of the date on which the golden finials were installed by Sevappa Acyuta, i.e. Acyutappa Nāyaka, the son and successor of Sevappa, viz. Aṅgīras, Kārttika Paurṇami, Samumyavāra, Rohiṇī (whose English equivalent is, Wednesday, 19 November 1572), are given in this epigraph. Soṇādrinātha has been described here as belonging to the Kāśyapa *gotra* and well-versed in the Śaivāgamas.[38]

RAGHUNĀTHA NĀYAKA (c. CE 1600-34)

Raghunātha Nāyaka was the most illustrious of the Tañjāvūr Nāyakas and his court flowered as a great cultural centre. He was a scholar and is said to have written a good number of *kāvyas*, *prabandhas* and *yakṣagānas* in Sanskrit and Telugu.[39] He was an authority on music and his benefactions to learning and patronage of pundits must have made his name so familiar in the land as to attract other learned men to his court.[40] He was succeeded by his son Vijayarāghava Nāyaka.

Rājacūḍāmaṇi Dīkṣita, the illustrious son of Ratnakheṭa Śrīnivāsa Dīkṣita, was patronized by Raghunātha Nāyaka on whom he wrote the poem *Raghunāthabhūpavijaya*. He was the disciple of his elder step-brother Ardhanārīśvara. His contribution to various fields of Sanskrit literature is remarkable.[41] Some of his works are *Tantraśikhāmaṇi*, a commentary on *Jaimini-Sūtras*; *Rukmiṇīkalyāṇa*, a poem in ten cantos; *Śaṅkarābhyudayam*, on the life of Jagatguru Ādiśaṅkara, etc.[42]

---

[37] *ARE*, 425 of 1928-29.

[38] *ARE*, 1928-29, pt. II, para. 69, p. 86.

[39] V. Vriddhagirisan, op. cit., p. 108.

[40] Ibid.

[41] C.S. Sundaram, op. cit., p. 177.

[42] Ibid., p. 178.

GOVINDA DĪKṢITA

Govinda Dīkṣita was a Kannada brāhmaṇa who is remembered even today as a very great scholar and who served the Nāyaka rulers of Tañjāvūr very loyally for many decades. The Dīkṣita played a very prominent part in the good administration of the country and it may be said that his fame eclipsed even that of the Nāyakas.[43] The existence of numerous villages and streets besides other memorials named after him stand testimony to his greatness and to the regard which the people and the rulers had for him.[44]

There are conflicting opinions with regard to Govinda Dīkṣita's tenure as minister during the era of the Nāyakas of Tañjāvūr. One school of thought suggests that Govinda Dīkṣita was minister to the first three Nāyakas of Tañjāvūr — Sevappa, Acyutappa and Raghunātha (CE 1532–1633), while another school of thought, which takes its stand on the evidence of literary works and stone inscriptions, considers that Govinda Dīkṣita could not have been minister to Sevappa, the first of the Tañjāvūr Nāyakas; that Govinda Dīkṣita is mentioned only in the records of Acyutappa and Raghunātha.[45]

According to B. Natarajan, Govinda Dīkṣita was born in CE 1515 and was perhaps not a minister in the formal sense to Sevappa Nāyaka, but was his chosen advisor right from CE 1532 when they met till CE 1580 when Sevappa Nāyaka passed away.[46] He was an active and enlightened prime minister (*pradhānī*) and Acyutappa Nāyaka (right from CE 1560 when he became the *yuvarāja*) and played an even greater part as *pradhānī* to Raghunātha Nāyaka till CE 1616 or 1620 for many years in the first phase of his rule as *yuvarāja* and *rājā*.[47] Govinda

[43] V. Vriddhagirisan, op. cit., p. 113.

[44] Ibid.

[45] B. Natarajan, *Advaita Vidyāchārya Mahārāja Saheb Bhagavān Śrī Govinda Dīkṣita*, Kumbakonam, p. 49 (date of publication not given).

[46] Ibid., p. 75.

[47] Ibid.

Dīkṣita's career as prime minister came to an end in the first part of Raghunātha's reign, perhaps around CE 1620.[48]

In addition to being a very great administrator, Govinda Dīkṣita was also a profound scholar. He is known as Advaita *vidyācārya* and his son Yajñanārāyaṇa Dīkṣita states that he was not only proficient in the Advaita philosophy, but had a thorough knowledge of the six systems of philosophy (*ṣaḍ-darśanas*).[49] Veṅkaṭeśvara Dīkṣita (or Veṅkaṭamakhi), another son of this great minister mentions that his father re-established the Advaita School of Philosophy of Śrī Śaṅkara and that he was an elder contemporary of Appaya Dīkṣita.[50] He is said to have written commentaries on the *Jaiminīya Sūtras* and *Kaumārila Darśana* (a commentary on Kumārila Bhaṭṭa's *darśana*). He was also very proficient in the science of music — Veṅkaṭamakhi says that the *Saṅgīta Sudhā* was in reality, written by his father.[51] Govinda Dīkṣita was an authority on the Dharmaśāstras and also a permanent court of arbitration.[52] An inscription found in the inner wall of the second *gopura* of the temple in Paṭṭīśvaram (near Kumbakonam) registers his administration of even-handed justice.[53]

It is very interesting to note that there is a Sanskrit inscription consisting of two verses dated Śāka 1502 (CE 1580) found in the Aruṇācaleśvara temple in Tiruvaṇṇamalai in praise of Sevappa Nāyaka. These two verses are by Govinda Sūri, who, styling himself as a dependent of Sevappa Bhūpa, expresses his gratitude for favours received, by composing

[48] B. Natarajan, op. cit., p. 75.

[49] V. Vriddhagirisan, op. cit., p. 121.

[50] Ibid.

[51] Ibid., pp. 121-22.

[52] Ibid.

[53] Ibid., pp. 121-22; *ARE*, 257 of 1927 and *ARE*, 1926-27, pt. II, p. 117.

verses in praise of his patron.[54] As a portion of this record is damaged, it is not possible to determine the exact contents of the particular verses and there are no details relating to the pedigree of the poet.[55] In all probability, the author of these verses is identical with Govinda Dīkṣita.[56]

Yajñanārāyaṇa Dīkṣita was one of the eight sons of Govinda Dīkṣita who has won immortal fame by his works *Sāhityaratnākara, Raghunāthavilāsa Nāṭaka* and the *Alaṁkāra Ratnākara* and he also performed the *Sāgnicitya* and the *Sarvatomukha* sacrifices.[57] Veṅkaṭamakhin alias Veṅkaṭādhvari or Veṅkaṭeśa Dīkṣita was one of the sons of Govinda Dīkṣita. He was a Mīmāṁsā scholar and composer of the *Vārttikabharaṇam,* a commentary on the *Tūpṭīkā* of Kumārila which is classified along with other important works on Mīmāṁsā.[58] He also wrote the *Karmānta Vārttika,* a commentary on a portion of *Baudhāyana Śrauta Sūtras, Śulba Mīmāṁsā,* a treatise on Vedic trigonometry and also *Saṅgīta Sāmrājya.*[59] He is best known for his famous treatise on music known as *Caturdaṇḍīprakāśikā*. Rājacūdāmaṇi Dīkṣita, the author of *Rukmiṇī Pariṇayam,* and Nīlakaṇṭa Dīkṣita, a grand-nephew of Appayya Dīkṣita, were his students.[60] Veṅkaṭamakhi was a minister of Vijayarāghava Nāyaka.

---

[54] *ARE,* 1928-29, pt. II, p. 87.

[55] Ibid.

[56] Ibid.

[57] V. Vriddhagirisan, op. cit., p. 122.

[58] Ibid.

[59] Ibid.

[60] Ibid.

9

Later Pāṇḍyas

AS SEEN in Chapter 5, Māravarman Kulaśekhara I (CE 1268–1308) was the last illustrious Pāṇḍyan ruler. Soon after his death, in CE 1310-11, there was an invasion by Malik Kafur, the general of Allaudin Khilji, the Sultan of Delhi, into the Tamil country. Later, another invasion of the Tamil land occurred in CE 1323. The history of the Pāṇḍyas, during and after the Muslim invasion, was one of a dynasty which was fading out of history by slow degrees.[1] The Pāṇḍyas could not prevent the establishment of the Sultanate of Madurai, nor could they, at a later date, prevent the spread of the Vijayanagara into what was originally the Pāṇḍyan country. The Vijayanagara monarchs did not do any harm to the Pāṇḍyas and allowed them to rule freely a small track of land near Tirunelveli south of Madurai.[2]

Some of the rulers of the later Pāṇḍyan kings were also scholars. The Pudukkoṭṭai plates state that Varatuṅgarāma Pāṇḍya was "famous like Bhoja" (in literary capacity) (*bhoja iva*).[3] Aḷagaṉ Perumāḷ Abhivīrarāma alias Śrīvallabha was a great Tamil scholar who translated the Sanskrit poet *Naiṣadham* into Tamil called *Naiḍadham*. He wrote the *Kūrma Purāṇa* and *Kāśī Kāṇḍam* in Tamil.[4]

---

[1] N. Subrahmanian, *History of Tamilnadu* (*to AD 1565*), Madurai, 1985, p. 234.

[2] N. Sethuraman, *The Later Pāṇḍyas*, 19th Annual Congress of the Epigraphical Society of India, Tiruchirapalli, 1993, p. 1.

[3] *TAS*, vol. I no. 1, p. 69.

[4] N. Sethuraman, op. cit., p. 10.

The Daḷavāy-agrahāram plates mention that Abhivīrarāma Pāṇḍya also known as Ativīrarāma and Śrīvallabha was very learned in the Tamil language (*kalaṣodhbhava jiṣṇuvāṇi tadbhūṣaṇaśca*).[5] Many of the epigraphs of the later Pāṇḍyan kings also refer to the grant of land to scholars. The Śrīvilliputtūr plates of Abhivīrarāma Pāṇḍya dated CE 1552 records that this ruler made the village of Kṣīrārjunapura into an *agrahāra* named Parākrama Pāṇḍyapura and granted it free of tax to eminent scholarly brāhmaṇas. The new name seems to have been conferred on it after the name of the king's father and would appear to have already been granted earlier to the brāhmaṇas by his predecessors.[6]

A copper-plate record dated CE 1581 registers a grant made by Abhirāma Sundareśa Varatuṅgarāma, son of Kulaśekharadeva Parākrama Pāṇḍya, of the village Śoḷaiseri alias Nayināragāram as an *agrahāra* to brāhmaṇa scholars under the new name Śivagāmasundarī-caturvedimaṅgalam, in honour of his queen.[7] The Daḷavāy-agrahāram plates of Varatuṅgarāma Pāṇḍya dated CE 1582 also records a grant of a village named Muruganeri to a brāhmaṇa donee named Candraśekhara, son of Chokkappa Paṇḍita of the Kāśyapa *gotra*, *Baudhāyana Sūtra* and Yajus *śākhā*. The donee was a doctor.[8]

The Pudukkoṭṭai copper-plate grant of Śrīvallabha and Varatuṅgarāma Pāṇḍya dated CE 1583 states that the villages of Pudukkoṭṭai, Iḷuppaiyaḍippaṭṭi, Vaḷaṅgaimigāman and Śivakalaiyakkaruchchi were granted by these kings to a number of learned brāhmaṇas of various *gotra*s and *śākhā*s.[9]

---

[5] *TAS*, vol. I no. XIII, v. 17, p. 137.

[6] *TAS*, vol. I no. IX, pp. 109-13.

[7] *ARE*, 1932-33, A. no. 9.

[8] *TAS*, vol. I no. IX, vv. 19-28, pp. 121-22.

[9] *TAS*, vol. I no. I, vv. 41-61, pp. 69-71.

The Daḷavāy-agrahāram plates of Varatuṅgarāma Pāṇḍya, dated CE 1588 states that this king also called as Vīra-Pāṇḍya and Abhirāma Sundareśvara set up many villages for brāhmaṇas. He also granted the village of Silarippaṭṭi to Govinda Bhaṭṭa, son of Udayam Bhaṭṭa, who was a student of *Ṛgveda*.[10]

Another copper-plate grant, the Daḷavāy-agrahāram plates of Ativīrarāma Pāṇḍya dated CE 1595, states that in the thirty-third year of the reign of Ativīrarāma Śrīvallabha (CE 1595), prince Abhirāma alias Ativīra granted at the request of Rāmakṛṣṇappa Nāyaka, the village of Nandikkurcci under the name Ativīrarāmapura to a number of brāhmaṇas.[11] A Sanskrit lithic inscription found in the *mahāmaṇḍapa* of the Viśvanāthasvāmin temple at Tenkāśi dated CE 1615 records that King Varaguṇa Śrīvallabha set up on the bank of the River Citrā, an image of Gaṇeśa named Yajñeśa during a sacrifice and there presented to the sacrificial priests an excellent *agrahāra* named Abhiṣekapura situated in front of the deity at Tenkāśi.[12]

It would not be out of place to make a mention of the contribution of the Marāṭhās to the field of education. The Marāṭhā rule in the Tamil country began in CE 1678 when Veṅkājī, the half-brother of Śivājī became the ruler of Tañjāvūr. It came to an end in CE 1855 when the last king Śivājī II died leaving no sons behind and the state was taken over by the British government by the Doctrine of Lapse.

Although the Sanskrit inscriptions of the Marāṭhā rulers do not speak much about the patronage given by these kings to education, it is well known from other sources that the Marāṭhā kings of Tañjāvūr were great patrons of scholars. Many of the kings of this dynasty were eminent scholars and

---

[10] *TAS*, vol. I no. XII, vv. 15-17, p. 129.

[11] Ibid., vv. 24-30.

[12] *TAS*, vol. I no. XIII, vv. 22-29, pp. 137-38.

authored many works on diverse subjects which included Āyurveda and music. Their court became the centre of literature and art. Here was an enormous literary output in Sanskrit, Telugu and Tamil and it embraced every form of composition: epics, dramas, romantic pieces, burlesques, treatises on medicine, astrology and music.[13]

These kings granted a number of *agrahāras* to learned brāhmaṇas where they could pursue their scholarly activities in peace. Shāhjī II's love for learning was so great that in CE 1693, he renamed Tiruviśanallūr as Shāhjīrājapuram and gifted it to forty-six learned men of his court. This village was the seat of scholarship in languages, literature, philosophy and medicine throughout the Marāṭhā period and some of the most distinguished men were Telugus.[14] The Marāṭhā rulers also invited many of their own countrymen speaking the Marathi language and planted a considerable colony of Marāṭhā and Gurjara brāhmaṇas in the Tañjāvūr kingdom.[15]

---

[13] *TAS*, vol. I no. XIV, p. 147.

[14] C.K. Srinivasan, *Maratha Rule in the Carnatic*, Annamalainagar, 1944, p. 370.

[15] K.R. Subrahmanian, *The Maratha Rajas of Tanjore*, Madras, 1928, p. 29.

Plates

i.

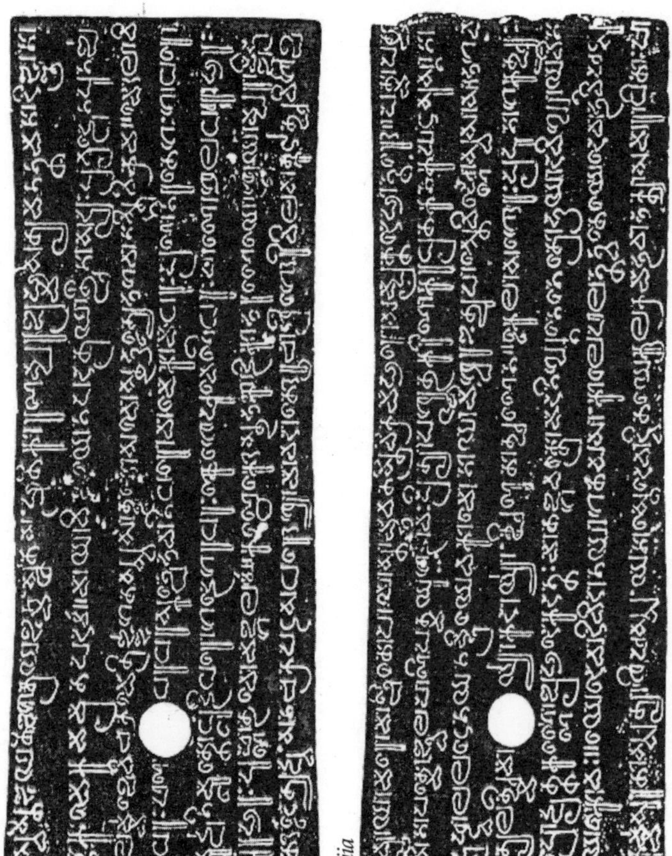

1. A portion of the Kaśākuḍi copper-plate grant of Nandivarman II Pallavamalla (*c.* CE 953-54).
(*Source: SII*, vol. II; *courtesy:* Archaeological Survey of India)

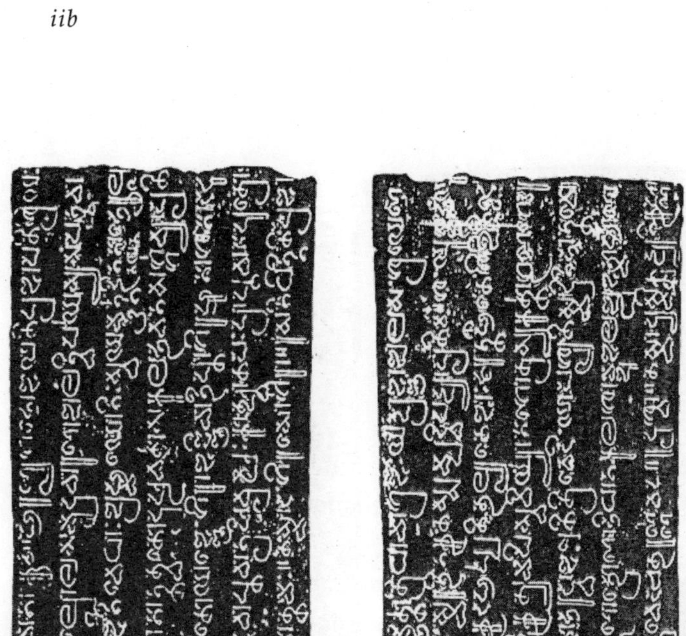

2. A portion of the Kaśakuḍi copper-plate grant of Nandivarman II Pallavamalla (*c.* CE 753-54).
(*Source: SII,* vol. II; *Courtesy:* Archaeological Survey of India)

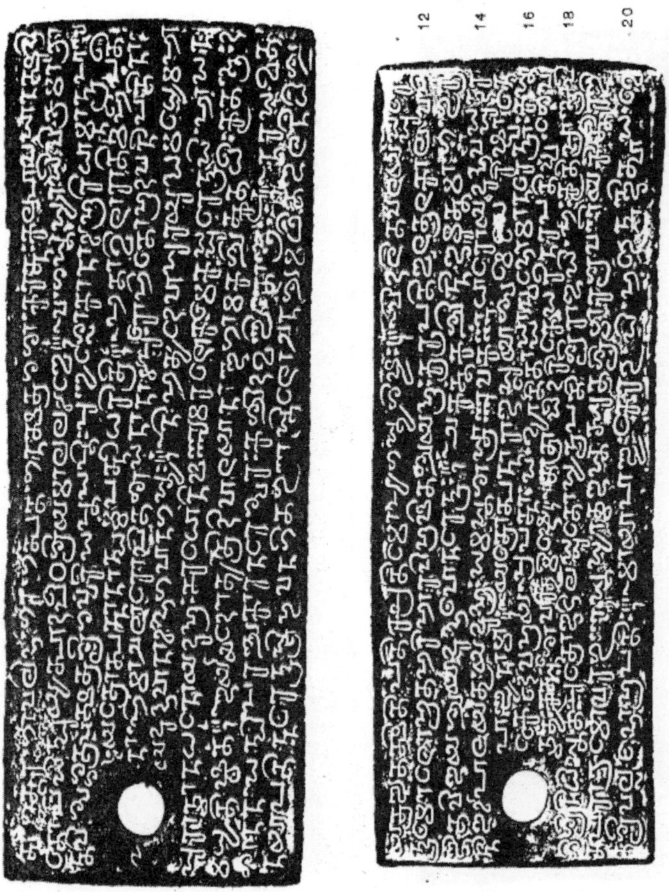

3. A portion of the Sinnamanūr copper-plate grant of Rājasiṃha II Pāṇḍya (c. CE 926-27).
(*Source: SII*, vol. III; *courtesy:* Archaeological Survey of India)

iiia

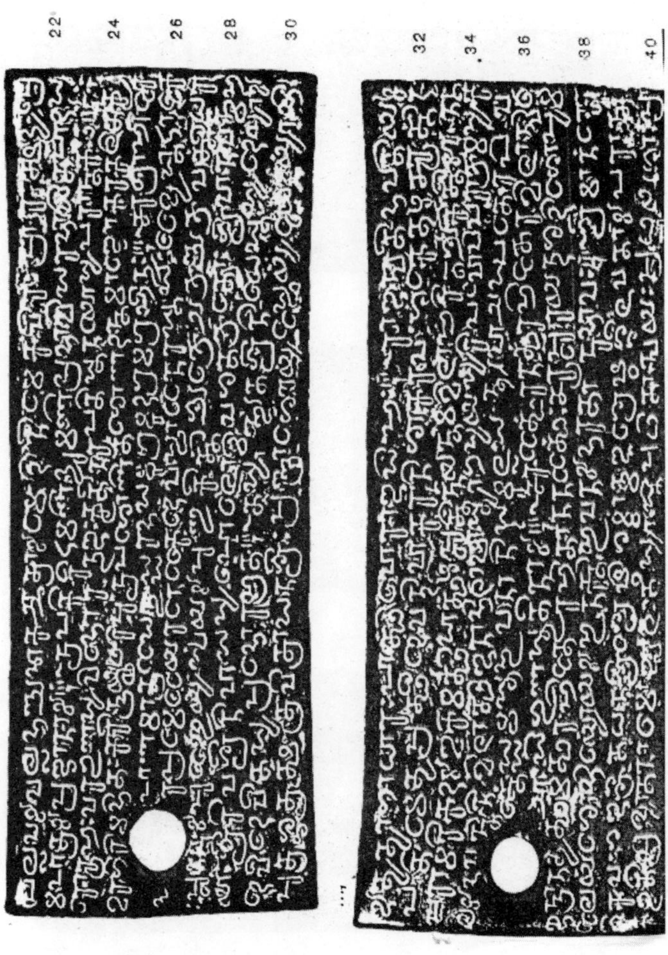

4. A portion of the Siṉṉamaṉūr copper-plate grant of Rājasiṁha II Pāṇḍya (*c.* CE 926-27).
(*Source: SII*, vol. III; *courtesy:* Archaeological Survey of India)

5. A portion of the larger Leiden copper-plate grant of Rājarāja Coḷa I (Sanskrit *praśasti* of the reign of Rājendra Coḷa I) (eleventh century CE).
(Source: EI, *vol. XXII;* Courtesy: *Archaeological Survey of India)*

6. A portion of the Śrīraṅgam copper-plate grant of the Vijayanagara Emperor Devarāya II (CE 1434).
(*Source: EI*, vol. XVIII; *Courtesy:* Archaeological Survey of India)

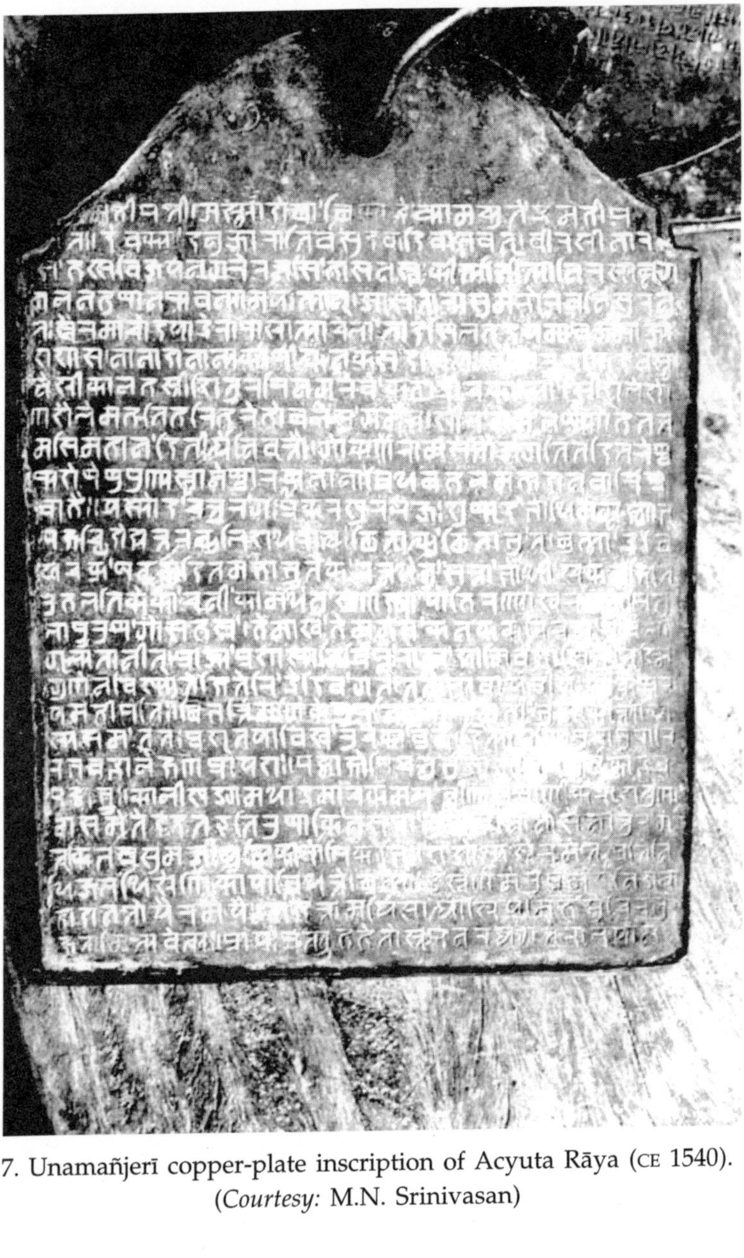

7. Unamañjerī copper-plate inscription of Acyuta Rāya (ce 1540).
(*Courtesy:* M.N. Srinivasan)

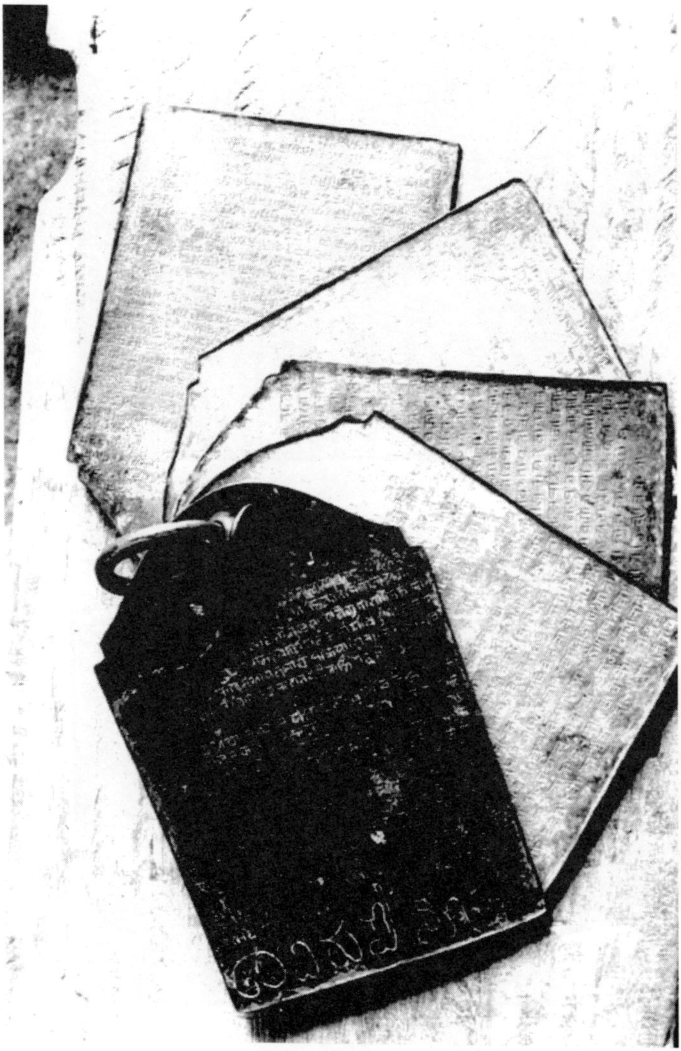

8. Unamañjerī copper-plate inscription of Acyuta Rāya (CE 1540).
(*courtesy:* M.N. Srinivasan)

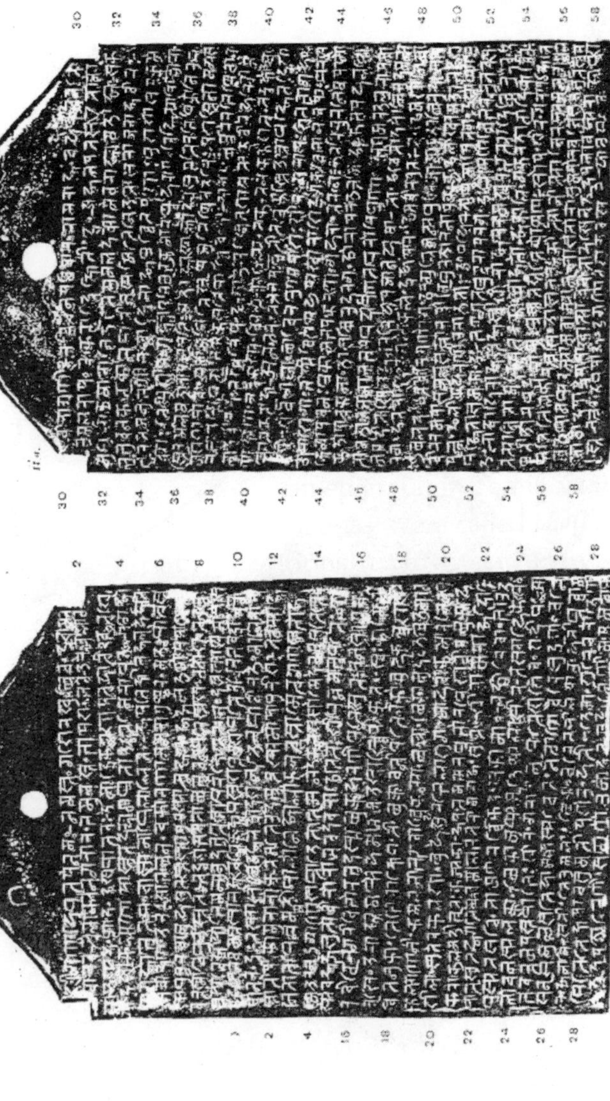

9. A portion of the Arivilimaṅgalam copper-plate grant of the Vijayanagara Emperor Śrīraṅgarāya II (CE 1577).
(*Source: EI*, vol. XII; *Courtesy:* Archaeological Survey of India)

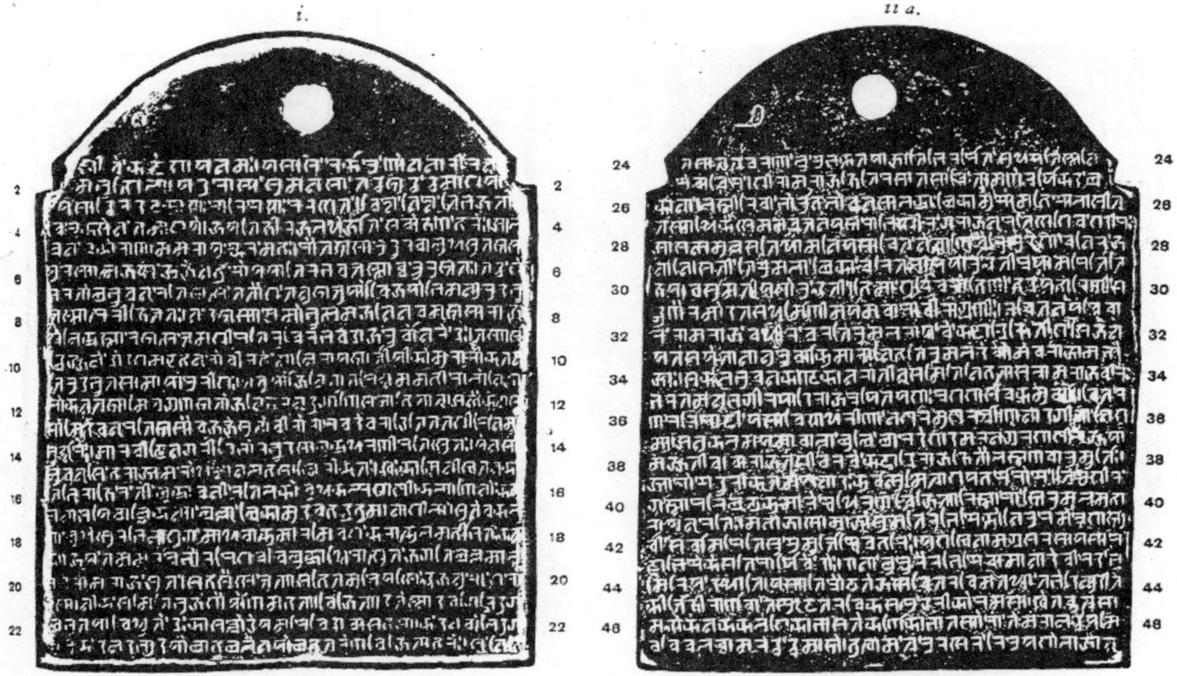

10. A portion of the Padmaneri copper-plate grant of the Vijayanagara Emperor Veṅkaṭa II (CE 1598).
(*Source: EI,* vol. XVI; *courtesy:* Archaeological Survey of India)

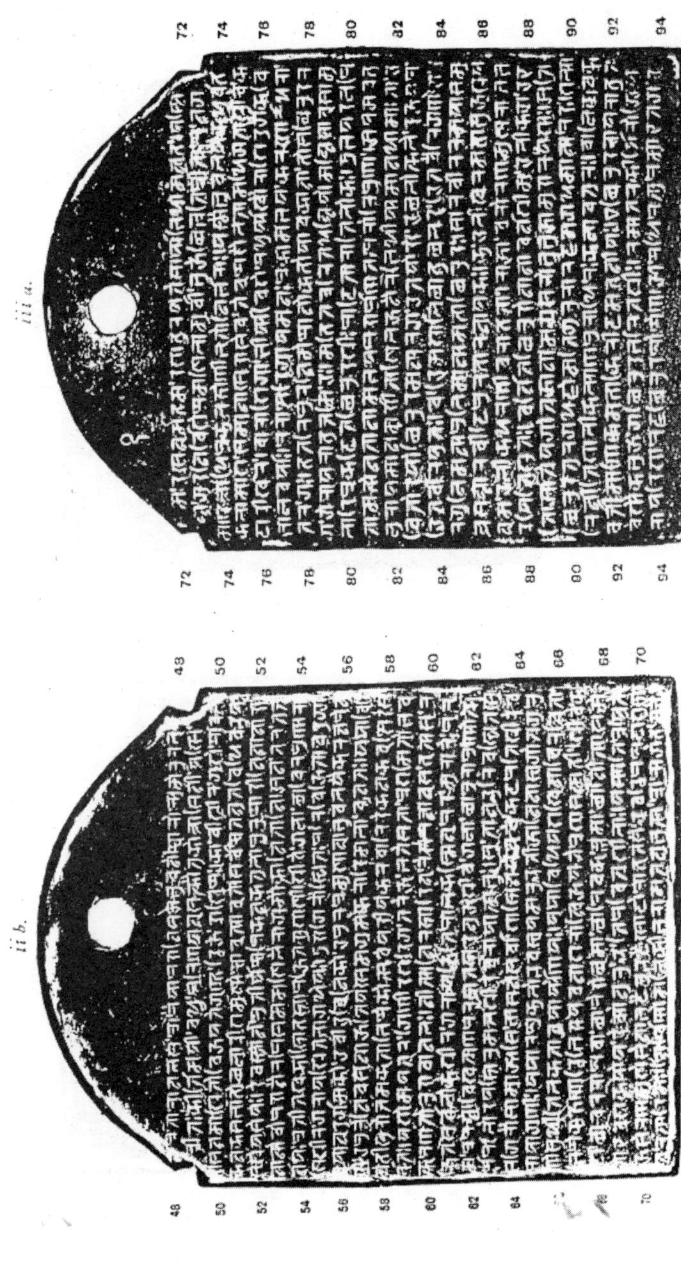

11. A portion of the Padmaneri copper-plate grant of the Vijayanagara Emperor Veṅkaṭa II (CE 1598).
(*Source: EI*, vol. XVI; *Courtesy:* Archaeological Survey of India)

12. *Kailāsanātha Temple, Kāñcīpuram*

13. *Inscriptions, Kailāsanātha Temple, Kāñcīpuram*

14. Varadarāja Perumāḷ Temple, Tribhuvanai

15. *Varadarāja Perumāḷ Temple, Tribhuvanai*

16. *Venkaṭeśa Perumāḷ Temple, Tirumukkudal*

17. Veṅkaṭeśa Perumāḷ Temple, Tirumukkuḍal

Bibliography

Epigraphical Sources

Annual Reports on Epigraphy

Epigraphia Carnatica

Epigraphia Indica

Indian Antiquary

Pallavar Cheppetukal Muppatu (Thirty Pallava Copper-plates), Madras, 1967.

Pandiyar Cheppedukal Pattu (Ten Pandyan Copper-plates), Madras, 1967.

South Indian Inscriptions

South Indian Temple Inscriptions

Travancore Archaeological Series

Uttankita Sanskrit Vidya-Aranya Epigraphs (vol. I)

Literary Sources

SANSKRIT

Abijñānaśākuntalam of Kālidāsa, tr. M.R. Kale, Delhi, 1994.

Alaṁkārasūtra of Rājānaka Śrī Ruyyaka (with the *vṛtti* Alaṁkārasarvasva of Mankhuka and commentary by Samudrabandha on the latter), ed. T.S. Ganapati Sastri, Trivandrum, 1915.

Amarakośa, ed. Satyadeva Mishra, Varanasi, 1972.

Avantīsundarīkathā, ed. K.S. Mahadeva Sastri, Trivandrum, 1954.

Avantīsundarīkathāsārā, ed. G. Harihara Sastri, Madras, 1957.

Bāṇa's Kādambarī, ed. M.R. Kale, Delhi, 1968.

Daśakumāracarita of Daṇḍin, tr. M.R. Kale, Delhi, 1997.

Gadyakarṇāmṛta of Śākala Vidyācakravartin, Madras, 1981.

Gajaśāstra of Palakapya Muni, ed. K.S. Subrahmanya Sastri, Tanjavur, 1958.

Madhuravijayam of Gaṅgā Devī, tr. S. Tiruvenkatachariar.

Mattavilāsaprahasana, ed. N.P. Unni, Trivandrum, 1974.

Nānārthārṇava-Saṁkṣepa, ed. T. Ganapati Sastri, Trivandrum, 1913.

The Raghuvaṁśa of Kālidāsa (Cantos I-V), tr. M.R. Kale, Bombay, 1925.

TAMIL

Koil Oḷugu, ed. Krishnaswamy Ayyangar, Tiruchirapalli.

Nālāyira Divya Prabandham, ed. Venkataswami Reddiyar, Madras, 1981.

Śilappadikāram, tr. V.R. Ramachandra Dikshitar, Oxford, 1939.

Secondary Sources

Altekar, A.S., *Education in Ancient India*, Banaras, 1951.

Das, S.K., *Educational System of Ancient Hindus*, Calcutta, 1930.

Gopalan, R., *History of the Pallavas of Kanchi*, Madras, 1928.

Gopinatha Rao, T.A. (ed.), *Copper-plate Inscriptions Belonging to the Sri Sankaracharya of the Kamakoti-Pitham*, Madras, 1916.

Gopinatha Rao, T.A., *History of the Sri Vaisnavas*, Madras, 1923.

Govindasamy, M.S., *The Role of Feudatories in Later Cola History*, Annamalainagar, 1979.

———, *The Role of Feudatories in Pallava History,* Annamalainagar, 1965.

Gupta, D.K., *A Critical Study of Dandin and His Works*, Delhi, 1970.

Gurumurthy, S., *Education in South India*, Madras, 1979.

Janaki, S.S., *Gadyakarnāmṛta*, Madras, 1981.

Kane, P.V., *History of Dharmaśāstra*, vol. II pt. 2, Poona, 1941.

Keith, A.B., *History of Sanskrit Literature*, Delhi, 1996.

Krishnamachariyar, M., *History of Classical Sanskrit Literature*, Delhi, 2009.

Krishnan, K.G., *Studies in South Indian History and Epigraphy*, Madras, 1981.

———, *Karandai Tamil Sangam Plates of Rajendra Cola-I, ASI, No. 79*), New Delhi, 1984.

———, *Inscriptions of the Early Pandyas (c. 300 BC to 984 AD)*, New Delhi, 2002.

Krishnaswami Ayyangar, S., *Evolution of Hindu Administrative Institutions in South India*, Madras, 193

———, *Sources of Vijayanagara History*, Madras, 1919.

Leela Shantakumari, S., *History of Agraharas (Karnataka, 400-1300)*, Madras, 1986.

Macdonell, A.A., *A History of Sanskrit Literature*, Hyderabad, 1935.

Mahalingam, T.V., *Inscriptions of the Pallavas*, New Delhi, 1988.

Majumdar, R.C. (ed.), *The History and Culture of the Indian People* (vol. 6: *The Delhi Sultanate)*, Bombay, 1990.

———, *History and Culture of the Indian People,* vol. 7: *The Mughal Empire,* Bombay, 1994.

Minakshi C., *Administration and Social Life Under the Pallavas*, Madras, 1975.

———, *The History Sculptures of the Vaikunthaperumal Temple Kanchi* (*Memoirs of the Archaeological Survey of India*), New Delhi, 1940.

Mishra, Satyadeva (ed.), *Amarakośa*, Varanasi, 1972.

Mookerji, R.M., *Ancient Indian Education*, London, 1947.

Mores, G.K., *The Kadamba Kula*, Bombay, 1931.

Nagaswamy, R., *Tiruttani and Velanjeri Copper Plates*, Madras, 1979.

———, *The Esalam Copper-plates of Rajendra Cola I*, Bulletin De L'Ecolencaise, D'Extreme-Orient, Tome LXXVI, Paris,1987.

———, *Studies in Ancient Tamil Law and Society*, Madras, 1978.

Natarajan, B., *Tillai and Nataraja*, Madras, 1994.

———, *Advaita Vidyacharya Maharaja Saheb Bhagavan Sri Govinda Dikshita*, Kumbakonam.

Nilakanta Sastri, K.A., *The Pāṇḍyan Kingdom (from the Earliest Times to the Sixteenth Century)*, Madras, 1972.

———, *The Coḷas*, Madras, 1984.

———, *Studies in Cola History and Administration*, Madras, 1932.

Raman K.V., *Early History of the Madras Region*, Madras, 1959.

———, *Some Aspects of Pāṇḍyan History in the Light of New Discoveries*, Madras, 1974.

———, *History of the Pandyas* (Tamil), Madras, 1977.

———, *Sri Varadarajaswami Temple, Kanchi,* New Delhi, 1975.

Ramesh, K.V., *Indian Epigraphy*, New Delhi, 1984.

Sarkar, H., *The Kampaharesvara Temple in Tribhuvanam*, Madras, 1974.

Sadasiva Pandarathar, T.V., *History of the Later Colas*, Annamalainagar, 1949.

Sankaranarayanan, S., *Rare Facets of Ancient History and Culture*, vols. I and II, New Delhi, 2009.

———, *The Viṣṇukuṇḍins and Their Times*, Delhi, 1977.

Sathyanathier, R., *Studies in the Ancient History of Tondaimandalam*, Madras, 1987.

Sethuraman, N., *The Later Pandyas, 19th Annual Congress of the Epigraphical Society of India*, Tiruchirapalli, 1993.

Sreedhara Menon, A., *A Survey of Kerala History*, Madras, 1998.

Sivaramamurti, C., *Epigraphical Echos of Kalidasa*, Madras, 1944.

———, *Indian Epigraphy and South Indian Scripts, Bulletin of Madras Government Museum*, vol. 3 no. 4, Madras, 1966.

Srinivasan, C.K., *Maratha Rule in the Carnatic*, Annamalainagar, 1944.

Subrahmanian, K.R., *The Maratha Rajas of Tanjore*, Madras, 1928.

Subrahmanian, N., *History of Tamilnadu* (to AD 1565), Madurai, 1985.

———, *History of Tamilnadu* (AD *1565-1984*), Madurai, 1977.

———, *Sangam Polity*, Madurai, 1980.

Sundaram, C.S., *Contribution of Tamil Nadu to Sanskrit*, Chennai, 1999.

Sundaram, P.S. (tr.), *Tiruvalluvar: The Kural*, New Delhi, 1990.

Swaminathan, S., *The Early Colas: History, Art and Culture*, Delhi, 1998.

Venkatraman, K.R., *Hoysalas in the Tamil Country*, Annamalainagar, 1950.

Articles

Balasubramanyam S.R., "Kopperunjinga — His Life and Times", *JMU*, vol. IX no. 3 and vol. X no. 1, pp. 40-98.

Buhler, G., "The Indian Inscriptions and the Antiquity of Indian Artificial Poetry", *Ind. Ant.*, Feb. 1913.

Chhabra, B.Ch., N. Lakshminarayana Rao, and M. Ashraf Hussain: "Ten Years of Indian Epigraphy (1937-46)", from *Ancient India (Bulletin of the Archaeological Survey of India)*, no. 5, January 1949, p. 57.

Diskalkar, D.B., "Dravidian or South Indian Inscriptions", *JIH*, vol. XXXIV, p. 173.

Gurumurthy, S., "Popular Education in Ancient South India from Inscriptions", *JMU*, vol. LI no. 1, January 1979, pp. 19-28.

———, Medical Science and Dispensaries in Ancient South India as Gleaned from Epigraph, *JHS*, V, 1970.

Harihara Sastri, G., "Kharapata and Muladeva", from *Asutosh Memorial Volume*, Patna, 1926-28, pp. 224-27.

Harihara Sastri, G. and V. Raghavan, "The Hanumad Viṁśati of Lakshmikumara Tatacharya", *JOR*, XVIII.

Krishnan, K.G., "Sanskrit in Inscriptions of Tamil Nadu" from *"Svasti Sri": Chabbra Felicitation Volume*, New Delhi, 1984.

———, "Cola Charters: Socio-Economic Aspects", *Tamil Civilization* (Journal of the Tamil University), vol. 3, nos. 1-2, 1985, pp. 71-74.

Mahalingam, T.V., "The Accession of Nandivarman Pallavamalla, *JIH*, vol. XXXVI, pt. II, August 1958.

Minakshi, C., "Elephant Love in Pallava History", *QJMS*, vol. 28, 1937, pp. 290-92.

Nagaswamy, R., "Mahendra's Inscription at Tiruchirapalli: A Study", *JOR*, vol. 7, pp. 135-38.

Narasimhachar, R., "Bhāmaha and Daṇḍi", *Ind. Ant.*, 1912.

Natarajan, D., "Saivism under Rajaraja: A Study", from *Rajaraja the Great — Seminar Proceedings*, Bombay, 1987.

Nilakanta Sastri, K.A., "The Kodumbalur Inscription of Vikrama-Kesar", *JOR*, vol. 7, 1933, pp. 1-10.

———, "Sanskrit Learning in the Cola Empire," *JOR*, vol. 9 pt. I, 1937, pp. 1-2.

———, "Education in the Tamil Country," *Indian Culture*, vol. I pt. I, pp. 85-88.

Raghavan, V., "The Bharatasamgraha of Vidyachakravartin", *ABORI*, vol. XIV, pp. 256-57.

Ramachandran, T.N., "The Royal Artist, Mahendravarman — I", *JOR*, vol. 7, pp. 219-45 and 303ff.

Ramesh, K.V., "A Pallava Charter and Two Copper Medallions from Peddamudiyam" from *Sri Rama Chandrika* (*Prof. Oruganti Ramachandraiya Festschrift*), Delhi, 1993, pp. 117-21.

Ramesan, N., "The Vesanta Grant of Pallava Simhavarman", *TASSI*, 1960-62 (vol. 6, Silver Jubilee Volume), pp. 85-96.

———, "The Kumaradimangalam Plates of the Pallava King Nandivarman III", *Shri Mallampalli Somasekara Sarma Commemoration Volume*, Hyderabad, 1976, pp. 193-205.

Sankaranarayanan, S., "A Pallava Inscriptional Poem in Sanskrit", *ALB*, vol. 55, 1991, pp. 71-90.

———, "Sanskrit Education in Ancient Tamil Country (An Epigrapihical Survey)", *ALB*, vol. 57, 1993, pp. 7-33.

———, "Sanskrit Education in Ancient Karnataka (*Epigraphical Survey*)", *ALB*, vol. 58, 1994, pp. 100-24.

———, "Pradipaka: A Forgotten Varttika (from Tamilnadu on the Sarirakabhasya of Sri Samkara)" *ALB*, vol. 62, 1998, pp. 109-23.

———, "The Bhagavadpadiyam Sariraka Bhasyam in the Colamadevi Epigraph: More Light", *ALB*, vol. 64, 2000, pp. 105-35.

———, "Sriharsa and Kāñcīpuram: Their Forgotten History Traced", from *Rare Facets of Ancient History and Culture*, vol. I, New Delhi, 2009.

Sircar D.C., "South Indian Epigraphy — Its Value as Source Material in South Indian Studies", *Dr. T.V. Mahalingam Commemoration Volume*, Mysore, 1990, pp. 183-90.

Srinivasan, P.R., "Gangadharashtakam in Pallava Inscription from Tiruchirapalli" from *'Śrīnidhiḥ': Perspectives in Indian Archaeology, Art and Culture* (*Shri K.R. Srinivasan Festschrift*), Madras, 1983, pp. 431-35.

Subrahmaniam, T.N., "The Dalavaypuram Copper-plate Grant of Parāntaka Vira Narayana Pandya", *TASSI* (1962-65), pp. 1-31.

———, Pallannkoil Jaina Copper-plate Grant of Early Pallava Period, *TASSI*, (1958-59), vol. IV, pp. 41-48.

Subrahmaniam, T.N. and P.R. Srinivasan, "The Sivakasi Copper-plate Grant of Vīra Pāṇḍya", *TASSI* (1962–65), pp. 33-52.

Subramanian, V.S., "Characteristic Features of Sanskrit Inscriptions (South Indian Studies)", *Dr. T.V. Mahalingam Commemmoration Volume*, Mysore, 1990, pp. 191-205.

Journals

Indian Journal of the Indian Research Institute, Calcutta.

Journal of Ancient Indian History, Calcutta.

Journal of the Epigraphical Society of India, Mysore.

Journal of Indian History, Trivandrum.

Journal of the Madras University, Madras.

Journal o f the Orient Institute, Baroda.

Journal of Oriental Research, Madras.

Journal of Tamil Civilization, Tanjavur.

Quarterly Journal of the Mystic Society, Bangalore.

Sri Venkateswara University Oriental Journal, Tirupati.

The Indian Historial Quarterly, Calcutta.

Index